A QUESTION OF LEADERSHIP

A QUESTION OF
LEADERSHIP
Gladstone to Thatcher

PETER CLARKE

HAMISH HAMILTON · LONDON

HAMISH HAMILTON LTD
Published by the Penguin Group
27 Wrights Lane, London W8 5TZ, England
Viking Penguin a division of Penguin Books USA Inc.,
375 Hudson Street, New York, New York 10014, USA
Penguin Books Australia Ltd, Ringwood, Victoria, Australia
Penguin Books Canada Ltd, 2801 John Street, Markham, Ontario, Canada L3R 1B4
Penguin Books (NZ) Ltd, 182–190 Wairau Road, Auckland 10, New Zealand

Penguin Books Ltd, Registered Offices: Harmondsworth, Middlesex, England

First published 1991

Copyright © Peter Clarke, 1991
The Acknowledgements on page 335 constitute an extension of this copyright page

Filmset in Monophoto Bembo
Printed in Great Britain by Butler & Tanner Ltd, Frome and London

A CIP catalogue record for this book is available from the British Library

ISBN 0-241-13005-0

CONTENTS

for Emily and Libby
born 4 July 1974
to explain what happened
before Mrs Thatcher's premiership

INTRODUCTION

How much difference does leadership make in politics? Our experience in Britain during the 1980s gives new pertinence to this question. So much has now been written about Thatcherism that we are in danger of supposing that the political impact of Margaret Thatcher has been not so much striking as unique. But though it has been remarkable, it has not been unprecedented. There is a certain symmetry in starting with Gladstone, who was the first British statesman to grapple with a democratic style of government, and ending with Thatcher, who, both consciously and unconsciously, echoes some of the classic themes of Victorian politics.

This book consists of a dozen or so biographical studies of some major figures in the making of British politics during the last century. Nine of the subjects served as Prime Minister at one time or another. One of the others (Hugh Gaitskell) was a party leader who would almost certainly have become Prime Minister had he not died prematurely. Three others were not leaders of major parties, though conceivably each might have become leader, and it is a point of interest in itself to discover why they did not. If Bonar Law was posthumously dismissed – admittedly prompted by the occasion of his interment in Westminster Abbey alongside the Unknown Soldier – as 'the unknown prime minister', in a sense Joseph Chamberlain, Hugh Dalton and Aneurin (Nye) Bevan appear here as the antithesis, since their considerable contribution to the course of party politics was anything but anonymous.

Richard Crossman's diary gives one piquant insight here. Talking to Dalton, just before Attlee's eventual retirement in 1955, he naturally gave vent to his own feeling that leaders and deputy leaders were 'always pretty contemptible. Why shouldn't Nye convince himself that he is too big a man for these jobs?' To which, of course, the superannuated Dalton roared his concurrence: 'That's the kind of job for which I've never felt any jealousy of the man who occupies it. Ernie Bevin, I and others aren't going to be little Attlees. Why can't Nye feel the same?' There is some evidence that in time Bevan did so; and even if there may be a whiff of sour grapes about such comments, there is a substantial point behind them. If not every prime minister is a titan, so there are major politicians who never, as Disraeli put it, 'climbed to the top of the greasy pole'.

This is true of one of the half-dozen biggest figures in British politics during the last century. In paying tribute to Joseph Chamberlain, Churchill caught it exactly: 'Above him in the House of Lords reigned venerable, august Lord Salisbury, Prime Minister since God knew when. Beside him on the Government Bench, wise, cautious, polished, comprehending, airily fearless, Arthur Balfour led the House of Commons. But "Joe" was the one who made the weather.' For it is one sign of the stature of a political leader whether he – or she – succeeds in setting the agenda of politics. The big issues in politics have changed in every generation, usually in this way. Here is one theme of this book and one criterion for determining whom to write about.

It also explains the fact that one essay is about a man who was never himself a political leader. By the middle of the twentieth century, the management of the economy had become crucial in government policy, in political argument and in electoral competition. The name which is linked with this sea-change is not, however, that of a politician but that of the author of a famous book which concluded: 'the ideas of economists and political philosophers, both when they are right and when they are wrong, are more powerful than is

2

commonly understood. Indeed the world is ruled by little else.' Now the claim which John Maynard Keynes made here is itself highly disputable. In the period of Keynesian triumphalism which lasted until the end of the 1960s, it was often naïvely supposed that he was 'right' in this general claim as well as in his own economic teaching. And though since then it has become fashionable to make the equally crude contention that he was 'wrong', an exception in this one respect has often been made, so as to hold him responsible for the allegedly deleterious economic consequences of Keynesianism. In Part Three of this book we see politicians grappling with a new agenda – one with which their predecessors were innocently unfamiliar, as Winston Churchill, who spanned both eras, feelingly indicated. Part Two helps explain the nature of the transition.

If setting the agenda of government is one strategic theme of this book, the other is the problem of mobilizing political support. Without this, nothing can get done in democratic politics and the finest potential for statesmanship will run to waste. If leadership is partly a question of vision about the direction in which policy ought to be developed, it is also a matter of projecting electoral appeal and putting together a winning coalition of effective support. It is a problem which can be tackled in very different ways, with the stress falling, for example, on rational persuasion, on executive efficiency, on charismatic oratory, on party organization, on institutional power-broking or on high-political scheming.

It can still be argued that some leaders are born great, some achieve greatness, and some have greatness thrust upon them. Salisbury owed much to birth; Churchill and Neville Chamberlain were not handicapped, on the whole, by their paternity and the political openings it brought. Both of them, however, grafted to achieve their personal goals, and in this they matched self-made men like Joseph Chamberlain, Asquith, Lloyd George and Bevan. Politicians who succeeded to the leadership by happening to be in the right place at the right time may seem less interesting; and I have not chosen to write about Lord Rosebery or Sir Henry Campbell-

Bannerman or Andrew Bonar Law or Sir Alec Douglas-Home. But with Attlee and, in important respects, Thatcher, who were both initially lucky to get where they did, we again find that Shakespeare's insights have worn well. There is indeed a tide in the affairs of men, which, taken at the flood, leads on to fortune. And if not, not. What distinguished Attlee, in making the post-war consensus, and Thatcher, in unmaking it, was that they took their chance when it was given to them.

Attlee, at any rate, would not have been a great leader except in his own particular historical circumstances. He was swimming with the tide and buoyed up personally by it. Others have attempted to swim against the tide, with mixed success. Joseph Chamberlain was on the whole unsuccessful in achieving his constructive aims. Lloyd George enjoyed seventeen continuous years in office up to 1922 – and seventeen years out of office from then until 1939. Churchill's career, and Macmillan's with it, turned from frustration to ascendancy only with the crisis of 1940. Bevan and Gaitskell, after achieving high office relatively young, were then doomed to an uphill struggle which turned into a losing battle, with a potential victory snatched from them by death.

The politicians who have left the most significant mark have been those whose own outlook and gifts chimed in with the contemporary mood, anticipating rather than simply echoing it, because they were able literally to speak to the concerns of the people. Joseph Chamberlain perhaps found his touch in linking Unionism with imperialism. Lloyd George made the fiscal issue into popular politics before the First World War. Neville Chamberlain struck a chord with middle England for a time in the 1930s, just as Macmillan increasingly found an appropriate way to voice the new consensual Conservatism of the affluent society. But the two most consistent and successful exponents of this style of politics, each with a peculiar blend of radicalism and conservatism, each effective in bringing popular authority to bear in re-shaping the agenda of statecraft, have been Gladstone and Thatcher.

This book has a recurrent theme but it is not a schematic

analysis of leadership. It remains biographical in focus in more than one sense, since it was sometimes an important new biography which moved me to write about these particular people. The selection of subjects thus has an arbitrary element, but while there is no call to justify omissions, one or two deserve a word. The prominence given here to Salisbury means that Disraeli appears fleetingly as his predecessor and Arthur Balfour is seen chiefly as his uncle's lieutenant. Ramsay MacDonald and Stanley Baldwin, who dominated British party politics in the years 1923 to 1937, would obviously have been worth more extended study in a different book. More recently, Harold Wilson and Edward Heath played major roles in the events surveyed in the final sections of this book, even though neither is featured in my chapter headings.

One of the chapters is defined thematically – 'The Decay of Labourism and the Demise of the SDP' – though each section within it focuses on particular individuals. This seemed the right approach to a recent crisis in party politics with inevitable haunting echoes of earlier episodes. It is clear that the propensity for centrist politicians to peel away from parties of the Left has seldom made an enduring mark. The Liberal Unionists, albeit reinforced by the forceful presence of Joseph Chamberlain, could not in the end resist assimilation by the Conservative Party. Lloyd George almost suffered the same fate, and many of his Coalitionist followers succumbed completely. Even the prestige of Ramsay MacDonald could not save National Labour from withering away as a parasitic remnant. The leadership of famous names, with established radical credentials, was plainly not enough to sustain an independent appeal nor to ward off the embrace of Conservatism.

Indeed, there is a stock speech which has always been a favourite of politicians defecting in this way. The Liberals first heard it from the Palmerstonians in the 1860s, and as Liberal Unionists in the 1880s some of them turned it back upon the Gladstonians. The old Liberals flung it at the new Liberals in the early 1900s, and the Asquithians and the Lloyd Georgians rehearsed it on each other in the 1920s. The Labour Party was regaled with it from the MacDonaldites in the

1930s, and the dust has been blown off it from time to time ever since. The notes for the speech go something like this:

– deep regret at sad moment – strong ties with party in which brought up – lifetime of service, proud of achievements – great leaders of yesterday, Gladstone/Keir Hardie/Attlee, etc. – but now would turn in graves – betrayal of finest traditions – *I have not changed, party has changed* – heavy heart, sleepless nights, no alternative, etc.

This speech has usually been followed, at no long interval, by a venomous assault on the old party, acting as a sort of purification ritual in which the old self is cast off and the rectitude of the new allegiance publicly confirmed. In this perspective, it is surely worth asking whether the SDP was doomed to fail, whether it died from swallowing its own propaganda, whether it simply sustained Conservatism by other means, and whether the outcome turned on personal factors – in short, on leadership.

One other fact has influenced me in deciding whom to write about and how – the existence of a good private diary. Five of these leaders were themselves diarists: Gladstone, Neville Chamberlain, Dalton, Macmillan and Gaitskell. In addition, Asquith wrote intimate letters in a similar genre and Lloyd George's mistress kept a diary. The diaries of Beatrice Webb and Virginia Woolf supplied me with incidentally pertinent passages. Following Dalton and Gaitskell, the modern Labour Party has bred a generation of diarists in Barbara Castle, Roy Jenkins, Tony Benn and – most illuminating for my purposes – Richard Crossman. There is no doubt that these diaries offer an unusually vivid source of some of the more elusive personal aspects which would otherwise go unrecorded. Such insights alert us to a final theme of this book: the irreducibly personal and particular circumstances which are one factor in explaining historical events.

Historians commonly offer two sorts of explanation, which can be termed structural and contingent. Structural explanations need not be deterministic but they emphasize what was likely to happen – on the whole, in the long run, in one guise or another, at one juncture or another – according to an explicit or implicit scheme of causation based on observed regularities, analogies, patterns, cycles, trends or tendencies. Such an approach involves generalization, which in turn necessarily depends on abstraction of what can be generalized from what seems unique, anomalous, trivial, or just messy, in its own particular context. An extrapolation of this approach would lead us to a rigorously scientific methodology, which is obviously appropriate to the physical world. Without such bold simplification, it will be said, there can be no scientific progress and Newton's speculations would therefore end with the trajectory of a single apple. Yet is this really the core of history?

Contingent explanations, which seek to recapture the complex play of causation in specific instances, are surely necessary to answer a different sort of historical question: not what we can learn from the past in general but how we can understand what actually happened in particular. The point here is not that we should discount structural constraints, but that we should recognize the interlocking of different chains of cause and effect. Such understanding will not arise from dismissing what is unique, or excluding what is anomalous, or ignoring what is trivial, or discounting what is just messy. We will thus acknowledge the futility of striving for the elegant simplicity of predictable replication as encoded by rigorous science in a field where such a model is inappropriate. In history we have to settle for the subtle complexity of real life as captured by a more plastic art, and one, moreover, which allows for the crucial role of the individual in an appropriate historical context.

It is not enough for a historian to tell this to his readers; he must show it to them. This is what I attempt to do in tackling my theme. How do we explain success – or failure – in setting the agenda of government and in mobilizing the necessary political support? Is it, in fact, a question of leadership?

PART ONE
VICTORIAN VALUES?

THE COLOSSUS OF WORDS.

(*Punch*, 13 December 1879)

I

GLADSTONE:

THE POLITICS OF MORAL POPULISM

Victorian Britain looks like a society hell-bent upon expansion. The population of England and Wales, which had been 9 million at the time of the first census in 1801, had doubled by 1851 and was to double again in the next sixty years. The British Empire was expanding at a rate of 100,000 square miles a year throughout the nineteenth century. If the economy, as it now seems, did not achieve an annual growth rate of 3 per cent before the 1830s – more belatedly than we used to suppose – this locates the unprecedented expansionary thrust of industrialization squarely in the Victorian era. In a society which threatened to burst apart at the seams, the question of political stability was posed with new urgency. In retrospect it may not seem remarkable that British society adjusted to the stresses of industrialization, that acute class conflict was averted, that an aristocratic system of government was steadily democratized, and that the Liberal and Conservative parties rode out these great changes. At the time, however, when none of this could be taken for granted, successful leadership required not only courageous decision-making but also considerable discernment of the possibilities of the situation.

The career of William Ewart Gladstone, four times Liberal Prime Minister, spans these great changes. He was indubitably part of the upper crust – Eton and Oxford and a landed estate had seen to that – and he professed lifelong aristocratic attachments. His early career, moreover, had been as a Tory and an insider, stepping precociously from a pocket borough into Cabinet office in Sir Robert Peel's Government. Only the split in the Conservative Party in 1846, when the Peelites insisted on repealing the Corn Laws in the teeth of Tory backbench opposition, had cast Gladstone adrift. It was an improbable background for a man who was to become known as 'the People's William'. The key which will decode this enigma is not so much that of class as of religion.

Gladstone himself had a theological outlook which was manifested alike in his private life and his public life. For all his High Churchmanship, he clung to the evangelical doctrines of his youth with their characteristic language of providence, sin, conscience, atonement, and judgement. In his private life he went through periods of stress which he analysed in primarily religious terms and which we may analyse in primarily sexual terms. His marriage can fairly be called happy as well as long-lasting; but there are passages in his diary on matters which he kept from his wife. To be sure, she knew in general about his night rescue work. Indeed, everyone in London seems to have known that, both as Chancellor of the Exchequer and later as Prime Minister, he would set out from Downing Street late at night and make contact with prostitutes.

Part of this was straightforward philanthropy, as pure as it was imprudent. But Gladstone's excitement in such encounters is testified by the self-flagellation he secretly recorded afterwards. And with one reformed courtesan, Laura Thistlethwayte, his relations severely taxed the boundaries of discretion during his first Government. In his old age he offered his son and pastor the assurance that he had 'never been guilty of the act which is known as that of infidelity to the marriage bed'. This has the ring of Gladstonian authenticity in its precise and emphatic vagueness. It is surely to his credit that he recorded his temptations and to the credit of his family that these records – so obviously open to misconstruction – were preserved. There is thus abundant evidence of the precarious compromise Gladstone effected, during a crucial phase of his career, between the strong drives of his nature and the peculiar disciplines of his moral code.

In his public life he was less tormented, less unsure of himself. Yet although on many issues he was the embodiment of a restless politics of conscience, he also displayed a deep streak of quietism about the workings of society and the proper role of the state. He dismissed the postulate of inherent human progress as mere trifling with the pervasive problem of sin. 'I believe in a degeneracy of man, in the Fall – in *sin* – in the intensity and virulence of sin,' he declared late in life. His efforts to make politics into a branch of theology did not secularize salvation by making it into a goal for this world rather than the next. Instead he saw the role of conscience chiefly as bearing witness against the evils of the world – preferably the outside world. He was, more than any other single person, the architect of a fiscal constitution founded upon Free Trade; he abhorred what he called 'construction', meaning interventionist meddling by government. The acceptance of individual responsibility was a divine injunction with inescapable implications. 'What is meant by being responsible?' he demanded. 'It is meant that we expose ourselves to the consequences flowing from our actions.'

If he was free after 1846 to make a series of uneasy accommodations with the Whigs, his High Church Anglicanism continued to mark him off from the mass of Nonconformists who were so prominent in the coalescing Liberal alliance – not yet quite a party – with which Gladstone worked in the 1860s. Yet the unlikeliness of his background was turned to account with superb finesse. Even the extreme defence he had once made of the Established Church was because he had 'clung to the notion of a conscience, in the State', not simply clung to its temporal power or endowments, and had relinquished this position only when the whole idea of a confessional state had become untenable; instead he eventually developed a broader-based politics of conscience and discovered common ground with Dissent in the process.

The issue of the franchise came to dominate British politics in the mid-1860s. What was at stake was the basic qualification for a vote in the boroughs (the counties were virtually left out of this argument), which since 1832 had been defined as occupation of dwelling worth £10 a year. One complication here is that, then as now, house prices and rents varied so much between regions. Even so, it makes sense to ask, who was this famous £10 householder? The general answer is that he was a shopkeeper – hence not only the talk of 'shopocracy' but the use of the trade boycott to exert pressure from below during elections. But in a period when the Liberal Party was reaching out to fresh sources of popular support among the artisans, it came face to face with the fact that its potential constituency was arbitrarily bisected by the £10 qualification. It could neither satisfy its radical supporters nor hope to mobilize its full potential support except by broadening the franchise. This was the test issue of the sincerity of the parliamentary leaders, whose plaudits for 'the people' otherwise sounded very thin.

Gladstone was the leader who passed this test with flying colours, and thereby laid the foundation for nearly thirty years of political supremacy. As Palmerston's Chancellor of the Exchequer, Gladstone embarrassed the Whig premier in 1864 with a debating intervention that could not be retracted: 'And I venture to say that every man who is not presumably incapacitated by some consideration of personal unfitness or of political danger is morally entitled to come within the pale of the Constitution.' Now personal unfitness might exclude many men, and political danger conceivably more, and Gladstone might protest privately that his words were 'neither strange nor new nor extreme'. None of this affected the import of his declaration, seen clearly enough in the universal opinion in clubland that 'he had broken with the old Whigs and placed himself at the head of the movement party'. What struck home was Gladstone's claim, all the more characteristic for being unpremeditated, about 'morally entitled', which shifted the whole argument on to a new premise. With Palmerston's death in 1865, Reform became a practicable issue and Gladstone, by now the Liberal leader in waiting, became one of its sponsors.

During the debates on the franchise in 1866, Gladstone greeted the working men as 'our own flesh and blood'. In making this political judgement – on which his career hinged – he was following his own star and found himself working with the grain of social change. If the forces of popular radicalism were to function inside the system, what they needed was a charismatic leader with gilt-edged credentials in Westminster and Whitehall. In Gladstone they found what they were looking for. 'Swimming for his life, a man does not see much of the country through which the river winds,' he wrote in his diary in 1868. Yet he was surely right to back his hunch about a process which it has taken the skill and insight of modern social historians to make us comprehend properly.

If market forces proved a great engine for the generation of wealth during the process of industrialization, this wealth was very unevenly distributed. A gulf between rich and poor was immemorial, but such divisions became dynamic when driven by a more highly geared economic machine. Admittedly, we should be wary of regarding this model of mechanized industrialization as representative of mid-nineteenth-century Britain as a whole. Economic historians have demonstrated how slowly the new technologies became generally diffused outside the industrial heartland of Lancashire and the West Riding of Yorkshire. The use of steam power in great factories, with their vast proletarian workforce, remained peculiarly characteristic of the Lancashire cotton industry well into the Victorian period. But it was this picture which made an indelible impression on Frederick Engels when he lived and worked in Manchester, and it was his friend Karl Marx who made the claim:

Forces of production and social relations – two different sides of the development of the social individual – appear to capital as mere means, and are merely means for it to produce on its limited foundation. In fact, however, they are the material conditions to blow this foundation sky high.

The viability of the new industrial society depended on whether class relations were characterized by antagonism or accommodation. In the 1830s and 1840s class conflict had stood out as the keynote, with widespread involvement of labouring men in movements of radical protest. In particular, Chartism expressed a popular demand for the vote which was seen as the lever with which to topple an exploitative governing class, whether aristocratic or bourgeois. Yet increasingly from the middle of the century the perspective of class harmony became conventional and its rhetoric persuasive. An article in the first number of the *Cotton Factory Times*, the Lancashire operatives' newspaper, put it in these terms in 1885:

I can look back to a time when the relationship that existed betwixt employer and employed was not such as we find it now ... Fifty years ago the outlook was dark and uncertain ... A gulf has been bridged over wide as the poet's dream of chaos; and the knitting together of units, that now form a strong brotherhood, has been one of the results.

In the same year, a reunion of Chartist veterans – some of them intransigent 'physical force' men in their day – took place in a Halifax temperance hotel. Their speeches were now full of self-congratulation on forty years of progress and their dinner ended with a vote of thanks 'to Mr Gladstone and his government for passing into law those principles which we have endeavoured during a long life to enjoy'. Whatever had happened? Various answers are possible, depending on whether the question is formulated in terms of the success of the Gladstonian style of politics within Victorian society or in terms of the failure of the working class to act as the executors of Marx's prophecy by blowing the foundations sky high.

The emphasis on failure has been characteristic of a tradition in labour history which insisted that working-class consciousness and organization 'ought' to have taken a prescribed form. Yet though in nineteenth-century Lancashire we see the data on which the Marxian analysis was based, we also see a social structure which displayed an evolutionary resilience which confounded its supposed revolutionary destiny. It now seems clear that Lancashire cotton workers settled down within a social system marked by stability, harmony, deference and paternalism, rather than by class conflict. The operatives sensed that industrial capitalism was there to stay and had to be lived with. Their outlook was rooted in the experience of factory work, and there is no need for an idyllic rendering of its paternalist aspects. Inequality and subordination were of the essence, but it was the internalization of authority by the working class which made the relationship work without resort to coercion. One can point to a conscious effort at manipulation from above after about 1850. But the process was instinctive and piecemeal, making an accommodation with laissez-faire and the ethos of self-help, with plenty of give and take. The growth of trade unions in the cotton industry did not mark an intensification of the class war so much as an institutionalization of class feelings within a framework of industrial conciliation. The co-operative movement was given a viable commercial form through the work of the Rochdale pioneers – a hard-headed compromise between the ethic of communitarianism and that of the corner shop.

Religion may often have been the inspiration of the new paternalism, and stewardship its language, but its economic functions can hardly be ignored – it was a paying proposition. Employers thus succeeded in focusing loyalty on themselves, their families, and their factories, using philanthropy and patronage, outings and picnics, parades and festivals as the means. The stability of the factory neighbourhood, reinforced by company-owned housing, made for a tight-knit sense of community. Denominational allegiance, moreover, was often a further tie between bosses and operatives, either through conscious choice by employers, or prudent calculation by employees, or maybe some more complex chemistry of affinity and conformity. All told, such openings for leadership by an enlightened élite indicated not only social realities but also pregnant political possibilities.

If this was the picture in Lancashire, the world's first industrial society, it is not likely that working men elsewhere stood in the vanguard of radical change. The problem of their apparent docility has been approached in another way. Here the concept of 'the labour aristocracy' has been invoked to explain the differentiation of a privileged section of manual workers, and hence to explain away the lack of class-consciousness among the proletariat as a whole. Capitalism, on this reading, was able to buy off the potential leaders of the working class, whose subsequent conservatism played an indispensable role in sustaining the status quo. In this form the argument has several weaknesses, which have been so incisively exposed in recent years that it is tempting to conclude flatly that there never existed a labour aristocracy capable of playing the mighty historical role assigned to it. Other social historians, however, have succeeded in developing and refining – and thus rescuing – the concept, by setting it to work on a useful but less heroic task of interpretation.

Especially in the engineering industry, the labour aristocrats can be found alive and well, as can be seen in the distinctive life-style of the skilled men, both in the workplace and outside. They emerge as men with a pride in their craft, cliquish in protecting their skill at work, and often unsympathetic to the unskilled labourers with whom they were in closest contact. They were, however, strong trade unionists, ready to fight for the due reward of their own skill, and their ethos was no simple capitulation to bourgeois values or emulation of upward social mobility. The respectability which the artisans wanted was to be achieved within their existing way of life, not by stepping out of it. Admittedly, this sort of status gratification had the function of allowing labour aristocrats to come to terms with structural inequalities in society at large. But their ideology, combining thrift and temperance and collective self-help, was of their own making; it was not an imposition from above as social control. In short, they

18

were respectable radicals. If their respectability set them apart from the 'rough' working class, so their articulate political radicalism distinguished them from the apathetic or deferential labourers. What the artisans yearned for was recognition of their aspirations as moral citizens.

These perspectives are surely convergent. The mid-nineteenth-century working class did not 'fail' to become revolutionary; instead it succeeded in making its own culture and its own politics, with its own heroes, including Gladstone. We need to make an imaginative effort to reconstitute the experience of ordinary people from within, in its own terms, as it was lived out in a unique historical situation, rather than resort to the tired stereotypes of 'class'. The fact is that there are some striking continuities in the popular radical tradition, with its emphasis upon the political roots of evil and misery, and its plea for the regeneration of a corrupt constitution by drawing upon the virtues of 'the people'. The co-operator William Thompson encapsulated this tradition in the 1840s with his denunciation of 'the feudal and theological systems, the systems of force and fraud'. For it was this well-worn Hobbesian language of 'force and fraud' which had long summed up the critique of what radicals called 'old corruption'. Nowadays we would naturally call it the Establishment, whether in church or state: an interlocking power élite with fingers in every pie worth fingering. This radical critique was extended in the nineteenth century to the unholy coalescence between a traditional landed aristocracy and a new commercial aristocracy, equally parasitic in nature. The essence of populism is to challenge 'establishment' values by appealing instead to the good sense and right thinking of ordinary people. Such perspectives indicate links between Chartism and Gladstonian Liberalism – and, in due course, the early Labour Party – in a way which the conventional terminology of 'class' may sometimes obscure. We need to pay attention to the way such terms were used at the time.

In 1839 John Stuart Mill was ready to maintain that 'the

19

motto of a radical politician should be government by means of the middle for the working classes'. This might be thought a safe enough strategy, since it left political decisions in the right hands and avoided the risks of democracy. We should not, however, be misled by Richard Cobden's statement of 1849, that his object was to 'place as much political power as he could in the hands of the middle and industrious classes', into supposing that he regarded the two as synonymous. For Cobden was not using two synonyms for the middle class but rather describing two classes. When mid-Victorian radicals used the term industrious classes they were trying to accommodate skilled industrial workers, in particular, within their concept of 'the people'. Presumably the industrious classes might, like the subsequent working class, be held to have 'belied their name', but Cobden's hopes of them are hardly in doubt.

The campaign which he and John Bright had led to repeal the Corn Laws apparently achieved its specific object in 1846. Cobden well recognized that the Anti-Corn Law League, the vanguard party of the Manchester bourgeoisie, represented one élite pitted against another – as one of his supporters put it, 'the owner of ten thousand spindles confronted the lord of ten thousand acres'. But the League's class character constrained its radicalism on broader issues so that Cobden's more ambitious strategy of an attack on what he liked to call feudalism soon faltered. In the aftermath of repeal, therefore, Cobden began looking to a wider electorate than that enfranchised in 1832 to force the pace of progress – albeit looking with his customary lack of sentimentality. 'The extension of the franchise must and will come,' he confided to Bright in 1851, 'but it chills my enthusiasm upon the subject when I see so much popular error and prejudice prevailing upon such questions as the Colonies, religious freedom and the land customs of our country.' If Cobden was the Marx of the middle classes, he too needed to brace himself against constant disillusionment.

It would be naïve to discount entirely the influence of economic conditions, which, in the long mid-nineteenth-century boom, generated an atmosphere favourable to class conciliation. Average real wages in the mid-1860s stood 20 per cent higher than a decade previously. Working-class institutions like trade unions and co-operative societies offered Liberals reassurance about the kind of self-improvement that had taken place and that could, therefore, be expected to underpin future experiments in citizenship. It was in this context that Gladstone took his own leap in the dark. 'Please to recollect,' he explained to one of his aristocratic associates, 'that we have got to govern millions of hard hands; that it must be done by force, fraud or good will; that the latter has been tried and is answering ...' If force and fraud, by the 1860s, had had their day, the Gladstonian strategy of good will (tempered with fraud, so critics have always alleged) would have to bear the brunt.

'Rochdale,' Gladstone declared, ' has probably done more than any other town in making good to practical minds a case for some enfranchisement of the working classes.' At the time he was arguing for lowering the franchise qualification from £10 to £7, which would prudently incorporate the Liberal artisan while leaving 'the residuum' outside the pale of the constitution. But in fact a Dutch auction between the parties in 1866–7 meant that the Second Reform Act gave the vote to all householders in the boroughs. This was not a fully democratic franchise – it notably excluded women and also young men living in the parental home – but household suffrage inaugurated mass politics in Britain. The political parties now had to project their appeal beyond Westminster.

In seeking to do this, of course, Gladstone could look to the example of popular tribunes like Cobden and Bright; great meetings in the open air had been a common feature of the Chartist agitation; but Gladstone in his own person united two traditions of politics when he stepped out of the cosy conventions of Westminster to go on the stump. Though his syntax remained labyrinthine, with ambiguous sub-clauses qualifying almost every statement, it was Gladstone's charismatic force and presence which won the day – and the hearts of his audience. Strong and vigorous, endowed by nature with not only a commanding eye but also a loud voice, he took to this new style of oratory like a duck to water – literally so on one famous occasion when he held 10,000 men spellbound on Blackheath in the pouring rain. Truly can it be said that Gladstone brought the whole of the Liberal Party under his mighty umbrella. He alone could, without self-consciousness or incongruity, hob-nob with the old Whig families and sing evangelical hymns with Nonconformist deputations. He alone was a hero simultaneously to Treasury mandarins for displaying an unparalleled grasp of financial principle, and to trade unionists for showing that 'An Honest Man's the Noblest Work of God'.

Liberalism can be seen as an optimistic creed. This is true of party political Liberalism, with a big 'L', but even more of doctrinal liberalism, with a small 'l'. 'Most of the great positive evils of the world,' John Stuart Mill asserted in 1863, 'are in themselves removable, and will, if human affairs continue to improve, be in the end reduced to within narrow limits.' The positive side of the Liberal ideal was to invoke self-help and the voluntary principle as the true means of promoting progress. This in turn meant leaving a great deal to individual responsibility and judgement, for good or ill. Newman put the objection to a philosophical liberal position here with some precision: 'Liberalism is the mistake of supposing that there is a right of private judgement, that is, that there is no existing authority on earth competent to interfere with the liberty of individuals in reasoning and judging for themselves.'

The alternative conception was stated unequivocally, and equally abstractly, by John Morley, who singularly exem-plified fidelity to all three persons in the Liberal trinity: Cobden, Gladstone and Mill. Liberalism, according to Morley, 'stands for the subjection to human judgement of all claims of external authority, whether in an organized Church, or in more loosely gathered societies of believers or in books held sacred'. The free-thinking tone of such a claim must have been rather jarring on the ears of those Nonconformists who were commonly dubbed the backbone of the Liberal Party. To some extent mutual anti-clericalism helped paper over this crack, as did a common emphasis upon conscience. But the liberal synthesis was less doctrinally consistent than Liberals (with a big 'L') liked to suppose. There was always some tension between the overriding force of Gladstonian moral imperatives and the ordinary Liberal belief in trimming back the functions of the state.

The doctrine of voluntaryism sometimes consorted uneasily with the politics of conscience. The philosopher T.H. Green attempted to resolve this dilemma in a way which he found philosophically compelling and which we may find psychologically revealing. 'When we speak of freedom,' the argument went, 'we do not mean merely freedom to do as we like irrespective of what it is we like. We mean the greatest freedom on the part of the citizens as a body to make the most and best of themselves.' Green had reached this view by 1881 in a public lecture on 'Liberal legislation and freedom of contract'. The opportunities for state intervention which this doctrine suggests were to give Green a posthumous reputation, still repeated in some quarters, for fathering a collectivist approach towards a Welfare State, although these implications were really fathered upon Green, and he himself had never meant to move so far. But that he was moving away from any tolerably strict definition of voluntaryism is surely evident. In 1873 he had declared that 'the drink curse is altogether too big a thing to be dealt with by individual effort alone'. In this field at least, higher claims than mere liberty had to be asserted, albeit by the citizens as a body. There survives a splendid vignette, dating from the following year, of Green in conversation with a friend, dwelling 'with great disappointment on the use made by the workmen of their half holiday and shorter hours. He even said that he thought it was better that they should not have a half holiday, but should be kept constantly at their work so that they should not have time to drink.' This too might be called a compelling suggestion.

What really united Gladstone and his followers was not a

narrowly defined doctrinal conformity but an irrepressible temperamental activism which infused their common creed. He himself observed in 1877: 'The vital principle of the Liberal Party, like that of Greek art, is *action*.' Though the party came to be denounced as a 'machine' controlled by 'wirepullers', its nature was essentially otherwise. It was an animal whose pedigree lay in the extra-parliamentary agitations for reform which had played a crucial part in politicizing Victorian Britain. These pressure groups, each exhibiting a relentless concentration on a single issue, were dismissed as 'faddists'. But they succeeded in leaving an enduring mark upon the style of Liberal politics, even while failing to achieve so many of their declared objectives. The fact is that conscience is an explosively unstable ingredient in politics. Irreconcilable claims made in the name of conscience constantly threatened to blow the Liberal Party asunder, yet the politics of conscience also proved to be the means of uniting it.

The struggle for the repeal of the Corn Laws was the paradigm for all subsequent pressure-group activities. It was emulated by the Liberation Society, with its aim of disestablishing the Church of England, and by the United Kingdom Alliance, intent on stifling the drink trade, as well as by labour and Irish organizations, committed to their own sectional ends. The Anti-Corn Law League had everything to commend it, especially when seen in retrospect – efficiency, money, moral enthusiasm, a leader of genius, a well-argued case and, above all, success at the end of the road. The myth of the League's efficacy in fact depended on the ambiguous ending to its campaign of electoral intervention. But its activities had transmitted the thrill of power to those who participated, as Cobden shrewdly appreciated. 'I hardly know what to suggest but shall merely offer my opinion of the necessity of *doing something*', he had written at one juncture.

All pressure groups relied on the self-sustaining effect of their own efforts for the cause to keep up momentum and morale. The minority of zealots at least convinced themselves that their fervour weighed heavier than mere numbers. One temperance man reflected in 1898: 'When the others are smoking and drinking in public-houses and clubs the tee-totallers are hard at work canvassing and winning the election.' But the faddists faced an inescapable dilemma. Part of their difficulty was that each group was built around a single issue, yet members were seldom single-minded in pursuing it. Membership overlapped, suggesting the pull of this *kind* of commitment upon the activists. Accused of being 'men of one idea', they had to admit that 'in truth we have too many'. Even when denied satisfaction from the Liberals on one allegedly overriding issue of principle, they usually found other pressing reasons for voting Liberal regardless. 'Our misfortune,' commented an agent for the United Kingdom Alliance, in 1874, 'is that the majority of our friends are such ardent Liberals that temperance politics must bend to circumstances.'

The more ruthless electoral strategies had to be abandoned because the faddists were not in practice ready to risk helping the Tories, who emerged ever more clearly as their real enemies. As one Nonconformist put it in 1872: 'We regard the Liberal party as represented by Mr Gladstone to be squee-zeable, and capable of being "educated" up to our views.' So it was always a question of trying to bring the Liberal can-didate up to the mark rather than exercising a truly inde-pendent influence. What did they get for their pains? As it turned out, the repeal of the Corn Laws was an unrepeatable coup for these methods of agitation. The Nonconformists never put their stamp upon the educational system, the Church of England remained obdurately established, and the pubs stayed open. Well before the end of the nineteenth century, all these great causes had become more or less enme-shed within Gladstonian Liberalism, with which they showed irresistible affinities. So the integration of the faddists into the Liberal Party seemed inescapable. They had nowhere else to go. Moreover, Liberalism needed their energies. The result was to give Nonconformist and temperance demands a new status within the Liberal programme – but to make these demands subservient to the party's general scheme of priorities.

'In the great business of unwinding the coil of life & establishing my freedom,' Gladstone wrote in his diary on 29 December 1875, 'I have made some progress by resigning the leadership, selling my house (needful for pecuniary reasons) and declining public occasions.' It was his sixty-sixth birthday; he had been in public life for over forty years; he had remoulded the Treasury as Chancellor of the Exchequer; he had become the leader of a fully-unified Liberal Party, which had denied the Conservatives a parliamentary majority for nearly thirty years; he had served as Prime Minister for a full Parliament (1868–74), during which Liberal legislation hallmarked the establishment of the mid-Victorian consensus. The extension of the franchise to an important section of the working class and the recognition of the legitimacy of working-class organizations, the dissolution of the claims of a confessional state and the achievement of religious equality, the entrenchment of Free Trade and of a minimalist approach to the role of government, were salient features of this consensus, and almost every aspect of it was linked with the name of Gladstone. Never did a political leader have better reason to look forward to a well-earned retirement – so much so, in fact, that he went on looking forward to it for much of the next twenty years.

By the time of his next birthday, the eirenic tableau of the return to the plough – or axe in Gladstone's case – was already falling apart. 'My desire for the shade, a true and earnest desire has been since August rudely baffled: retirement & recollection seem more remote than ever,' he admitted at the end of 1876. What had happened in August, of course, was the composition (initially in bed during an attack of lumbago) of his pamphlet *The Bulgarian Horrors and the Question of the East*. Once seized of the iniquity of the treatment of the Christian population of Bulgaria by their Turkish oppressors, Gladstone was unstoppable, lumbago or no lumbago, retirement or no retirement, recollection or no recollection. 'Future Retribution. *From this I was called away to write on Bulgaria,'* was the docket found on a bundle of Gladstone's papers.

'Politics are at once a game and a high art,' Gladstone once wrote. His genius lay in his ability to impose order by successfully asserting the primacy of great national issues which at once restored the Liberal Party's unity and reinforced his own authority. He was not unmindful of the fact that the different sections of the party had first come together in 1859, not on any mundane domestic issue, but in high-minded support of the Italian nationalists in their struggle against their Habsburg rulers. Nor was he unconscious of his own strategic political instinct, as an autobiographical note, written after his retirement, sufficiently demonstrates. Though modestly doubting 'that Providence has endowed me with anything which can be called a striking gift', he in fact went on to claim 'an insight into the facts of particular eras, and their relations one to another, which generates in the mind a conviction that the materials exist for forming a public opinion, and for directing it to a particular end'. The first example he gave was the renewal of the income tax in 1853, when he was Chancellor of the Exchequer. (This fastened responsibility for the restraint of state expenditure within moral peacetime limits directly upon the citizen as taxpayer.) A second was the cry for the disestablishment of the Irish Church, with which the establishment of his own leadership of the Liberal Party was accomplished in the 1868 General Election. Inevitably, the crusade for Irish Home Rule, which he proclaimed in 1886, splitting his party in the process, was another example. Finally, the strategy for an attack upon the House of Lords in 1894, in which he was thwarted by his Cabinet colleagues, completed the list.

The Bulgarian campaign is a notable omission, yet it became the most distinctive of all Gladstone's dominating causes. What was it all about? World-weary Whigs and Tories, versed in the old diplomacy, were disdainful about efforts to link the periodic maltreatment of the subject nationalities of the Ottoman Empire with the fitful lapses of the great British public into bouts of moral indignation. Gladstone himself waited until journalists like W.T. Stead had primed public opinion. He was thus slow to rise to the occasion, or to snatch his opportunity (whichever gloss one prefers to put on it). Once risen, however, this was undoubtedly the big occasion, the big snatch. Lord Granville and Lord Hartington, to whom Gladstone had consigned the awkward job of running the Liberal Party, found themselves on the sidelines. 'I acted under a strong sense of individual duty without a thought of leadership,' Gladstone recalled in old age; 'nevertheless it made me leader again whether I would or no.'

Gladstone's politics of conscience swept over the heads of the Whig leaders to make an irresistible appeal to the Liberal rank and file. He made their repressed, chapel-going flesh creep with stories of atrocities against their fellow-Christians in exotic places, beside which the artisans' own immediate trade-union grievances about jobs and prices seemed like the small change of agitation. The Nonconformists suddenly found a bigger bee in their bonnets than disestablishment; the temperance faddists discovered the difference between the small beer of prohibition and the heady wine of Gladstone's oratory. He sadly concurred with them in observing that Lord Beaconsfield and his Tory Government were unmoved to intervene; he invited them to draw their own conclusions; he accepted the Queen's reluctant commission to form another Government in 1880.

Gladstone's keen speculative interest in electoral sociology helped him to unearth encouraging precedents for the fact that the humble and meek made the warmest response to the appeal he articulated. 'Did Scribes and Pharisees or did shepherds and fishermen yield the first, most and readiest converts to our Saviour and the company of his Apostles?' he demanded pointedly. Gladstone pitched his claims high, in a way that his critics have never been able to stomach. 'What about your Gladstone?' Clemenceau asked during one of the longueurs of the Versailles Conference. 'What sort of man was he?' 'He was a very great man,' Lloyd George replied, to which the Conservative leader Bonar Law added, 'He was a very great humbug.' Is it so simple?

In 1876 Gladstone himself justified his emergence on the grounds that it was 'in a noble cause, for the curtain rising in the East seems to open events that bear cardinally on our race'. A year later he considered that 'the part assigned to me in the Eastern question has been a part great and good far beyond my measure'. By December 1878 the case was even more compelling. He realized now that the past three years, 'instead of unbinding and detaching me, have fetched me back from the larger room which I had laboriously reached'. But he could also detect 'the marks of the will of God' in the way that this had happened.

For when have I seen so strongly the relation between my public duties and the primary purposes for which God made and Christ redeemed the world? Seen it to be not real only but so close and immediate that the lines of the holy and the unholy were drawn as in fire before my eyes. And why has my health, my strength, been so peculiarly sustained? All this year and more – I think – I have not been confined to bed for a single day. In the great physical and mental effort of speaking, often to large auditories, I have been as it were upheld in an unusual manner and the free effectiveness of voice has been given me to my own astonishment. Was not all this for a purpose: & has it not all come in connection with a process to which I have given myself under clear but most reluctant associations. Most reluctant: for God knoweth how true it is that my heart's desire has been for that rest from conflict & from turmoil which seems almost a necessity for a soul that would be prepared in time to meet its God for eternity.

What would Bonar Law have made of such a passage? He might have said drily that Gladstone was not alone in sensing something pretty peculiar about the whole business. Twentieth-century medical science would not seek supernatural explanations for the reinvigorating physical effects of wholesome activity upon a basically healthy man in his late sixties; nor for the self-sustaining improvement in morale which attended the successful accomplishment of self-assigned tasks, with a gratifying degree of public acclaim. It was Lord Moran, as Churchill's doctor, who took the view that the best therapy for his elderly patient, in making a plucky recuperation from the odd stroke here or there, was to continue as prime minister. 'I was in body much much below par,' Gladstone noted of one oration, 'but put on the steam perforce.' He then spoke for two and a half hours, showing them all that the old man was not finished yet, not by a long chalk, even if he grimly noted: 'It ought to have been *far* better.' Longer too? But perhaps this was an occasion when he was upheld in an insufficiently unusual manner, when the effectiveness of voice given to him fell somewhat short of the freedom which would have enabled him to astonish himself once more. Even by his own exacting standards, however, Gladstone's activities were a remarkable example of what could be achieved by a man whose fixity of purpose liberated him from the stress and tension of ordinary political concerns and enabled him to forge ahead, sustained by a single-minded conviction of his own rectitude. To ask whether he was really prompted by Providence or simply fuelled by adrenalin is in a sense irrelevant.

On 24 November 1879 he set off for Midlothian, the new constituency which he had decided to contest and with which his name was henceforth memorably linked. In the course of the next two weeks he delivered thirty speeches as well as short addresses to the crowds who besieged him at the railway stations along the line of his pilgrimage. By his own reckoning, he had audiences totalling 86,930. The cult of Gladstone had already reached new heights when charabanc parties of pilgrims to his Flintshire country house watched him felling trees on his estate and collected the chips as souvenirs. But whole forests must have been felled to supply newsprint to the provincial press which devoted column upon column to verbatim reports of his speeches, especially during his successive whistle-stop campaigns.

If the Midlothian campaign was functionally equivalent to our own beloved photo-opportunities as contrived media events, it was a cut above them in intellectual content. Several dozen cuts, in fact, for Gladstone's distinctive ability surely lay in harnessing charismatic force to the development of a rationalistic appeal to the electorate. By articulating the discussion of great national issues in this way, Gladstone made a reality of the Liberal conception of active citizenship, making a direct personal assault upon the emotions of his immediate constituents and an indirect dialectical claim upon the judgement of his wider constituency throughout the country. Little wonder that he wrote at the end of 1879 that for the past three and a half years he had been 'passing through a political experience which is I believe without example in our Parliamentary history'. He considered that 'the battle to be fought was a battle of justice, humanity, freedom, law, all in their first elements from the very root, and all on a gigantic scale. The word spoken was a word for millions, and for millions who cannot themselves speak. If I really believe this then I should regard my having been morally forced into this work as a great and high election of God.'

Gladstone wrote to a colleague at the beginning of the Bulgarian campaign: 'Good ends can rarely be attained in politics without passion: and there is now, the first time for a good many years, a virtuous passion.' Not for Gladstone a Liberalism derived from cool libertarian logic! His appeal was to temperaments capable of excitement by virtuous passion, especially to what became known as 'the Nonconformist Conscience'. Here was no cynical exercise in manipulation; Gladstone's conviction in the unassailable rectitude of his position burnt as strongly as that of his most earnest admirers. He was constantly alert, in his reading of scripture, in case 'another of those minute but striking Providential adjustments which I have often had to remark' should lie encoded in the psalm for the day. He harboured no doubt that God 'takes sides in that conflict between virtue and vice, which incessantly prevails in the world'. There was plentiful evidence for the Fabians' later complaint against Gladstonianism that 'a Liberal reform is never simply a social means to a social end, but a campaign of Good against Evil'. Despite his tortured circumlocutions, what Gladstone conveyed was a blinkered simplicity of vision about politics, tinctured with a distinctive moral authoritarianism. As a young boy, so it is recorded, W.T. Stead exclaimed: 'I wish that God would give me a big whip that I could go round the world and whip the wicked out of it.' His future career as a Gladstonian journalist was already ordained.

Gladstone did not simply return to the leadership: he assumed it provisionally and on special terms – his own. He continued from year to year, staying only so long as there remained great national causes to settle which not only justified but demanded his continuation. Hence he refused to act as a party leader in the ordinary sense, choosing almost arbitrarily which responsibilities to exercise and which to saddle upon others. He maintained his formidable reading and devoted a remarkable amount of time to his own literary productions. In effect, it was a compromise. Gladstone agreed to go back to Downing Street in 1880 so long as it was only part-time and temporary and with the dirty work foisted on to others. Yet the arrangement was even more peculiar since, on this basis, he served simultaneously until past the age of seventy-two as not only Prime Minister but also Leader of the House of Commons and Chancellor of the Exchequer. If he played God in his own Government, Gladstone was licensed by his sense of calling. He became the prophet as statesman: the Ayatollah of Victorian Christianity.

Gladstone's vision of politics is interesting in itself; but it becomes so significant in understanding Victorian Britain when we link it with the popular support which he managed to mobilize behind his great causes. His moral populism stands as both the key to his political effectiveness and the great paradox of his career. When John Ruskin visited the Gladstone country house, Hawarden Castle, in October 1878, its master declared: 'I am a firm believer in the aristocratic principle – the rule of the best. I am an out-and-out inequalitarian.' This was the landed gentleman who had been left by his father, bloated on the profits of Liverpool's investment in slavery, a distinctly wealthy man. It was also the churchman whose peculiar and intense religious views had found expression through the Oxford Movement.

Like Newman, Gladstone fastened upon the great text of St Augustine, *Securus judicat orbis terrarum*. Here was a standard of judgement which suggested that the settled verdict of the whole world must prevail. It suggested, 'not that, for the moment, the multitude may not falter in their judgement', as Newman put it in his *Apologia Pro Vita Sua*, but, in his own case, 'that the deliberate judgement, in which the whole Church at length rests and acquiesces, is an infallible pre-scription and a final sentence against such portions of it as protest and secede'. Newman acted on this precept, renounced Anglicanism, joined the Church of Rome, and ended his days as a cardinal. Not so Gladstone; yet his life too demands its apologia. For when Gladstone abandoned the high doctrines of his youth about the necessity for the state to be moralized by an institutional connection with a catholic church, he not only set about 'demoralizing' the state but looked beyond the Establishment for a source of moral unity. Augustine's precept became the basis for an appeal to the Concert of Europe as a secular proxy for the authority of the universal church. Gladstone thus appealed to 'the general judgement of civilized mankind' at the time of the Franco-Prussian War in 1870: 'It has censured the aggression of France; it will censure, if need arise, the greed of Germany. *Securus judicat orbis terrarum*'. Little wonder that he reached for the text again in 1877.

So far, so abstruse. Gladstone's ability to clothe his own recondite reasoning in language which made a clear, straight-forward demotic appeal was what transformed the situation. Moreover, he needed to make such an appeal because, among 'the classes', who might be expected to know their Augustine, 'the hardening crust of egotism and selfishness' had impaired 'the capacity of right judgement in large and most important questions'. Worst of all, a new social group – 'the class of hybrid or bastard men' – had arisen: hard-faced men scattered throughout all classes, united by 'the bond of gain' and deaf to social compunction. Disillusioned with the educated classes, let alone these unspeakable yuppies, Gladstone maintained that 'in judging the great questions of policy which appeal to the primal truths and laws of our nature, those classes may excel who, if they lack the opportunities, yet escape the subtle perils of the wealthy state'. Hence the tenor of the Midlothian campaign; hence too the comment of *The Times* that politics were now 'at the mercy of excitement, of rhetoric, of the qualities which appeal to a mob'.

The development of a distinctively Gladstonian style of politics from this point onward was self-consistent and self-reinforcing. The charge against Gladstone was that he relentlessly 'Bulgarianized' everything he took up. He saw little alternative once the class from which he had sprung steadfastly turned their backs on him. By 1885 he naturally identified 'class-preference' as 'the central point of what I call the lower & what is the now prevalent Toryism'. He thought that his opponents were 'warped by the spirit of class, but that few comparatively are aware of it', leading him to wonder if he might be 'warped by the spirit of anti-class' in the same unconscious way. 'My dislike of the class feeling gets slowly more & more accentuated,' he concluded, '& my case is particularly hard & irksome, because I am a thoroughgoing inequalitarian.'

Gladstone wrote this in May 1886, when a section of his own party had already broken with him over his proposal for Irish Home Rule. In the following month, on 28 June, the Grand Old Man entered Liverpool – '7 or 8 miles of processional uproar, and a speech of 1h. 40 min. to 5000 or 6000 people in Hengler's Circus . . . Once more my voice held out in a marvellous manner. "I went in bitterness, in the heat of my spirit: but the hand of the Lord was strong upon me."' He told his audience that 'it cannot be pretended that we are supported by the dukes, or by the squires, or by the Established clergy, or by the officers of the army, or by a number of other bodies of very respectable people'. Not just the landed interest, or even the bastard men, were against him now, but the professional classes too (though Gladstone offered a partial exemption of lawyers and doctors). His question, 'Are the classes ever right when they differ from the nation?', was met with cries of 'No'. 'Well, wait a moment,' Gladstone counselled. 'I draw this distinction. I am not about to assert that the masses of the people, who do not and cannot give their leisure to politics, are necessarily, on all subjects, better judges than the leisured men and the instructed men who have great advantages for forming political judgements that the others have not.' But this characteristically Gladstonian qualification heightened rather than impaired the force of his ringing declaration 'that upon one great class of subjects, the largest and most weighty of them all, where the leading and determining considerations that ought to lead to conclusion are truth, justice, and humanity, there, gentlemen, all the world over, I will back the masses against the classes.'

Gladstone's tentative essays in democracy in the 1860s received a new impetus with the Bulgarian agitation of the late 1870s. When the Establishment, from which he had sprung, showed itself impervious to Gladstone's appeals, he readily attributed this, in authentic radical style, to the fact that the Church of England was chained to secular corruption and high society choked with plutocratic gains. It had become clear to him by 1877 that 'the popular judgement, on a certain number of important questions, is more just than that of the higher order'. Gladstone could still, at this point, generally count on the support of those liberal intellectuals who, under the patronage of Mill, had made out the case for reform in the 1860s. Morley spoke for them when he claimed that, in future, 'the contest will lie between brains and numbers on the one side, and wealth, rank, vested interest, possession in short, on the other'. But whereas the intelligentsia, on the whole, exhibited the requisite virtuous passion over Bulgaria, when it came to Irish Home Rule in 1886 many of them fell by the wayside.

An oppressed nation rightly struggling to be free was one thing when it was to be found within the Habsburg Empire or the Ottoman Empire; but Gladstone's imaginative leap of sympathy in discovering, within the British Empire, 'a broad and black blot upon its history' was a tough demand on tender consciences which had bled for the Italians or the Bulgarians.

When he made his appeal 'to stand by the traditions of which we are the heirs in all matters except our relations with Ireland, and to make our relation with Ireland to conform to the other traditions of our country', he met with sudden incomprehension even among the educated classes. If there was now a division between brains and numbers, it was within the Liberal Party itself, when prominent academic liberals as well as Whigs defected to the Unionist cause. 'Never in the history of England was there such a consensus of intellect arrayed against statesmen as is now arrayed against Mr Gladstone,' wrote one apostate. Yet Gladstone's response – marking, perhaps, the primacy of a religious rather than a strictly intellectual sensibility – was a still more dogmatic asseveration of his populist convictions.

Gladstone saw himself as a statesman whose own conservative instincts were thwarted by a failure of intelligence and will on the part of the ostensibly Conservative Party. As he told the Duke of Argyll in September 1885, 'my first & great cause of anxiety is, believe me, the condition of the Tory party'. Adventurers like Lord Randolph Churchill were more pernicious in their influence than Radicals like Joseph Chamberlain. He mentioned these points, he told the Duke, '1. because out of such a Conservative party you will never get Conservative work, & specially 2. because these are the men who play directly into the hands of the extreme wing of Liberalism.' It aided 'the leaning of both parties to Socialism which I radically disapprove'. There is no reason to doubt him when, speaking of the leadership of the Liberal Party by Liberal Lords, he said: 'I keenly desire the continuance of this feature.' As it turned out, however, Gladstone had to strive for his higher conservatism by himself outflanking the Radicals.

Gladstone appreciated that 'the Liberal party as a rule draws its vital breath from great Liberal measures'. The settlement of the franchise in 1884–5, by extending the borough system of household suffrage to the counties too, fulfilled this claim. But, unlike the string of legislative triumphs in the first

Gladstone Government, the Reform Act was an isolated success in his second Government. Part of the trouble was that in the 1880s many of the social and economic measures proposed by his enthusiastic supporters were not such as he could support, least of all as a Prime Minister living on borrowed time.

At the end of 1881, it is true, Gladstone wrote that he had 'never closed a year more abounding in signs of what is termed prosperity'. Twelve months later, however, it was a different story: 'Another year of mercy and forbearance. Why encumbreth it the ground.' On the last day of 1883 there was a remarkable outpouring. 'My position is a strange one,' he wrote. 'A strong man in me wrestles for retirement: a stronger one stands at the gate of exit, and forbids. Forbids, I hope only for a time.' This was a delicately poised equilibrium, held steady through powerful countervailing pressures. Whereas Gladstone talked of 'the prolongations of cares & burdens so much beyond my strength at any age, and at this age so cruelly exclusive of the great work of penitential recollection', he also acknowledged that 'my political or public life is the best part of my life: it is that part in which I am conscious of the greatest effort to do and to avoid as the Lord Christ would have me do and avoid.' None of which made him a more amenable colleague. Poor Hartington! Poor Chamberlain! After six years of this regime, with the Prime Minister beginning a third term, both of them, each for his own reasons, decided that enough was enough.

Irish Home Rule thus became the last crusade. In June 1885 Gladstone's second Government disintegrated in a manner to which the Liberal Party was inured. No one saw it as a tragedy, least of all the Prime Minister. 'At 11.45 cleared out of my official room & had a moment to fall down and give thanks for the labours done & the strength vouchsafed me there: and to pray for the Christlike mind.' There is nothing here to support the idea that he was distraught at leaving office, or desperate to return at any price. Why, then, in the following year, did he bring down Salisbury's Conservative Government and bring forward his own Home Rule Bill, with the support of the Irish Nationalists under Parnell? The question-begging answer seems to be: because Salisbury refused to carry Home Rule as a consensual measure with the support of the Gladstonian opposition.

Perhaps Gladstone, who had learnt his trade in Peel's Cabinet in the 1840s, was being old-fashioned in entertaining such a notion. It is abundantly clear from his diary, corroborated by associated documents, that Gladstone was moving step by step towards a Home Rule scheme throughout the latter months of 1885, more or less oblivious to immediate electoral considerations or parliamentary arithmetic. By November 1885, before the General Election, which left Parnell holding the balance of power, Gladstone drew up the heads of his own scheme – the moment of truth at which Home Rule became his settled policy. In his own mind, it all irresistibly made sense. He came to see Home Rule as 'a source not of danger but of strength – the danger, if any, lies in refusing it'. Hence it was, he assured Tennyson, 'in the highest sense Conservative'. Gladstone, however, had little difficulty in discerning why the Conservative Party came to oppose it. 'My sons and I cut two trees,' Gladstone recorded on 10 December 1885, and later: 'Read Burke.' Was it the great philosopher of true conservatism, with his metaphor of the British oak, who prompted Gladstone's further reflections? 'Toryism in other days had two legs to stand upon: a sound leg, and a lame leg. Its sound leg was Reverence: its lame leg was Class-interest. Reverence it has almost forgotten. It no longer leans upon that leg. It leans now upon its lame leg, the leg of Class interest, more and more.'

Fortified, uplifted, the old man resolved his hesitations into a typically dynamic strategy. He proceeded to give substance to the general maxim which he had offered his Chief Secretary for Ireland in 1882 'that the least danger is in going forward at once. It is liberty alone, which fits men for liberty.' When Gladstone presented his Home Rule Bill to the House of Commons, he said: 'This, if I understand it, is one of those golden moments of our history, one of those opportunities which may come and may go, but which rarely return, or, if they return, return at long intervals, and under circumstances which no man can forecast.' The Bill was rejected by 341 to 311, much to Queen Victoria's relief, with Hartington and Chamberlain leading a decisive number of Liberals into the lobby against it. Gladstone noted in his diary that 'it is a serious mischief. Spoke very long: my poor voice came in a wonderful manner.' Nearly fifty years later, Victoria's grandson, King George V, told Ramsay MacDonald: 'What fools we were not to have accepted Gladstone's Home Rule Bill.'

It was the magic of Gladstone's name, as much as the merits of the Home Rule Bill, which kept the mass of the Liberal Party loyal to him. His followers were henceforth identified as Gladstonian Liberals, their creed as Gladstonianism; he had incontrovertibly created a party in his own image. If Gladstone, rising eighty, could no longer without impertinence be called 'the People's William', he now became 'the Grand Old Man'. There was no stopping him, as he claimed special authority to go on and on as a leader, still infused with a sense of mission but now lacking, as it seemed even to loyal followers, a sense of proportion. One of them rebuked Gladstone's efforts to 'Bulgarianize' the Irish issue by noting: 'To the sane Englishman Mitchelstown is not Batak; the Irish constabulary are not Bashi-Bazouks, nor Irish magistrates Turkish pashas.' Even the faithful Morley wrote ironically to a colleague, imploring him to 'be kind enough to lock up a certain G.O.M., and to bring the key away in your pocket'. But Gladstone remained, year after year, master of his party, in the country as much as in the Cabinet, and its irreplaceable leader.

It was in many ways a democratic party in ethos and outlook, a fit repository for the old Chartist and radical aspirations which had fed into it; yet it reflected few of the immediate grievances of its working-class constituency. Its leaders, as one social reformer put it, failed to exhibit 'for the East End docker the enthusiasm which they have rightly developed for the Connemara cottier'. To a remarkable extent, though, the working-class cult of Gladstone persisted, with his image venerated through a popular iconography of mass-produced busts and portraits, commemorative mugs and plates. When Keir Hardie first stood as an independent Labour candidate in 1888, though running against the Liberal Party machine, he campaigned on the slogan 'A vote for Hardie is a vote for Gladstone'. The last phase of his career exhibited more strikingly than ever Gladstone's authentic streak of political radicalism.

Yet he remained simultaneously a social conservative, with an ambiguity which only his complex personality could encompass. 'He is, and always was, in everything except essentials, a tremendous Tory,' was the affectionate observation of a political opponent, Arthur Balfour. Though some of Gladstone's Whig critics came to regard him as a class traitor, he regarded them as selfish – or worse. After all, the outcome of his life's work had been to perpetuate the rule of a high-minded liberal aristocracy by founding it upon the secure basis of popular consent. He reproached the Whigs who left him in 1886 for their culpable blindness to the consequences for social stability of a reactionary policy. Morley saw more deeply into the developments of these years, even as they were unfolding. Faced with the unpalatable intrusion of demands for social reforms at home, he remarked in 1885 that Ireland might act on all other issues 'like the sun on a fire in the grate'. The motivation of Gladstonian politics may have been straightforwardly moral, but the effect could not have been better achieved by the most cynical diversionary tactics. Hence, for the principled individualist Morley, Gladstone's Home Rule crusade, far from being a wild aberration, consistently subserved a valuable function – 'I look upon him as the strongest bulwark we have against all the strong socialist doctrine I hate.'

Gladstonian populism was in this sense the means of avoiding socialism under democracy. But the charismatic leadership on which this style of politics depended carried its own inherent perils. One was the risk that the old magic might cease to weave its spell upon the electorate, as the sorry experience of the Liberal Party after 1886 tended to confirm. Moreover, even the Grand Old Man, however prodigious, was mortal; he could hardly go on for ever, even if no one had the temerity to challenge him directly for the succession. 'His wisdom and his eloquence!' apostrophized a Gladstonian song, though the next line was more feelingly equivocal: 'Oh, who shall be his heir?' Above all, the peculiar dependence of the Liberal Party upon his presence increasingly sapped its own inner coherence and stored up intractable problems for a post-Gladstonian future. 'Talk of the Liberal party?' Morley said in 1891. 'Why, it consists of Mr G. After him it will disappear and all will be chaos.'

Lord Salisbury in the House of Lords, by Sydney Prior Hall (National Portrait Gallery)

2

THE AUTHENTIC VOICE OF CONSERVATISM:
LORD SALISBURY

When Clement Attlee, deep into retirement, was asked whom he regarded as the best prime minister in his lifetime, he replied at once: 'Salisbury!' It may seem a surprising choice. For Salisbury is the most consistently underestimated figure in modern British politics. He led the Conservative Party (jointly at first) for more than twenty years, of which he was Prime Minister for a total of fourteen, and during which he faced only one clear electoral defeat. Moreover, his career pivoted on two great measures of electoral reform which had been confidently expected, not least by himself, to mark the eclipse of his party. If the forces of Conservatism were more formidably marshalled at the end of the Victorian era than at any earlier point, the lion's share of the credit for apparently reversing the tide of history must belong to Salisbury.

He was born Lord Robert Cecil, the third son of the second Marquess of Salisbury, in 1830; he became heir to the title (as Lord Cranborne) only when his elder brother died in 1865, and he succeeded in 1868; but Salisbury is the name by which he is generally known. The Cecils were an ancient aristocratic family who had had their ups and downs since an earlier Robert Cecil acquired the earldom of Salisbury from his royal master, James I; but they had subsequently wormed their way up to a marquisate, and the great palace of Hatfield, twenty miles north of London, had been preserved. It was there, shortly before the introduction of the First Reform Bill, that

Salisbury was born. High among its delights, when he came to enjoy them as its master, was its fine library; and he was responsible not only for making it the first private house in England to be lit by electricity but also for building his own scientific laboratory. For Salisbury was egregious among his class in the depth and range of his intellectual interests. No bluff, clubbable, fox-hunting aristocrat, this large shambling man was a highly-strung patrician who slowly grew a shell of taciturn obliviousness as his protection against intrusion.

As a younger son, he supplemented a modest allowance from his father with a hard-earned and much-needed income from journalism. Salisbury did not enjoy writing; he wrote for money; but he needed the money; so he wrote often. The result is an unusually rich record of the political views of a highly intelligent member of the governing class, set down at a formative stage of a career which ultimately led to the premiership. We can make sense of Salisbury not just by watching how he acted but by observing his reasoning, articulated with ruthless candour behind a protective veil of anonymity.

Salisbury had no aspirations as a political theorist; but as an intellectual in politics he thought it natural to apply the conventional theoretical axioms of his day to the immediate practical issues of his day. For him, this meant absorbing the lessons of utilitarianism, which suited his temperament in scotching any high-flown rhetoric about 'the rights of man'. Instead, everything had to be justified in terms of its expediency. Consequences were thus the judge and jury in politics. 'The only principle upon which, in the present day, any thinking politician really acts, is "the greatest happiness of the greatest number",' he wrote in 1858. This explicitly utilitarian criterion about the ends of politics had ultimately led Bentham and his followers to conceive a democratic representative system as the means to achieve these ends. Every man would count for one; every one would aim at his own happiness and pursue his own interest; every interest would be represented and reconciled, as in a market; and the result would be felicity.

The novelty of Salisbury's position was that he used utilitarianism precisely in order to resist these democratic conclusions. His real affinity with Bentham – as with Hobbes or Hume or Marx – lay in the unsentimental view which he thought it prudent to take of human nature. He was conscious of 'how thin is the crust which the habits of civilization, however ancient and unbroken, draw over the boiling lava of human passion'. Salisbury saw self-interest as the mainspring of human motivation, and hence class conflict as the normal condition of society. He was therefore a utilitarian from the point of view of the privileged minority interests – the aristocracy, the propertied classes, the Church of England – which would naturally go under if democracy prevailed. The movement for Parliamentary Reform in the 1860s was, on this bleak reading of the situation, the signal for a final and desperate confrontation. 'The struggle for power in our day,' Salisbury wrote in 1862, 'lies not between Crown and people, or between a caste of nobles and a bourgeoisie, but between the classes who have property and the classes who have none.'

Salisbury's political outlook was cynical and tough-minded precisely because salvation was not to be achieved on this earth. His deep-rooted Christian beliefs were the one jealously protected compartment of his mind from which scepticism had been banished. His attachment to the Church of England was not an urbane recognition of the social utility of squire and parson sticking together: it was an unshakeable commitment. Christianity gave him a calm sense of fatalism in the face of an inscrutable providence, quite different from the intrusive interventionism of the Gladstonian conscience. Salisbury's faith therefore licensed extreme wordliness in the affairs of this transient, imperfect world, where a choice of evils was the only way to make the best of a bad job.

It is little wonder that Salisbury emerged as one of the most forthright opponents of Reform in 1866–7. He saw the conflict as 'a portion of the great political struggle of our century – the struggle between property, be its amount small or great, and mere numbers'. His reading of the course of English history left him in no doubt as to what the result of a large extension of the franchise would be. 'As each rival class or party saw its opportunity,' he reasoned, 'it has made the House of Commons an instrument for establishing its own supremacy.' This process seemed to him so natural that there was no need to postulate sinister designs or peculiar rapacity on the part of the masses who were now agitating for the vote. 'It is not to be supposed that the working-classes, more than any other classes, would commit an act of glaring robbery unless they had some very strong motive to do so, and something in the nature of a pretext to cover from the eye of their own consciences the nudity of the operation,' Salisbury affirmed. 'But this reservation, though edifying and necessary to make, is wholly beside the question.'

The fact is that this sort of utilitarianism irresistibly posed the issue in such terms. Robert Lowe, who emerged as Gladstone's leading critic on the Liberal benches, in working from similar premises, arrived at similar conclusions about the likely prospects. 'What must be the politics of people who are struggling hard to keep themselves off the parish?' he demanded. The obvious answer was socialism, if not at once then in due course, as soon as the democratic electorate found its voice. 'What man will speak acceptably to them except the man who promises somehow or other to re-distribute the good things of this world more equally, so that the poor will get more and the rich and powerful will get less?' Lowe might be thought a natural ally for Salisbury, and so he was in a purely negative and obstructive role; but the very different views of society which inspired them tell us a lot about the difference between a Liberal and a Conservative cast of mind.

Lowe's was, for all its anti-democratic fervour, a Liberal case against Reform. For him the essence of the problem was education. His vision of a meritocratic society gave an elevated role to an educated élite, recruited through competition; he favoured 'fancy franchises' which would give extra votes based on educational qualifications as his solution to the problem of brains and numbers. What he feared was the rule of the untutored mob. His fallback position, once reform became a *fait accompli*, is captured by his famous remark on the need 'to compel our future masters to learn their letters'. Thus although Lowe opposed the 1867 Bill he still – like most Liberals – instinctively believed in progress, given the correct structural reforms. Salisbury's pessimistic view of human nature in an imperfect world licensed no such hopes. He dismissed Lowe's schemes as devices projected by and for bookworms; and, when the chips were down, the bibliophile of Hatfield yielded to the third Marquess. Salisbury's intractable class view of the issue was founded not on bright ideas about education but on the rock of property.

Salisbury may have been atavistic about the interests he was defending, but he was thoroughly up to date in the conception of government which he put forward. 'The chief object of government, in England at least, is the protection of property.' So far, so traditional. But Salisbury was no Burke, peering back into the mists of time to discern a partnership not only of the living but of the dead. Instead Salisbury, brisk and businesslike, was not afraid to take the war to the Reformers, with their bourgeois ethos of Manchesterism, by adopting the joint-stock company as his model of representative government. Its constitution, he asserted, 'is that which is dictated by common sense, viz. that each man should have as many votes in the government as he has shares in the concern'. In business, the notion that 'two day-labourers shall outvote Baron Rothschild' would not be entertained for a moment!

Yet in politics, as Salisbury incredulously observed, this was the imminent prospect. He could barely comprehend how members of the governing class could contemplate letting power, possession and property slip through their fingers. Throughout the Reform debates, Salisbury was assiduous in calculating the likely effect of the franchise proposals which were so light-heartedly advanced by his densely innumerate colleagues. He went back to the laboratory bench to check the formula on which this highly dubious experiment was to be conducted. As early as 1860 he published a list of thirty-four boroughs where it was calculated that the current

Liberal proposals for Reform would double the electorate. Since most returned two members, this accounted for fifty-five MPs in all. Gloomy with foreboding, Salisbury counted fifteen Conservative MPs returned at the previous election for these boroughs, 'in which, therefore, Conservative seats will probably be lost'. It was not just that the writing was on the wall: the arithmetic was there too.

It was, however, not a Liberal Government which finally passed the Second Reform Act in 1867, but a Conservative Government led in the House of Commons by Disraeli. Salisbury had initially been a member of it – his first Cabinet post – but his resignation was a wholly characteristic action. 'I am not "testifying" or any nonsense of that kind,' he explained to a friend, 'I am trying to kill the Bill – or failing that to take the sting out of it: and I shall continue to take any opportunity that offers for contributing to that end.' Disraeli had approached Reform as an issue that now had to be settled, preferably in a way that would salvage the maximum advantage for his own party while simultaneously inflicting the maximum discomfiture on Gladstone. This meant that a minority Conservative Government had to be kept in office by creating such a fog of ambiguity about its intentions that no clear issue would emerge on which to vote it down.

Such tactics were meat and drink to Disraeli: poison to Salisbury. Disraeli juggled with no less than four schemes of Reform, all pointing in different directions, balancing the radical connotations of household suffrage with the off-setting conservative qualifications of fancy franchises. It was only when Salisbury sat up all night doing the sums for himself that he discovered the horrible truth: that 'in small boroughs the addition is large and the counterpoise small, in the large boroughs, where we are hopelessly over-matched, the counterpoise is large and the addition small'. To a believer in the utilitarian calculus of self-interest, the game was up.

Yet the fact is that the Conservatives went on to snatch victory from the jaws of defeat. True, Salisbury's account of his calculations came to Lord Derby, the Prime Minister, as a bombshell. 'The enclosed, just received, is utter ruin,' he wrote to Disraeli. 'What on earth are we to do?' The answer, as it turned out, was to put on a bold front, to shrug off Salisbury's resignation as a little local difficulty, to concoct further proposals on the back of an envelope (the so-called 'Ten Minutes Bill'), to go back to the drawing-board with household suffrage, and, in the end, to pass a Bill which made a reality rather than a mockery of this irresistible phrase. Not only that, but Disraeli blandly went on to claim that household suffrage had been the Conservative strategy all along. 'No one else has been sufficiently master of his countenance to repeat this wonderful defence,' was Salisbury's caustic comment.

If Disraeli achieved a short-term parliamentary triumph in passing the 1867 Reform Act, however, did he perhaps purchase this at the price of the long-term electoral disaster for the Conservative Party which had so cogently been predicted? True, Gladstone won the 1868 General Election, the first to be fought under the new suffrage. But even in the small boroughs which Salisbury had singled out for special concern, the Liberals did not sweep the board to the extent that he had feared. On the list which he had printed in 1860, he had not supposed that any of the fifteen Conservative MPs he identified could count on surviving a reduction of the franchise line from a £10 to a £6 limit. In the event, in 1868, with no limit at all left on household suffrage, the boroughs on his list still returned sixteen Conservative MPs.[1] At the next General Election in 1874, moreover, a Conservative majority was secured for the first time for more than thirty years.

The Conservatives kept their end up in the boroughs, even the large boroughs, with a particularly impressive per-

---

[1]Salisbury's list appears in Paul Smith (ed.), *Lord Salisbury on Politics* (Cambridge, 1972), pp.141–2. I have compared it with the election results for 1859 and 1868, as given by J. Vincent and M. Stenton (eds.), *McCalmont's Parliamentary Poll Book, 1832–1918* (Brighton, 1971), which suggests that Salisbury may have missed two Conservatives in 1859. The figures are:

1859	17 Cons.	37 Libs.	1 Peelite	55 total
1868	16 Cons.	42 Libs.		58 total

formance in Lancashire. This was the great unexpected feature of the results; but in explaining the Conservative success we have to look not only at what the Second Reform Act changed but at what it did not change. If all the noise came from the boroughs, the English counties were like the dogs that did not bark in the night. For in the counties there had been no drastic revision of the franchise. The ancient forty-shilling freehold qualification was prudently left undisturbed by Disraeli's Reform Act, which meant that power continued to rest in the hands of a traditional landed hierarchy. The stereotype of borough politics as axiomatically Liberal turned out to be somewhat misleading. But the stereotype of county politics as Conservative was not only true to life before the Second Reform Act but thereafter remained the same – only more so. In the last three General Elections before Reform, the English county seats were Conservative by a steady two-to-one margin; in 1868 this rose to three-to-one and in 1874 to more than five-to-one.

So the game was not up, after all. The resilience of a deferential social structure had withstood constitutional tinkering. If Salisbury made no bones about what he saw as the Conservative surrender in 1867, he was not the man to despair of the situation, however regrettable. It was a part of his Conservatism to distil the bitterness of defeat into the bloody-mindedness of resistance. 'The evils of the measure itself, dangerous as we think it, are not necessarily irremediable,' he wrote within months of the new legislation. 'If the probability arises that the newly-admitted classes will combine to abuse their power, the classes who are threatened may combine on their side in self-defence; and, if their mettle were to equal to that of their assailants, the conflict would be far from desperate.'

Salisbury's willingness to rethink his position in the light of the changed situation marks his maturity as a Conservative statesman. Although his fundamental conceptions showed great consistency, no one thought less in terms of a blueprint than Salisbury. His own exercises in political arithmetic in the 1860s had been rational essays in foresight which were then confounded by events in ways that were not fully foreseeable. He did not need Derby to tell him, in a retrospective admission in the House of Lords, that the Reform Act had been 'a leap in the dark': Salisbury had himself anticipated this famous phrase. As far back as 1860 he had written: 'The leap which the House of Commons is taking with such philosophic calmness is a leap absolutely in the dark.' But if it was irrational to leap in the dark, it was sensible to make the best of a fortunate landing. Salisbury's pragmatic willingness to adapt his strategy left him ready to take advantage of unforeseen contingencies. He thus became the living exemplar of Marx's dictum that men make their own history but do not make it just as they please.

In adjusting to the kind of mass politics which he had feared, Salisbury's essential insight was that the party of reform creates the party of resistance. 'Hostility to Radicalism, incessant, implacable hostility, is the essential definition of Conservatism,' he had written in 1859; after 1867 the problem was to redirect the hostility. He came to believe that established interests might still be preserved if popular government could be brought under effective discipline. He overcame his reluctance to resume an active role in the affairs of the Conservative Party and paved the way for a reconciliation with Disraeli, the 'artless dodger' of many a scornful article. Salisbury realized that the imminent threat of political radicalism could be turned to good account. As early as 1862 he had conceded that 'a little Radicalism is a very useful thing for the purpose of keeping in check the natural selfishness of the classes who are the tenants of power'. Not only that: the tenants also needed to be shocked out of their indolence. Even the success of Gladstone's Midlothian campaigns was a cloud in which a silver lining could be detected. Hence Salisbury's remark to Disraeli in 1880 that 'many of our friends want frightening'. In 1882 Salisbury was to be found proclaiming to the new-fledged National Union of Conservative Associations 'that those who wish to preserve greatly outweigh those who wish to destroy, but the difficulty is to awaken the Conservative classes to a sense of the danger in time to repel active assailants of our institutions'. He had long dreaded 'the strong, steady, deadly gripe of the trades' unions', and he suspected Radicals of making a cottage industry out of the manufacture of grievances. The natural voice of the country was Conservative: the problem was to make sure that it was heard – and heard, moreover, in the level tones of common sense rather than in imitation of Radical stridency.

Disraeli, who died in 1881, was a hard act to follow. As Conservative leader in the Commons, he may have had the uniquely bad record of losing six General Elections and winning only one. But he went out on a high note, lending some plausibility to Lord Randolph Churchill's subsequent verdict: 'Failure, failure, failure, partial success, renewed failure, ultimate and complete victory.' Since the best heroes are usually dead heroes, Disraeli's reputation flourished posthumously as never in his lifetime. The party did not immediately turn to Salisbury. His claims to lead in the House of Lords were those of hereditary prescription as well as native ability; but it took the unfolding crises of the next five years to make him master of his party. Meanwhile Salisbury had to endure the lacklustre leadership of the Commons by Sir Stafford Northcote and the gadfly insubordination of Churchill. It is not surprising that there remained in some sections of the party a hankering after the old leader's dash and sparkle, whereas Salisbury's sober consistency of purpose made a different appeal altogether. Churchill, the nakedly self-seeking younger son of the Duke of Marlborough, saw his chance in leading a brat pack of backbenchers against Northcote and the respectable leadership, ostensibly clutching at the Disraelian legacy. When he began musing about 'Elijah's mantle' and the identity of a fit successor – 'whoever he might be' – few people doubted whom he presumptuously had in mind.

What Churchill did was seize upon the phrase Tory Democracy, attach it to Disraeli's name, and suggest that it represented the true strategy for the party. As an ideological coup, this proved both brilliant and durable, as can be seen from the way Disraelian imagery posthumously took on a mythical status in Tory hagiology which it has never lost. 'Disraeli started the idea of the Tory Democracy and Lord Randolph proclaimed it,' Iain Macleod asserted in 1954. 'Lord Randolph's son today is the head of a team of ministers that is trying to put it into practice.'

On dispassionate inspection, however, the evidence suggests that Disraeli had no such strategy. The 1867 Reform Act was not conceived as a democratic initiative; the Disraeli Government of 1874–80 looked in vain to its leader for a policy of social reform with working-class appeal. In the age of Gladstone and Disraeli, welfare issues were simply not big politics. But just as Gladstone developed a style of moral populism to consolidate his mass following, so Disraeli successfully refurbished the popular image of the Conservative Party in ways that helped neutralize class conflict. With the death of Palmerston in 1865, the patriotic stance with which he had been identified was open for appropriation by the Conservatives. As one of Disraeli's colleagues immediately told him, 'now the lion is dead' their task was 'to persuade the public that we are the right parties to roll ourselves upon the lion's skin'.

Here was a challenge to which Disraeli rose with assurance, projecting the Conservatives as the national party, ready to embrace a broad national following. Though there were some striking examples of working-class support for the Conservatives after 1867, these occurred mainly in Lancashire, where popular Protestantism inflamed sectarian divisions not unlike those of modern Ulster. With this sort of politics the traditional Toryism of 'Church and King' could cope reasonably well. What was new was the growth of middle-class support for the party, as the expanding residential suburbs came to offer the Conservatives a new electoral hinterland, far removed from the conventions of the rural Tory shires. If Disraeli was the passive beneficiary of such trends, Salisbury showed a keener appreciation of what was happening. 'I believe there is a great deal of Villa Toryism which requires organization,' he observed in 1882. Here was the role for party organization, and the Conservatives were lucky at this juncture to have a principal agent like Captain Middleton, a man who brought a naval sense of discipline and rank to his task. It seems that 'the Skipper' had never actually risen above lieutenant in the service, but he now seized his chance to run a tight ship. Imposing order from the top down, he created an efficient political machine which put muscle behind Salisbury's leadership.

The new National Union of Conservative Associations, which Churchill tried to use as his launching pad, purported to work on the opposite principle, organizing the party from the bottom up. Even so, it represented Tory Democracy only in a certain highly restricted sense. The term itself was in any case notoriously elastic, as in Churchill's magnificently empty declaration: 'The Tory democracy is a democracy which has embraced the principles of the Tory party.' In the National Union it was not really the working class but the middle class which benefited from the fitful exercises in *perestroika* and *glasnost* which created a nominally elective party organization. Only in the top-heavy oligarchy that was the old Tory party could this have been passed off as democratization. The result was to make the party more faithfully representative of the possessing classes in general instead of simply the landed interest. The maturing trend of Salisbury's views pointed in the same direction, albeit his line of approach was different.

'My opinions are not such as would enable me to work heartily with the moderate Liberals – and it is only under their lead that a Conservative party in the future could be formed,' Salisbury told a colleague in 1868. 'Pure "squire" Conservatism is played out.' At this stage he had envisaged no active role for himself in a transformation of Conservatism which he saw as inevitable. Yet, as things turned out, he became if not the architect then the clerk of works of reconstruction. Instead of a fusion of moderates under Liberal leadership, the Whigs and their allies were eventually brought under Conservative leadership – his own. What Salisbury wanted was a principled reconstruction of parties, consolidating the natural forces of conservatism against those of radicalism. 'Among men, the old, the phlegmatic, the sober-minded, among classes, those who have more to lose than to gain by change, furnish the natural Conservatives,' he reflected in 1872. He had the patience to play a waiting game, swallowing his frustration that the Whigs, though fellow-members of the propertied classes, for so long failed to see which side their bread was buttered on.

For the second time in his career, the outcome turned on electoral reform. It was virtually inevitable that, having achieved household suffrage in the boroughs in 1867, the Liberals would press on, as soon as the opportunity offered, with its extension to the counties. The Conservatives, to be sure, had weathered the assault of the borough householders with remarkable resilience; but the swamping of the forty-shilling freeholders, the yeomen of England who for centuries had stood foursquare in the counties, was another matter. Wherever would the Tories be without this stolid and stead-fast backing? Looking back in the 1890s, Salisbury dwelt justifiably on the general expectation that once the Liberals 'got the mass of the English people within the boundary of the suffrage the first desire of the latter would be to upset the institutions they found here'. By then, not only he but the Radicals knew better: 'The result has turned out exactly the other way.'

Salisbury's part in assuring this happy outcome was twofold. First he established his authority in the party as the man to strike a deal with the Liberals on Reform. When he went to negotiate at 10 Downing Street, Gladstone noted that Salisbury 'took the whole matter out of the hands of Northcote, who sat by him on the sofa like a chicken protected by the wings of the mother hen'. Churchill was simply shut out of the negotiations altogether. Everything was settled at the summit, with Salisbury using the bargaining counter of the House of Lords' veto to impose a redistribution scheme which took the Liberals' breath away. This involved drastic remodelling of the ancient representative system – essentially introducing single-member constituencies of equal size. In subsequent operation, this structure permitted the Conservatives to enhance their parliamentary representation not only through the larger number of county seats that were created but also through the middle-class suburban divisions which were carved out of the big cities.

If Salisbury did not precisely foresee all the results, nonetheless he acted shrewdly to squeeze the most out of a situation which he had not created. The same is true of his other stroke of wary opportunism in consolidating the Conservative position. For in 1885–6, faced with Gladstone's dramatic proposal for Irish Home rule, Salisbury succeeded in marshalling a decisive majority in defence of the Union. It was no surprise that he himself took up a Unionist position. He had already staked out the ground in 1883 with his general claim: 'The dangers we have to fear may roughly be summed up in the single word – disintegration.' When the Whigs defected to his side, it was no more than he had anticipated for twenty years; when Joseph Chamberlain and his Radical supporters also proved unable to swallow Home Rule, the Unionist cause received an uncovenanted bonus. In this crisis the rising younger leaders who had made such a splash in the early 1880s – the Radical Chamberlain and the Tory Democrat Churchill – were marginalized as Gladstone and Salisbury confronted each other, eyeball to eyeball. Just as the Liberals now became a Gladstonian party, so the Unionist alliance henceforth bore the distinctive stamp of Salisbury's leadership. This was not exactly the political reconstruction he had long sought; but he accepted it as the best he was likely to get; he made it easy for the Liberal Unionists to serve under him; and he created out of these materials a party of resistance which enjoyed an unprecedented degree of mastery.

If Salisbury was ultimately proved right about the sharpening of class divisions in British politics, he was wrong in thinking that the possessing classes would lag behind the lower orders in their mobilization. It was an asymmetrical process, with a disproportionately strong rally of property to the Unionists' side, thus tipping the electoral scales in favour of Salisbury (though against his prognostications). After 1886 he was virtually Prime Minister for life, running his governments on an easy rein and giving plenty of jobs to members of his own family. He showed a studied tolerance of Liberal Unionists like Chamberlain, whose support was worth paying for and whom he rewarded with the Colonial Office in 1895.

As a minister, Salisbury's attention was overwhelmingly occupied with foreign affairs. He upheld the traditional lines of British foreign policy, eschewing both a Gladstonian lapse into moralism and a Chamberlainite lurch into jingoism. He was deeply uneasy over the initiatives to which the restless energy of Chamberlain committed the Unionist Government. A reckless foreign policy had long seemed to Salisbury a natural concomitant of domestic demagogy. When the Boer War offered his Government the opportunity of cashing in with a khaki election, Salisbury was disdainful. Even though the Unionists gained a great popular victory at the polls in 1900, he remained mistrustful, speculating morosely 'that the Reform Bills, digging down deeper and deeper into the population, have come upon a layer of pure combativeness'. Such people might vote Conservative but they knew nothing of Conservatism as he understood it.

Joe Chamberlain's vision of an interventionist state, at home and abroad, was alien to the wisdom with which Salisbury had sought to contain the challenge of democracy. His record, like that of Queen Elizabeth, began to tarnish in his last years, with a *fin-de-siècle* weariness in face of the eruption of intractable problems which he bequeathed to his successors. He reproved the callow enthusiasm of one member of his family by saying: 'You are like Joe, who again is like Randolph.' But the old man had the good sense not to provoke Joe with the patient lecture which he had once given to Randolph:

We have so to conduct our legislation that we shall give some satisfaction to both classes and masses. This is specially difficult with the classes – because all legislation is rather unwelcome to them, as tending to disturb a state of things with which they are satisfied. It is evident, therefore, that we must work at less speed, and at a lower temperature than our opponents.

This was not a thrilling political creed but in Salisbury's hands it was highly effective. He recognized its negative force, claiming to rank himself 'no higher in the scheme of things than a policeman – whose utility would disappear if there were no criminals'. He knew that the country was going to the dogs; his aim was to retard this process. His mind-set is revealed in the way he once assessed the battle – maybe a losing battle – to preserve the Establishment: 'they had kept church rates alive for thirty years, and with their numbers they could keep them alive ten years longer; at any rate, they might keep tithes twenty years after that, and endowments twenty years longer still. That brought them to fifty years, and that period was something in the life of a nation.' He was no rhetorical reactionary indulging in nostalgia but a prescient politician steeled to act in deadly earnest. He saw the Conservative opportunity even in the hour of Liberal triumph. 'The army of so-called reform, in every stage of its advance, necessarily converts a detachment of its force into opponents,' he wrote as early as 1869. 'The more rapid the advance the more formidable will the desertion become, till at last a point will be reached where the balance between the forces of conservation and destruction will be redressed, and the political equilibrium be restored.'

Salisbury's confidence in this analysis turned out to be well-founded. Matched for most of his career against the titanic figure of Gladstone, he withstood and outwitted the Grand Old Man with a grim tenacity which ultimately paid off. Whereas Churchill wanted to ape the Radicals in method and outbid them in policy, with a flagrant demagogic appeal designed to set up Toryism as a rival brand of populism, Salisbury refused to play this game at all. He thought such antics merely alienated the sort of voter he was after. He sensed all along – but let on only in his old age – that 'Mr Gladstone's existence was the greatest source of strength which the Conservative party possessed'.

Salisbury's achievement was practical, not theoretical, as a party leader rather than a political thinker. Yet he did more than any other Conservative leader to endow his party with a coherent vision of Conservatism. 'If circumspection and caution are part of wisdom, when we work only upon inanimate matter, surely they become a part of duty too, when the subject of our demolition and construction is not brick and timber, but sentient beings, by the sudden alteration of whose state, condition and habits, multitudes may be rendered miserable.' So wrote Burke, whose writings have often been taken as a foundation text of conservative thought (with a small 'c'). Salisbury was ideally placed by birth, position, temperament and aptitude to stamp such sentiments as Conservative with a big 'C'. 'The perils of change are so great, the promise of the most hopeful theories is so often deceptive,' he once wrote, 'that it is frequently the wiser part to uphold the existing state of things, if it can be done, even though, in point of argument, it should be utterly indefensible.' Salisbury succeeded beyond his own gloomy expectations, at the price of more than one ruthless reappraisal of strategy and priorities, in upholding the existing state of things throughout his lifetime. In the 1860s, with his fervent commitment to the Confederate cause in the American civil war, he used to suffer from nightmares, imagining his bedroom invaded by nocturnal insurgents – Federal soldiers, perhaps, or leaders of a revolutionary mob. But in his old age he slept more soundly. He did not die on the barricades, nor in the last ditch, but at Hatfield House, where he had been born.

THE BIRMINGHAM PET.

"*I have received hard blows, and I have endeavoured to return them.*"—Mr. CHAMBERLAIN at Birmingham, July 9, 1906.
"*His blows are like the stroke of steel,*
His words like burning wine."
—Extract from the "Celebration" Song sung at Birmingham.

(*Westminster Gazette*, 11 July 1906)

60

3

JOSEPH CHAMBERLAIN:
THE FIRST MODERN POLITICIAN

Joseph Chamberlain failed to reach the top of the greasy pole, but he had a more decisive influence upon the course of British politics than most men who succeeded in becoming Prime Minister. He came from a moderately prosperous London family who settled in the Islington district of Highbury, where young Joe was brought up. But he himself made his fortune and his political career in Birmingham, where he was sent as a young man to develop a new American patent for manufacturing screws. The business boomed; Chamberlain retired from it at forty a wealthy man. He built a huge mansion for himself in a Birmingham suburb and gave it the name 'Highbury'. In an age when the top politicians were known by the names of their houses – usually country seats set amid rolling acres – Highbury was to become as much of a name to conjure with as Hatfield. It was a mark of how far Chamberlain had come.

Modern biographers of Chamberlain and his family have often been scathing about the supposed bad taste of Highbury. Perhaps it is understandable that Sir Keith Feiling, writing the life of Neville Chamberlain in the 1940s, should have held that it exemplified 'the hideous roomy Victorian-Gothic style, with a vast hall of arches, stained glass and inlaid woods'. But the wheel of fashion has turned again since this dismissive assessment was made. One suspects that if Highbury were still standing today it would be a centre of pilgrimage for the

Victorian Society; the fine orchid houses which Joseph Chamberlain built to supply him with his inevitable button-hole – as much a trademark as his monocle – would be a distinctive heritage feature, perhaps even the focus of an appeal to save them for the nation. As things turned out, Highbury was eventually bought by the corporation of Birmingham for the sort of municipal development which Chamberlain had pioneered as mayor in the 1870s, and it was pulled down to make way for the new with a lack of sentimentality of which he would have approved. The house that Joe built did not even outlast the British Empire, the other enthusiasm of his later years.

As a Unitarian, Chamberlain was well placed to channel Nonconformist grievances into political dissent. His first steps in Birmingham politics thus centred on the schools issue, which was coming to the boil during Gladstone's first Government. Chamberlain's objective was a national system of free and unsectarian education and he quickly extended the agitation of his Birmingham supporters into a National Education League, pledged to contest those clauses of the Liberal Education Act of 1870 which arguably favoured Church schools. Half of the substantial sums of money needed to found the League came from Chamberlain's family and he himself naturally became its president. At this stage he spoke the unflinching language of faddism and militant Dissent. 'I would rather see a Tory Ministry in power than a Liberal Government truckling to Tory prejudices,' he wrote to a colleague. Yet he himself seems to have lost his religious faith in 1875 as a result of the death of his second wife. 'After trying to find an explanation of the "great mystery",' he later explained, 'I gave it up once for all, satisfied that there was quite enough to occupy me in this life without bothering about what is to come afterwards.'

It was on the foundations of the Education League that Chamberlain decided in 1877 to build the National Liberal Federation – 'with headquarters at Birmingham and the League officers as chief cooks,' as he explained the plan to John Morley. Chamberlain was as good as his word. He helped to give the Liberal Party a form of organization which nominally invited the participation of all supporters and in fact produced a highly professional party machine. His methods, it was said, involved the Americanization of British politics, with the introduction of a party caucus to control the machine at ward and constituency level.

Chamberlain found Birmingham to be an ideal power base. A city of small workshops, it stood for the characteristic values of mid-Victorian radicalism: an ethic of work and self-reliance combined with hostility to privilege and patronage. In Chamberlain's conception, class conflict was not something that occurred between masters and men within Birmingham, but was a challenge by the Birmingham ideal to the power of the landed aristocracy with its headquarters at Westminster. Salisbury was to become a particular target, as representing a class 'who toil not neither do they spin'; but Hartington, the heir to the Duke of Devonshire, who was nominally the leader of the Liberal Party during Gladstone's withdrawal in the late 1870s, was little better. Hence Chamberlain's hopes for the NLF: 'I think this may become a very powerful organization, and proportionately detested by all Whigs and Whips.'

Chamberlain was a thoroughly modern politician in his conception of party politics. For example, it is nowadays a common ploy by party activists to assert the power of the party machine over the parliamentary leadership, whose statesmanship allegedly consists in ignoring the aspirations of their rank-and-file supporters. How, then, can the claims of the party organization, working in the name of democracy, be asserted except by the threat of deselection, so as to purge the elected representatives? This is certainly how Chamberlain saw things. Party, in his view, was an engine of power, fuelled by popular enthusiasm. The control of the party belonged with its grass-roots activists, whose time and money earned them a clear right to have their voice heard. The policy of the party had to be such as won their consent and commitment. Programmes and proposals of a clear-cut, wide-ranging character were the essence of democratic politics since they were the means of enlisting electoral support. Majorities were what counted, within the party or in the country at large, and it was no good seeking to march at the pace of the slowest man. That way, nothing would ever get done. The proper role of Government, therefore, was an active one, with purposeful progress towards stated objectives. These were the views for which Chamberlain stood throughout his career, whatever his other vicissitudes.

Chamberlain made civic pride into part of the Birmingham gospel, propagating an ideal of municipal activity premised on the ability of a great democratic city to govern itself with energy and dignity. He served as mayor from 1873 until his election to Parliament in 1876. 'I think I have now almost completed my municipal programme and may sing Nunc Dimittis,' he wrote with satisfaction. 'The Town will be parked, paved, assized, marketed, Gas-and-Watered and *improved* – all as the result of three years' active work.' This was not a cheese-paring conception of local government but a vigorous conduct of the ratepayers' business which involved heavy investment in the infrastructure. Moreover, the programme needed to be driven through by the usual means, which meant bringing his supporters into line. His newly organized Liberal caucus imposed its will on Birmingham city politics; and when some of the old councillors complained in 1876 that they were being asked to conform to party policy by voting against their consciences, Chamberlain's retort was characteristic: 'I don't care about their consciences.' He was not, in any sense of the word, a nice man. He was ruthlessly straightforward, despising subtlety and sophistication as much as he scorned Tory nonchalance and Whig indolence.

'By temperament he is an enthusiast and a despot,' wrote Beatrice Potter in her diary in 1884 – not the voice of a hostile critic or a political opponent but of a highly perceptive young woman who was deeply but ambivalently attracted to him. She reported his commendation of America: 'Cultured persons complain that the society there is vulgar; less agreeable to the delicate tastes of delicately trained minds.' But he judged it preferable for the ordinary worker, and his earnest hope of moving along similar lines in Britain was undeniable. And yet, Beatrice Potter recorded, 'running alongside this genuine enthusiasm is a passionate desire to crush opposition to his will, a longing to feel his foot on the necks of others, though he would persuade himself that he represents the right and his adversaries the wrong'. It was essentially this sort of personal revulsion against his domineering instincts which led her, despite a strong sexual attraction, to resist his advances. She asked him outright, 'You don't allow division of opinion in your household, Mr Chamberlain?' After some prevarication, his answer was 'No'. So was hers. She became, instead of the third Mrs Chamberlain, the one and only Mrs Sidney Webb; and, though not without subsequent pangs, she did not regret her decision.

Still at a personal level, one cannot ignore three unfortunate episodes involving Chamberlain's honour. One was the Crawford divorce case in 1886, which effectively blighted the prospects of Sir Charles Dilke, Chamberlain's rival for the leadership of the Radicals. Dilke collaborated closely with Chamberlain and relied upon him to help refute the damaging allegations of Mrs Crawford – 'three in a bed' – which were an obvious threat to his political career. Yet there were indications of prior dealings between Chamberlain and Mrs Crawford of which no satisfactory explanation was ever offered. Though the charge against him here is probably unprovable either way, the fact remains that a charge was made.

So, too, with that other politico-sexual scandal of the period, *O'Shea* v. *O'Shea*. The implication of the Irish Nationalist Leader, Charles Stewart Parnell, in this divorce case in 1890 destroyed his reputation. In this sense it finished the job of character-assassination which had misfired the previous year; the evidence purporting to link him with organized crime in Ireland, gleefully printed in *The Times*, had been exposed in 1889 as the work of the forger Pigott, and thus nothing more than a Unionist 'dirty tricks' campaign. As the most prominent Unionist, and one who had egged on Salisbury's Government in making a meal of the Pigott letters, Chamberlain had a lot at stake. 'He who smashes Parnell smashes Parnellism,' Chamberlain had been assured – by none other than Captain O'Shea, whose clandestine association with Chamberlain over both the Pigott affair and the divorce case provokes suspicion. Again, it cannot be proved exactly what Chamberlain was up to. Finally, as Colonial Secretary, Chamberlain left many questions unanswered about his role in the Jameson Raid, as will be seen. In none of these three murky episodes is there a properly documented case against Chamberlain. The evidence simply does not survive. And who, one is left wondering, saw to that?

It is unlucky to find oneself in a compromising position, since innuendo is often unselective in its targets. Once is wholly understandable; twice is rather unfortunate; three times is quite unfathomable. Such incidents suggest that Chamberlain was ambitious, not over-scrupulous in his choice of methods or associates, and adept at concealing a smoking gun. He was a man who won respect rather than trust or affection. Salisbury once asked: 'Does anyone love Mr Chamberlain?' His determination to get his way was legendary. Though not lacking in personal charm, he seldom exhausted himself on the business of conciliating his colleagues, preferring to browbeat them into submission. If he found himself frustrated by the constraints of a charmed circle, in which the aristocratic politicians held all the aces, he knew that he had a card up his sleeve in the force of party opinion outside. In 1885 he hoped to 'sweep the country', fighting on popular electoral issues with which, he confidently predicted, 'the Tories will be smashed and the Whigs extinguished'. The next twenty years duly saw a trail of smashing and extinguishing; but if Chamberlain was as good as his word in making things happen, they did not always happen according to plan. For though he was an irresistible force, twice he had the misfortune to encounter an immovable object. The first time it was the Liberal Party and the second it was the Conservative Party.

★

In the uneasy coalition of Liberal politics in the 1880s, Gladstone's position was in itself the key to whether the party would split. As Rosebery noted of the 1885 Cabinet: 'All ministers individually want it to break up and yet none want to break away from the rest disassociated from Mr G.' Chamberlain was prepared to tolerate the Grand Old Man's dominance as a sort of holding operation for radicalism. He had complacently told Dilke in 1876 that if Gladstone 'were to come back for a few years (he can't continue in public life for very much longer) he would probably do much for us and pave the way for more'. Nine years later, he was wearily reiterating that 'his reign cannot possibly be a long one and it is undesirable to have the remains of his great influence cast against us'. In the end, Gladstone's leadership outlasted Chamberlain's patience. His prediction in 1882 that 'the politics of the future are social politics' was squarely confronted with the inflation of Irish Home Rule as the apotheosis of Gladstonianism.

Rarely given to introspection or self-doubt, Chamberlain was the supreme man of action in politics. He steamrollered over opposition as Mayor of Birmingham, he blandly displaced one of the city's incumbent MPs in 1876, he shouldered his way into the Cabinet in 1880, and in 1885 he thrust his 'unauthorized Programme' before the electorate in more or less direct challenge to Gladstone. Under Gladstone the Liberal Party was like a people's crusade at the bottom and like a gentlemen's club at the top. Chamberlain had a more rationalistic approach to politics, seeking to build up mass political organizations around programmes which incorporated the demands of the membership. He mistrusted Gladstone's approach as a means of manipulating Radical feeling in order to perpetuate a Whig hierarchy of power.

The crisis of 1886, when Chamberlain broke with Gladstone over Home Rule, did not therefore come out of thin air, but neither was its impact predictable. Chamberlain knew that the fine print of rival legislative proposals on Ireland was not the real issue. He acknowledged that 'a large number, perhaps a majority, of Liberals will support *any* scheme of Mr

Gladstone's' and saw the need to protect his own political base. His own attitude had not been unsympathetic to the Irish in the way that Salisbury's was; but their fears of disintegration nonetheless struck some common chords. For Salisbury authority was a function of class, for Chamberlain it was a function of personality; but there was a similar strong-minded defensive reaction. The great Radical, who could not countenance a division of opinion in his own household, likewise had a forthright answer to the Irish Question – 'No'. He proved surprisingly susceptible to the claims of maintaining the authority of the Imperial Parliament, and once his teeth fastened into this bone of contention his stubbornness was truly dogged. Chamberlain therefore made the representation of Irish MPs at Westminster his sticking point. But issues of policy, as so often, were infused with those of personality, in a head-on clash with Gladstone; and steely ambition governed the way the game was played out, move by move.

Chamberlain, Hartington and Gladstone were each reluctant to give up the big prize: the prospect of a united Liberal Party under his own leadership. In the event, none of them secured their aims, Chamberlain least of all in aspiring to a pivotal position. Gladstone at least maintained Liberal legitimacy on the basis of Home Rule. The Tories were born Unionists and hence the natural opposition; the Whigs achieved Unionism as a long-delayed consummation; but Chamberlain really had Unionism thrust upon him. Unexpectedly separated from the Liberal Party, he had to make the best of his predicament. By 1887 he was indomitably outlining 'the possibility of a strong Central Party which may be master of the situation after Mr Gladstone goes'.

For a man who did so much to institutionalize political loyalties, Chamberlain had an appalling record of provoking party splits. When he and Gladstone parted company over Home Rule in 1886, the Liberal Party was doomed to nearly twenty years of futility. It did not recover until Chamberlain's proposals for Tariff Reform had had an almost equally disruptive effect upon the Unionists. Chamberlain did not feel unduly guilty. The struggle of parties was the struggle for policies; power and conflict were inseparable in his vigorous, tough-minded approach to politics. After 1886, of course, he changed his political bearings. Birmingham remained impressively loyal to him – all seven seats, which had been Liberal, were now carried for Unionism – and within the city the radical appeal of his sort of Liberal Unionism had to be maintained. But his general view of politics was accommodated to the needs of his alliance with the Conservatives. By 1894 he was telling his old sparring partner Hartington, now Duke of Devonshire, that 'the House of Lords seems to me to fulfil excellently the necessary duties of a second chamber'. It was, by this time, the confiscatory demands of Labour which alarmed the man who, ten years earlier, had asked, 'What ransom will property pay for the security it enjoys?'

As a centre party, Liberal Unionism never stood much chance. Its *raison d'être* was defence of the Union; but as long as Salisbury made himself the champion of this cause, and as long as Gladstone correspondingly continued to defy mortality for the sake of Home Rule, there was no room for a true third choice. A centre party must be able to say with conviction, 'A plague on both your houses'. And it must find a constituency which finds this an appealing sentiment and a plausible strategy. None of this was applicable to Chamberlain. He came to recognize his community of interest with the political right as the only means of exerting his leverage. By the 1890s his social perspective was undoubtedly undergoing change. It is, however, too crude to call this inconsistent with the proposition of some of his admirers that Chamberlain's radicalism remained undimmed.

Chamberlain, in short, had to apply his characteristic methods to a new problem. He had not become a Conservative but he recognized that he now had to work with the Conservatives. There were certain specific concessions he could extract from Salisbury as the price of his support – free education in 1891, for example. But Chamberlain's career as a domestic reformer was drawing to a close; inclination and prudence alike directed his attention towards imperial problems where his expansive instincts had long been at odds with Gladstonianism. and were much more in tune with the outlook of many younger Conservatives. Thus it became possible for him to enter a Unionist Government as Colonial Secretary in 1895. He was not the first Liberal Unionist to serve under Salisbury – Devonshire and the other Whigs had long been in the Cabinet – but Chamberlain's accession at once cemented the new political alignment and made him virtually the second man in the Government. Other Colonial Secretaries had come and gone during the nineteenth century without leaving much impression; but under Chamberlain the Colonial Office was where things happened. By the time he took office, the great age of territorial annexation may have been over. It remains true that it was during his eight years as Colonial Secretary that imperialism became big politics.

The Boer War of 1899–1902 was the climax of British imperialism. It represented not only the largest military commitment in furtherance of colonial ambitions but also the last major effort of its kind. But if it can be seen as the end of Britain's participation in the scramble for Africa, it can also be seen as the beginning of a self-conscious era of imperialism in British politics. For these are two different things. In the period when the partition of Africa was substantially completed, popular support for expansion had played little part in the process. Indeed the official mind, closeted in the Foreign Office or the Colonial Office, was fearful that the masses might prove indifferent to empire. The cold-blooded quest for imperial safety was thus the preserve of aristocratic statesmanship, far removed from the hot-blooded spasms of democratic politics.

Chamberlain, by contrast, made a determined effort to square the diplomacy of empire with the force of public opinion. Like Gladstone, Chamberlain was essentially concerned with creating public opinion as well as responding to it. He had no qualms about seeking to politicize the conduct of colonial affairs, believing that only by enlisting popular interests in the empire could the democracy be educated to think imperially. He refused to accept that the people stood in the way of the sort of vigorous foreign policy which was necessary for national survival. As he told Balfour, 'I think a democratic government should be the strongest government from a military and imperial point of view in the world, for it has the people behind it.' His method was, as always, the frontal assault, appealing for support in the country in order to get his own way in the corridors of power. He found, however, that public opinion was not simply a lap-dog, with one ear cocked to his master's voice, but a rottweiler which could easily get out of hand.

The whole process thus acquired a momentum of its own. Salisbury was one of the last exponents of the old tradition of closed diplomacy, but he perceived clearly enough how the new rules of the game worked. The French, he noted in 1892, 'are always defending their worst proceedings by saying their Chamber won't stand this and won't stand that. It may be an advantage that we too should be able to flourish an inexorable Chamber in their faces.' Here was Chamberlain's opportunity in his handling of the developing crisis in South Africa. He did not invent the problem, which turned on a conflict between the imperatives of British expansion and the integrity of the two Boer republics. The fact that it was Gladstone who had effectively recognized the Boers' independence gave an ideological twist to the issue; the fact that the intractable Paul Kruger was the long-serving Transvaal president gave a personal twist; and the fact that the bucolic Boers now turned out to be sitting on the world's greatest goldfield gave an economic twist. Naturally, settlers poured into Johannesburg; and Chamberlain quickly took up the grievances of these Uitlanders, who, as British immigrants, lacked citizenship rights in the Transvaal republic.

There is little doubt that Chamberlain was prepared to uphold and extend British interests with a wholly new sort of vigour. Whether he was guilty of complicity in the Jameson Raid, which took place at the end of 1895, barely six months after he had taken office, is another matter. Precipitately launched by Cecil Rhodes as Prime Minister of the Cape

Colony, the raid struck directly at the Transvaal in an attempt to destabilize it. Had it succeeded, there is little doubt that Chamberlain was standing ready to follow up the advantage; but since it was a fiasco, he adroitly distanced himself from any connection with it. There is no surviving record of his direct prior involvement – 'I did not want to know too much,' he once said – and the messages that passed between Rhodes and his London associates may not have given a fair impression of Chamberlain's position. All of this remains ambiguous. But what is clear is that Chamberlain managed to suppress these vital telegrams, which might have proved revealing and would certainly have been embarrassing, when he himself sat as a member of the parliamentary inquiry which was set up. This was a magnificent effort in effrontery which guaranteed his political survival.

Chamberlain's chosen weapons were not those, in the first instance, of military force but of cleverly projected propaganda. The grievances of the Uitlanders constituted an issue with immediate appeal, and an explicitly democratic one at that. Here was a cause tailor-made for the old Radical. Twenty years previously, when Salisbury had subjected Chamberlain's methods to public scrutiny, he had distinguished 'the grievance of suffering', which was felt in good faith, from 'the grievance of strategy', which was the forte of Radicalism. 'Its characteristic is that the discontent it indicates is not cured but aggravated by concession,' Salisbury had explained. 'It is urged, not for its own sake, but for the sake of something that lies beyond. It is part of a great plan in which each move prepares the way for the move that is to follow.' It was Kruger who really needed this advice in the late 1890s as the Uitlanders' grievances became the crux of Chamberlain's negotiations with the two Boer republics. At every stage Chamberlain printed the dispatches from South Africa, carefully angled to give credence to his case and to prompt public support for his stand. This tactic also served to stymie his Radical critics, who felt they could hardly object to open diplomacy.

The policy was given a further dimension, not entirely of

Chamberlain's making. Sir Alfred Milner, appointed British High Commissioner in South Africa in 1897, had his own axe to grind. If anyone plotted a war, it was Milner, whose position as the man on the spot gave him such impressive credentials as a judge of the situation. His plan was to create a crisis in which Chamberlain would be compelled by events to take precipitate action. To this end Milner established undercover links with the South African press, which in turn fed the London newspapers with inflammatory stories of Boer malfeasance. Though the extent of Milner's stage-management was kept from him, Chamberlain too showed himself fully adept in the theatre of dissimulation. Having aroused an angry public opinion in Britain, he could point to it in his dealings with Kruger as a reason for a settlement on favourable terms. He had, in short, created his own 'inexorable Chamber'.

The Boers, however, remained generally unimpressed. They would not enter into this game nor abide by its rules. They did not acknowledge the reality of the Uitlanders' grievances, nor accept that free negotiations could remove them. Moreover, the chance of a negotiated settlement – which Chamberlain might well have been ready to accept – was continually being eroded by his own relentless propaganda. A position was reached where Chamberlain's policy of publicity captured him as its prisoner in its self-sustaining lurch onward. There came a point when it was simply too late to jump clear of the juggernaut. Thus 'Joe's War' became inevitable in 1899, though by this stage his fellow ministers were as firmly bound to the enterprise as Chamberlain himself. The media had kept the crisis on the boil; the Government was forced to act to meet the expectations which it had helped to raise. The flexibility of the old diplomacy, of which Salisbury was the great master, was no longer available once Joe had ostentatiously painted himself into a corner.

The Boer War may be attributed to the failure of the Government's diplomacy, but its political repercussions were to bring ample compensation. Despite early military setbacks, the war was initially popular at home. Salisbury, to be sure, had his qualms – 'we seek no goldfields', he said – but Chamberlain knew what he was seeking. In the Khaki Election of 1900 he found it: a mandate for his policy, a victory for the Government of which he was now the most prominent member, and an unanswerable personal vindication. The so-called 'pro-Boers', who denounced the war as immoral, included not only old Gladstonians like Morley but rising Radicals like Lloyd George. They were brushed aside as Chamberlain cashed in on the mood of popular jingoism. It is no coincidence that, as late as December 1901, Lloyd George could not get a hearing in Birmingham and had to be smuggled out of the Town Hall dressed as a policeman. The ex-mayor was well satisfied.

Contemporaries recognized that Gladstonianism was now buried along with the Grand Old Man. Moreover, this had implications for domestic as well as external policy. Chamberlainite imperialists tended to favour the big state at home as well as abroad. It is indicative of the new course in politics that the leading Fabian socialists should have declared themselves sympathetic to imperialism at this juncture on the same anti-Gladstonian logic. To Bernard Shaw – 'inveterately anti-Liberal, anti-Individualistic, anti-Jehovistic, anti-Independence-Liberty-Nationality and all the rest of it' – this made perfectly good sense. In his friend Sidney Webb, the war provoked a cooler response: 'It's not my show,' he would say. But to explain Beatrice Webb's much warmer commitment to Chamberlain's cause, we need to appeal to more than a persuasive analogy between imperialism and collectivism. She privately recorded having 'suffered years of pain, possibly from the same coarse inconsiderateness which others say he has shown towards the Transvaal'. When the chips were down, however, her 'tenderness for the man I loved & an almost exaggerated desire for his success & happiness' left her still susceptible to his personal magnetism.

Chamberlain was an accident-prone politician. At the summit of his achievements, during the Colonial Conference over which he presided in London in the summer of 1902, he sustained injury on a cab journey. He happened to be travelling down the Mall when one of the decorations, in place for the Coronation, accidentally fell, which caused the horse to shy, which led a strap to break, which released a heavy window frame, which caught Chamberlain awkwardly on the head. It was nothing more than a fortuitous chain of circumstances. While he was recovering in his hospital bed, the Cecils took the opportunity of reconstructing the Government; Salisbury resigned the premiership and his nephew Balfour slipped opportunely into his place. Chamberlain probably did not expect to become Prime Minister at this juncture, but it was his last chance, and sheer bad luck on his part to be *hors de combat*.

There were more deep-seated reasons why Chamberlain's hour of triumph proved to be transient, for the war brought in its train accumulating difficulties. When, in 1902, the Unionist Government introduced an Education Bill, which was politically sensitive for Nonconformists because it put a charge for Church schools on the rates, this touched a sore point for a man whose first steps in politics had been as the champion of Dissent on the schools issue. He now demanded why central Government could not supply the funds instead. 'Because your War has made further recourse to State grants impossible,' was the answer he received. So the war dictated the shape of the Education Bill; and the widespread unpopularity of the Bill, it seems clear, prompted Chamberlain to try to save the situation by launching an agitation for Tariff Reform.

Here too Chamberlain was in a sense faithful to his radical heritage. Temperamentally this was an iconoclastic challenge to doctrines of Free Trade which had prevailed for nearly sixty years. As long as Britain remained the workshop of the world, it was possible to insist – perhaps not even necessary to insist – that the performance of the economy was not a political issue. Laissez-faire was a precept sustained by an object lesson. With the coming of the twentieth century, however, problems which have since become familiar begin to intrude. Chamberlain was the first leading politician to propose a drastic method of averting the sort of national decline which he saw as otherwise inevitable.

It has sometimes been claimed that Chamberlain was still a Radical in that tariffs were designed to finance a programme of social reform. It is, of course, true that Chamberlain had committed himself to the provision of old age pensions in the 1890s, and this unfulfilled promise remained as a hostage to fortune. So it is not surprising that, when Lloyd George taunted him in the House of Commons in May 1903, Chamberlain should have retorted that tariffs might provide the revenue to pay for pensions. But, having opened up this exciting possibility, Chamberlain closed it down again in the following month. In a vain bid to conciliate the Duke of Devonshire, whose Free Trade scruples were much in evidence, Chamberlain proposed to juggle with the various food taxes so that no net increase in the cost of living would arise. Since the Liberals would in any case claim that the people's bread would cost more under protection, Chamberlain thus for once missed the chance of fighting back with a popular cry. And since the Duke in any case became the patron of the Unionist Free Traders, Chamberlain was yet again thwarted in a radical initiative by his old antagonists, the Whigs. (It is indeed a fine irony that having spent the declining years of the nineteenth century squabbling with them over who should run the Liberal Party, Chamberlain should have opened the new century with a fresh squabble over who should run the Unionist Party.) But if Chamberlain was deflected in his strategy, it was surely because social reform was not for him an end to which Tariff Reform supplied the means; if anything, the converse is true.

The origins of Tariff Reform lay in his wish to consolidate the Empire. Much of the subsequent ambiguity here lies in the fact that the single phrase 'Tariff Reform' came to cover so many different proposals. Imperial preference was at the heart of Chamberlain's scheme as launched in 1903; he was inconsistent over whether any revenue should be applied to social reform; and he was initially wary of sullying his imperial dream with what he called 'the squalid argument' for industrial protection. Other glosses on Tariff Reform left him cold. For retaliation – Balfour's brainchild – he claimed, 'I would never have taken off my coat.' As for the revenue aspect, this provided a useful argument for Tariff Reform in so far as it could be linked with the popular appeal of old age pensions. If social reform could sell imperialism to the British public, well and good. Chamberlain's priorities thus stand out clearly enough, and involved an implicit repudiation of the social radicalism of his earlier phase.

The fact is that Chamberlain maintained his original political style but charged it, during the last decade of his career, with a changed political content. He encountered the proverbial difficulty of putting new wine into old bottles – the bottles burst. His objectives were now those of imperialism abroad and social stabilization at home, with the link between them remaining problematic. The Tariff Reform campaign, therefore, remained true to the established Chamberlain style. It was bold, bald and brash; imaginative, creative, and innovative. He himself spearheaded the campaign with a carefully planned series of great meetings throughout the country. The Tariff Reform League was set up as a pressure group designed to bring the whole Unionist Party into line on the big issue. Its methods were those of the Education League and the National Liberal Federation, suitably brought up to date in the age of the gramophone, which could personalize the message from Highbury in hundreds of public meetings throughout the country. Chamberlain was ready to proclaim, at nearly seventy, that 'a fighting policy will have the best chance'. He was prepared to impose his policy on the Liberal Unionist organization with all the vigour of his old caucus methods, finally driving out the Whigs, and he hoped that the Conservative party could be treated likewise. He was adumbrating a new sort of politics for the right in Britain, resting on a calculated politicization of the masses, with strong overtones of populism and nationalism, and focused through his own charismatic leadership. There is no need to dub this proto-fascist to make the point that something funny was happening to the Tory party.

The content of Chamberlain's new programme was also remarkable. Though its ultimate ends may have been conservative, its means involved a radical assault on the conventional wisdom on economic policy. 'What is the whole problem as it affects the working classes of this country?' Chamberlain demanded. 'It is all contained in one word – employment.' The idea that the state had a responsibility here was, of course, anathema to the prevailing free market doctrine, which Chamberlain dismissed as 'a part of the old fallacy about the transfer of employment'. He brought his famous capacity for sarcasm to bear in caricaturing this view to an audience of working men: 'It is your fault if you do not leave the industry which is falling and join the industry which is rising.' Instead of sugar refining, jam; instead of the iron trade, mousetraps – 'You see how easy it is' – instead of the cotton industry, 'try doll's eyes'. He laid bare the assumptions of a self-acting system and its economic consequences in a way that adumbrates Keynes. 'You cannot go on,' he warned, 'watching with indifference the disappearance of your principal industries.'

The Tariff Reform initiative in some ways looks like a prescient endeavour to catch the wave of the future. What Chamberlain sought was a dynamic policy to forestall the polarization of classes. His impatient stabs at linking tariffs with social reform, in order to enlist working-class support for radical Unionism, were a recurrent theme. But his frontal assault upon laissez-faire was alien to the Conservative temperament, even though ostensibly directed against the Liberals as the defenders of Free Trade. 'The more I think of the matter,' wrote the son of the great Lord Salisbury to the son-in-law of the great Lord Salisbury in 1906, 'the more impressed I am with apprehension at the violent nature of the changes proposed. The whole of my Conservative training revolts against the catastrophical theory of politics.' The Tariff Reformers represented the emergence of a Radical Right whose messianic catastrophism was a mirror image of the ideological approach to the Left.

Their attempt to hijack the Conservative Party was superficially successful. In the years 1903–10 the Unionist Free Traders, initially led by the Duke of Devonshire, found themselves inexorably displaced from a position of influence within the party as, step by step, acceptance of Tariff Reform became the test of party orthodoxy. Numbering men like Sir Michael Hicks Beach, the Cecils and Winston Churchill, the Unionist Free Traders hardly lacked position, birth, brains or, for that matter, ambition. Yet their eclipse was total. Most of the old men went into disconsolate retirement. Some of the younger men – Churchill is the most prominent example – crossed the floor. But most of the sixty-odd MPs whom the Unionist Free Traders could muster at their zenith, late in 1903, eventually made their peace with Tariff Reform. The issue was really settled inside the party within twelve months of Chamberlain's first Tariff Reform speech in May 1903, which seemed at first to have caught the popular mood. Tariff Reform scored initial by-election successes and it was only from the beginning of 1904 that the electoral tide turned decisively in favour of the Liberal Party. The Chamberlainite policy thus appeared to have made great strides, and if it was temporarily checked by the electoral débâcle of 1906, the Unionist Free Traders were the real losers.

But Chamberlain's grand design ultimately failed. Within ten years of its spectacular launching it lay waterlogged in the shallows, scuppered by its own crew. The real cause of the trouble, according to Richard Jebb, a Tariff Reformer of extreme views, was that 'we were running a Radical policy in the name of Conservatism ... to suit our purpose, which was Liberal Unionist. We did it in good faith, but it was a fraud all the same ...' Insofar as it focuses attention unduly on the Liberal Unionists, this comment is misleading; but it is perceptive in indicating the tension between Chamberlain's radical initiative and authentic Conservatism. When, after its stunning electoral reverses in 1906, the Conservative Party eventually proclaimed Tariff Reform as its official policy, it showed that Chamberlain's original vision had almost slipped from view. Balfour's pragmatic approach, albeit taunted as pusillanimous and tainted with defeatism, succeeded in domesticating Tariff Reform for specifically Conservative purposes. In all this Balfour was true to the Cecil blood in his veins. As *The Times* commented in November 1907, Tariff Reform had been adopted 'because time and circumstance have made it the most potent engine for carrying out the traditional aims and policy of the party'. Even the hard core of Unionist Free Traders who withstood the 1906 elections found their position fatally undermined by the opprobrious social legislation of the Liberal Government. The appeal of Tariff Reform was now as an alternative source of revenue to the sort of progressive taxation which all right-minded Conservatives abhorred in the Free Trade Budgets of Asquith and Lloyd George.

These, then, were the lines of party division which underlay the conflict over the House of Lords in 1909–10. Its rejection of the 'People's Budget' of 1909 made a constitutional crisis out of the fiscal issue. Tariff Reform was the policy on which the Conservatives therefore fought the 1910 elections. Their failure to defeat the Liberals when carrying this banner made it a vulnerable commitment thereafter. Though in 1911 the Unionists elected a new leader, Bonar Law, who had made his reputation as an ardent Chamberlainite, he showed himself an even more fervent Unionist in his choice of strategy. With the re-emergence of the Home Rule issue, he was responsible for repudiating food taxes as party policy at the beginning of 1913. Without food taxes, imperial preference was impracticable, and, though Tariff Reform remained in name, it was now a ghost policy, or at most a nod towards industrial protection. For the Unionist Party, the defence of the Union against the threat of Irish Home Rule was its *raison d'être*; by comparison, Tariff Reform was only its hobby. It was eclipsed, therefore, by the logic of party priorities, which had in fact always governed its progress.

Chamberlain's health failed before he could bring his last campaign to a resolution. In 1906, at the age of seventy, he had a stroke from which he never recovered. The last eight years of his life form a moving and pathetic epilogue to the story of his career. Sequestered in Highbury, he was like Napoleon on St Helena; his legend was nourished by a faithful band of adherents but everyone knew that he had met his Waterloo. The stricken general continued to pour out a stream of admonitory messages to his troops. Almost his last public act was to urge the House of Lords to reject Lloyd George's Budget in 1909. This made good sense from the point of view of Tariff Reform but it was an ironic valediction for Radical Joe.

His strongest lifelong claim to a radical influence surely lies at another level. For what remained consistent from the Birmingham caucus to the Tariff Reform League was an effort at political mobilization of an innovative kind. He remained permanently convinced of the inherent virtues of unorthodox policies and methods, even though the Radical shibboleths of his early days were discarded one by one. In the last twenty years of his life he may have been on the Right rather than the Left. But not for him the Conservative appeal to a deferential clientele by an invocation of the traditional symbols of undisturbed hierarchy! Instead, Chamberlain was the first right-wing politician to seek to politicize a mass following and to present policies which enlisted behind them widespread popular grievances against the status quo. His problems are not our problems, his solutions can hardly be our solutions. In particular, the British Empire, to which he finally devoted his energies, has disappeared in a far from Chamberlainite manner: not with a bang but a whimper. For all that, Joseph Chamberlain is still the first major British politician whom we can recognize as our contemporary.

THE NEW CONDUCTOR.
OPENING OF THE 1917 OVERTURE.

(*Punch*, 20 December 1916)

82

4

ASQUITH AND LLOYD GEORGE:

MISALLIANCES

No family has been more closely associated with the fortunes of the twentieth-century Liberal Party than that of Herbert Henry Asquith. He himself led it for nearly twenty years, from 1908 to 1926, during which time, it must be said, it suffered catastrophic reverses. His daughter, best known as Lady Violet Bonham Carter, watched over its subsequent difficulties with much the same mixture of rueful impotence and faintly absurd proprietorial melancholy as that with which Toni Buddenbrooks observed the decline of her family. In the 1950s and 1960s, to be sure, her son Mark and her son-in-law Jo Grimond helped to light beacons of revival which, as the jealous guardian of the Asquithian tradition, she lived to see. Yet even she could not prevent her father's reputation from suffering an eclipse. This was largely a result of the overdue historical rehabilitation of the political creativity of Lloyd George in recent years – almost as though our estimation of the two men was bound to vary inversely, going up and down like counterweights.

In 1916 Asquith was replaced as Prime Minister by Lloyd George. The rift between them was institutionalized with the subsequent disruption of the Liberal Party. To most contemporaries, therefore, a favourable assessment of one implied an unfavourable view of the other. By the time the dust settled in the 1920s, Asquith and Lloyd George were both in the wilderness and Labour had filled the Liberals' former role as a party of government. There was plenty here to keep the animosities burning among contemporaries. Upon the personal rivalry between them, so it was held, hinged the destruction of their party. Subsequent historians, however, have often looked for structural reasons for these developments in explaining why the Liberal Party lost its room for manoeuvre and Labour, by contrast, acquired a far more solid and effective political base.

There is no doubt that the increasing polarization of politics along class lines squeezed the Liberals out in the end. But how far this was an inevitable development remains disputable. For there is good reason to argue that class had already emerged as the bedrock of voter alignments in the pre-war period, yet at this stage the Liberals were able to benefit from the process and Labour was contained. Maybe this was an inherently precarious situation, unlikely to last. But the fact is that it was only after 1916 that Labour made an effective independent bid for power – and it did so at a time when Asquith and Lloyd George had obligingly dealt the Liberal Party a series of stunning blows. To interpret the course of politics in these years simply in terms of structural causes is to overlook the role of contingency. There is, in fact, a story to be told, with an inescapable personal dimension, about two men who were curiously matched in their strengths and weaknesses.

Asquith remains a complex figure who, like the sphinx, keeps some of his secrets. It is easy enough to pile up the paradoxes about him. He came from Yorkshire Nonconformist stock, he was a scholarship boy, a self-made man; yet he became the embodiment of a patrician political style, took to London society, to bridge, and to rather more drink than was good for him. As a backbencher in the 1886 parliament he was, along with his friend R.B. Haldane, a leading hope of the progressive wing of the Liberal Party, and when in high office he was responsible for innovations in social and economic policy which many considered revolutionary in laying the foundations of a Welfare State financed through redistributive taxation. Yet he was deeply conservative by temperament, with an unimaginative and often legalistic cast of mind. He was a Liberal Imperialist and took Britain into the First World War; yet he became the champion of many Radicals who mistrusted militarism, conscription and power politics. His relations with most of his colleagues were purely formal and his manner often seemed constrained by a Victorian reserve; yet he could be relaxed and frivolous in the company of the young and, as will be seen, he came to depend on liaisons of a sentimental and somewhat indiscreet kind.

In part these conflicting images are those of past and present. A sterner, younger Asquith gave way to a more indulgent older man. As Keynes put it, 'the somewhat tight features, the alleged coldness of the aspiring lawyer from Balliol, were entirely transformed in the noble Roman of the war and post-war years, who looked the part of Prime Minister as no one has since Mr Gladstone'. The triumphs of Asquith's early career were thus the result of ability, ambition, and also a certain austerity which he later lost. In this respect his second marriage, to Margot Tennant in 1892, is clearly relevant but was not simply the cause of a new departure. She opened doors for him in creating a stylish social life which he certainly enjoyed, though it is a moot point whether 'the aristocratic embrace', as some suggested, smothered his radicalism. 'Asquith *qua* Asquith is a fine fellow, an honest man and a sincere Liberal,' thought the Liberal leader, Campbell-Bannerman. 'But Asquith *cum* Margot is a lost soul.'

If Asquith was an enigma, David Lloyd George has proved equally baffling. Keynes again supplies a memorable image. He doubtless spoke for many of his fellow-countrymen when he asked, 'who shall paint the chameleon, who can tether a broomstick?' But Keynes was not, of course, a fellow-countryman of 'this goat-footed bard, this half-human visitor to our age from the hag-ridden magic and enchanted woods of Celtic antiquity', and what baffled him was a 'flavour of final purposelessness, inner irresponsibility, existence outside or away from our Saxon good and evil, mixed with cunning, remorselessness, love of power ...' Keynes's conclusion, that 'Lloyd George is rooted in nothing', therefore, simply means that he was rooted in nothing which was familiar to a particular sort of highly educated Englishman. Yet what he was rooted in – the chapel culture of rural North Wales – can be explained perfectly well by the Welsh historian Kenneth Morgan, able to draw upon Welsh language sources in acting literally as his interpreter.

'I was brought up in a workman's home,' Lloyd George once claimed. Since he was addressing the Trades Union Congress at the time, it was a happy sentiment: but not, of course, one to be taken literally. The cottage-bred man from Llanystumdwy had in fact been brought up in the best cottage in the village, the home of his uncle, Richard Lloyd, a master cobbler. A non-smoker, a total abstainer, an unpaid pastor in a strict Baptist sect, Uncle Lloyd was a village elder who took in his two orphaned nephews, David and William George. With monstrous favouritism, David was singled out as the bearer of his hopes and allowed, unlike William, to call himself Lloyd George. He was assured of a decent schooling; no university, of course – Oxford or Cambridge unthinkable; but solid professional credentials, articled as a solicitor. It was the sort of career which was commonplace in French or American politics: the rise of a locally well-connected country attorney who championed a series of interlocking religious, educational, legal and political causes. Lloyd George was used to being pampered by his family and made it a lifelong habit. He exploited his brother by leaving him to run their law firm (Lloyd George and George), which provided an indispensable income to its sleeping partner. Only his wife Margaret failed to make enough fuss of him; and when he felt himself neglected and lonely in London he fell readily enough into the arms of other women. In his own Welsh-speaking, chapel-going, Liberal-voting community, Lloyd George was an insider who secured the local parliamentary seat at the age of twenty-seven; only when he got to Westminster was he an outsider.

What gave him prominence as a British politician was his

opposition to the Boer War. Many opponents of the war can fairly be called Little Englanders – a description which is comprehensively inappropriate for Lloyd George. He was no pure-minded pacifist but a combative and courageous orator, ready, as in Birmingham, to take the war into the enemy's camp. His Gladstonian self-righteousness struck a chord with C. P. Scott, the great editor of the *Manchester Guardian*, who helped give Lloyd George a platform. The *Manchester Guardian*, moreover, stood for a New Liberalism which was defined in terms of social democracy as well as political democracy and which looked for co-operation with the rising forces of Labour. As patriarchal a figure as Uncle Lloyd, Scott assumed the role of self-appointed conscience to Lloyd George, who played up magnificently because this represented one side of his nature. He once claimed that at the Day of Judgement he would say only one thing: 'Sir, I was a pro-Boer.'

Although Asquith was identified as a Liberal Imperialist at the turn of the century, he took no step which would mark a more permanent breach with the official Liberal Party. He steered a course better calculated to ensure him the reversion to the leadership than to further any strident doctrine of empire. In particular, Asquith followed Chamberlain around the country during the Tariff Reform campaign, making himself the leading champion of the Liberal case; it may have been a defensive and even conservative response to Chamberlain's economic radicalism but Free Trade was the cry on which the Liberals were to win their landslide victory in the 1906 General Election.

There was thus no real obstacle to Asquith taking office under Campbell-Bannerman in 1905, and as Chancellor of the Exchequer he carved out an unchallenged position as heir apparent. His work here quietly laid the essential groundwork for the more flamboyant initiatives which Lloyd George took as his successor, advancing beyond the essentially negative Free Trade consensus of 1906. It was Asquith who first moved towards a graduated income tax and who presented the Budget which first provided for old age pensions. It was, moreover, Asquith, as incoming Prime Minister, who appointed Lloyd George to succeed him at the Treasury in 1908. It was with the formation of this partnership at the top of the Government that the New Liberalism of social reform was given a real political cutting edge.

In one sense the Liberal Government took up social reform as a response, not to socialism, but to Tariff Reform. By the time Lloyd George became Chancellor of the Exchequer the issue had become clear. If the Liberals were to ignore social reform while in office, Lloyd George had warned, 'then would a real cry arise in this land for a new party, and many of us here in this room would join in that cry'. The new party, of course, would be Labour, which might then become 'a force that will sweep away Liberals amongst other things'. But the fact that advanced Liberals sometimes talked in this way did not mean that in their bones they believed it would really happen, and their electoral competition with their traditional opponents was more often at the front of their minds. When Lloyd George looked to the Old Age Pensions Bill 'to stop the electoral rot' in 1908, it was the threat from Unionism he had in mind.

Lloyd George introduced his first Budget in April 1909 and for seventy years, almost to the day, it set the strategy for the British fiscal system. It deliberately shifted the balance towards direct taxation, with heavy increases in death duties and a firm move towards a fully progressive income tax. As a means of raising revenue, these taxes proved highly successful, unlike the land duties which accompanied them. They were also intended to bear unequally on different classes, thus indicating the possibilities of redistributing income through fiscal policy. The class character of the Budget was central to its political inception and reception. When the House of Lords stood poised to reject it in the autumn of 1909, Lloyd George declared: 'The Lords may decree a revolution which the people will direct.'

Lloyd George, it is clear, did not plan his Budget as a means of leading the Lords into a trap. The revenue difficulties which confronted him were real and pressing. What with old age pensions and naval rearmament, a looming deficit foretold the end of the Gladstonian fiscal tradition. Being Lloyd George, he did nothing to play down the seriousness of the budgetary crisis, thus raising the stakes as regards its resolution. In this he was aided and abetted by the Tariff Reformers on the Conservative side. For them the bankruptcy of Free Trade finance was an irresistible argument for tariffs as the only way of finding new revenue. The strong men in both parties were happy to see the issue polarized in these terms. The Liberals had to prove through their Budget that social reform could be financed without abandoning Free Trade. The Unionists recognized that the Budget would pre-empt the appeal of Tariff Reform and therefore had to prevent it from passing.

The Budget was designed to appeal to the working classes while safeguarding the Liberals' historic constituency. Hence the rich were hit hard but earned incomes in the middle range came off lightly. Likewise political calculations underlay the rejection of the Budget by the Lords. This was not, as has often been implied, a suicidal impulse on the part of unsophisticated backwoodsmen, but a rational decision taken by Balfour with the interests of the Conservative Party at heart. Back in 1907 Lloyd George had called the House of Lords, with its tame Tory majority, Mr Balfour's poodle. And it had, after all, a perfectly lawful right to reject a Budget – especially one cobbled together for ulterior social and political ends. Naturally the Liberals denounced this as 'unconstitutional'. They would, wouldn't they? Although it was a high-risk strategy, the Lords' gamble was not wholly stupid.

The fact is, it nearly came off. If the Conservatives had actually won the 1910 elections – in which they gained ground from the Liberals – their claim that the Budget should not become law without reference to the electorate would have been vindicated. As things turned out, the Liberals used the popularity of the Budget to pay off old scores with the House of Lords, which had thwarted them so often in the past. In the 1910 elections the Liberals' new posture made many of their comfortable supporters uncomfortable; but they and their Labour allies achieved solid victories in industrial and working-class seats, notably in London and Lancashire. The link between social reform and Free Trade served to scotch Tariff Reform by removing its strongest electoral rationale. What mattered on both sides were the basic issues of social and economic policy, of which the constitutional issue was a refraction. Politics thus emerges as the real arbiter under an unwritten constitution.

Lloyd George's rhetorical triumph in selling his Budget to the voters could not, however, be repeated with National Insurance. His plan for health insurance was borrowed from Germany and amalgamated in a wide-ranging statute with the unemployment insurance scheme of his colleague Winston Churchill. But this was an administrative marvel rather than a popular success. Perhaps that is why in 1910 Lloyd George explored the possibilities of a coalition with the Unionists to carry this and other measures. Such a move had obvious attractions for him, not least in strengthening the Government's hand in negotiating terms for the scheme with the powerful private insurance companies. But harnessing the Conservative Party to the domestic programme of the New Liberalism would have been a breathtaking finesse, and it is not surprising that Lloyd George failed to pull it off. National Insurance was passed as a party measure but at the price of major concessions to the private insurance interests. 'Many men have tried to get their ideas through without associating themselves with party,' Lloyd George reflected in 1913, 'and they have always failed, because party government is an essential part of the government of this country.' Though he did not conceal his hankering after a party truce as an opportunity for constructive change, for the time being he accepted this constraint.

All told, the pre-war Liberal Government had not done so badly. True, this Government failed, like every Government, to solve the Irish problem, and, with less excuse, to address the issue of women's suffrage effectively. Asquith must be held culpable here; but by the same token he must be given credit for the successes of his Government. He was largely responsible for the strategic steadiness, the executive authority and parliamentary adroitness which helped it get most of its programme through. Its measures gave it a social-democratic dimension which was at once the means of containing Labour and of checking the electoral appeal of the Conservatives, who had now lost three General Elections in a row. This is the measure of what Asquith and Lloyd George had achieved; and the evidence that they intended to stick together can be summed up in one word – Marconi.

Lloyd George, always on the look-out for ready cash, had been given some shares in the American Marconi Company by his friend Rufus Isaacs, the Attorney-General; and, when questions were raised about Government contracts with the British Marconi Company, he kept mum while Isaacs assured the House of Commons in October 1912 that they had never traded in the shares 'of that company'. Poor Isaacs, of course, was found out; he had to go back to the House to explain the difference between this company and that company, a distinction with which Members were singularly unimpressed. But if the Attorney-General resigned, the Chancellor of the Exchequer would have to go too. This is surely why Asquith (who had more of an inkling about this and that than he let on) stepped in to protect them both; and with the Prime Minister behind them, they could all bluff it out and tough it out together. It is a revealing if not an edifying indication of how much Asquith and Lloyd George needed each other. Nor did the advent of the First World War disrupt their partnership. Despite the unease of Radicals like C.P. Scott over British foreign policy, Asquith's confidence that he could keep his Cabinet substantially intact turned out to be well-founded. True, the old Gladstonian Morley resigned on principle; but Lloyd George stayed, also on principle.

When Britain declared war in August 1914, her *casus belli* was the violation of Belgian neutrality by Germany. Lloyd George assured Scott that this had 'completely altered the situation'. Strategic priorities of a wider kind undoubtedly influenced Government decision-making, but the example of 'gallant little Belgium' had a peculiar force for the sort of

Liberals who had earlier opposed the Boer War. Lloyd George spoke for them when he claimed to have upheld on both occasions 'exactly the same principle, the principle of opposition to the idea that great and powerful empires ought to have the right and to use their right to crush small nationalities'. The Gladstonian propensity to translate international politics into issues of right and wrong was clearly at work here. It fostered a black-and-white view of events which is consonant with Lloyd George's switch to outright endorsement of the war. He could never be accused of supporting it half-heartedly. This was, indeed, the seed of subsequent disaffection with his Liberal colleagues. Once in, he was in up to his neck, while many of them seemed to be dabbling their toes at the edge.

Lloyd George thus pitched his claims high – perhaps too high. He first publicly declared his support for the war in September 1914 at the Queen's Hall, London, having endured his customary perturbation before a big speech, 'lying on the sofa', as a friend observed, 'yawning and stretching himself in a state of high nervous excitement'. Once on his feet, doubts fell away as Lloyd George pulled out all the stops, including the *vox humana*. He showed his audience 'the great peaks we had forgotten, of Honour, Duty, Patriotism, and, clad in glittering white, the great pinnacle of Sacrifice pointing like a rugged finger to Heaven'. Yet only a month previously he had privately told his wife that enlistment in a 'war on the German people' must not claim their son Gwilym – 'I am not going to sacrifice my nice boy for that purpose.' Perhaps, in a fast-changing situation, the charge of crude hypocrisy can be extenuated, but an uneasy impression remains.

The ironies of his position were not entirely lost upon Lloyd George. The war transformed his role in a series of bewildering steps. When he made an appeal for co-operation to the Trades Union Congress in September 1915, he began with a couple of jokes about his credentials. As Minister of Munitions, he announced, he must surely be 'the greatest employer of labour' to have addressed the TUC. With his tongue in his other cheek, he claimed to be a trade unionist himself, since as a lawyer he belonged to 'about the strictest, the most jealous, trade union in the world'. He vigorously repudiated any notion that he had simply sold out to the governing class which he had once scourged. But by December 1916 the radical spokesman of the Edwardian peace movement had become war leader in a government dominated by the Conservatives.

In making sense of the lives of Lloyd George and Asquith at this juncture, historians are now able to draw upon two remarkable sources. One is the diary of Frances Stevenson, Lloyd George's personal secretary and mistress; the other is the vast body of letters which Asquith sent to his confidante, Venetia Stanley. The strange death of Liberal England has become a cliché; the strange life of its leading custodians gives a new twist to the story. It is especially revealing in Lloyd George's case to have a record of this kind, since he was notorious for not writing letters, and he rarely put himself into what he put down on paper. What insights, then, do we gain from these documents?

Frances Stevenson's own position was never easy. An educated and independent-minded young woman, she was first engaged to teach Lloyd George's daughter. Like the heroine of a novel by H.G. Wells, she fell for a man twice her age; and when he offered her a post as his secretary in 1912 it was, as she later put it, 'on his own terms, which were in direct conflict with my essentially Victorian upbringing'. She made one effort to break away and, staying in Scotland at Christmas 1912, considered a proposal of marriage from a young man whom she had met on holiday. Lloyd George responded first by saying that he would not stand in her way, then, almost immediately, by doing so. He summoned her to London; something terrible had happened, he needed her, she returned. 'It was the Marconi scandal which was about to break,' she recalled – as indeed it was, though not until some weeks later. In the meantime Lloyd George's terms were accepted and Frances Stevenson became his 'darling Pussy'. Her affair upset her parents, who later tried to separate them – 'they think I am his plaything, and that he will fling me aside when he has finished with me – or else they think that there will be a scandal and that we shall all be disgraced'.

Frances Stevenson's confidence that the relationship would last triumphed on the first point. But the fear of scandal is a thread that runs through the story. Even in later years, they always had to be careful: careful not to go about in the Government car, nor to dine together in public; careful not to travel back and forth together too often between London and the Versailles Conference; always careful not to be 'too reckless' in going about together. Lloyd George believed that it was possible to defy respectability provided a certain homage was paid to conventions. 'There is much satisfaction in "doing" the world!' he exclaimed in 1915. So he shamelessly helped propagate a picture of himself as a conventional family man, despite Frances Stevenson's unease. He was virtually a bigamist, with his old wife back in Wales and Pussy in London. Moreover, he obviously thought Pussy should aspire to the same state in planning an empty marriage between her and one of his henchmen as the perfect front. But this was going too far and the bizarre idea was dropped.

One problem was to shuttle the Lloyd George family between his own house, his wife's house in Wales, Downing Street and later Chequers, with Frances Stevenson ready to disappear through the back door when they appeared at the front. These were not ideal arrangements but they avoided an overt domestic crisis. There was always the latent threat that Lloyd George's career, like Dilke's and Parnell's before it, would end in the divorce courts. By January 1916 Lloyd George claimed that he could face disgrace: 'I can understand Parnell now for the first time.' But Frances Stevenson remained happier that the issue should not be put to the test.

Frances Stevenson, of course, was more than 'the other woman'. She saw Lloyd George at work as well as at play, and observed him 'adopting flanking movements, so to speak, when a frontal attack is not likely to prove successful, "roping in" persons whose influence is likely to prove helpful or whose opinion counts for something, seeking out those who are "on the fence" and whose opposition would be dangerous, and then talking them round, using all the arts of which he is a past master'. She saw that charm was 'essential to a Lloyd George', and that he was hardly so innocent of craft as he seemed. 'No one ever convinced anyone by an argument,' he once said, and she saw how he would use all his personal wiles instead to gain a point. She saw too how 'he *distributes* his own nerves in a crisis', exhausting those around him but fortifying himself. These observations go to the heart of Lloyd George's effectiveness in politics.

The earliest letters from Asquith to Venetia Stanley, a daughter of the Liberal peer Lord Sheffield, date from 1910, but only in 1912 did the correspondence pick up. It was at this point that Venetia emerged from her schoolgirl role as his daughter Violet's friend and appeared in a new light to the Prime Minister. 'Suddenly, in a single instant, without premonition on my part or any challenge on hers, the scales dropped from my eyes,' he later recalled. It was, as he told her, when 'I made my great discovery of the *real* you'. This is a suggestive phrase, to be sure, and one which Edwardian fiction could endow with explicit sexual connotations. But the idea that Asquith was in any position to consummate his passion for Venetia must be discounted. Instead the affair blossomed and flourished (as it ultimately withered and perished) through the virtually daily series of letters he wrote her from the end of 1913 to May 1915. In July and August 1914 there was a second change of gear in the relationship, marked by an increase in the intensity of epistolary bombardment. The peak was reached in the spring of 1915. These dates, of course, coincide with two great crises: the outbreak of war and the imminent downfall of the Liberal Government.

Considered intimately, the liaison was not carried as far as might initially be supposed. But there was clearly more to it than was apparent to members of Asquith's circle, for all their ready acceptance that the Prime Minister, as he put it himself, manifested '(perhaps) a slight weakness for the companionship of clever and attractive women'. This served as his cover. It meant that his contacts with Venetia needed no apology provided nothing happened to flout the indulgence they were accorded by the two families and friends alike. Only when she started her course at the London Hospital did the arrival of a messenger, delivering letters from the Prime Minister to a trainee nurse, in itself cause eyebrows to be raised. The existence of the correspondence was acknowledged; but its frequency was masked by Asquith's practice of by-passing the official mail arrangements in Downing Street; and its content was certainly kept from prying eyes. 'Don't leave this on your table', Asquith enjoined.

The fact is that the correspondence cannot possibly be regarded as merely sentimental, and its erotic charge clearly signalled a threat to Margot Asquith's position. She liked to claim that 'he shows me *all* his letters & all Venetia's', but she also began brooding on 'the knowledge alas! that I am no longer young & I daresay – in fact I always observe – as men get older they like different kinds of women'. In Margot, Asquith had a loyal, vivacious, outspoken supporter, but he looked elsewhere for respite from public affairs. It is not very mysterious what Venetia had to offer Asquith. Aged twenty-seven in 1914, presentable, well-connected, good-natured and trustworthy, she was well qualified for an *amitié amoureuse*. What Asquith had to offer was a flattering degree of attention from a man of great eminence who was ready, indeed eager, to cut through the veils of discretion and formality. It was an implicit trade-off between sex and power.

The more taxing the political problems he faced, the more indiscreet Asquith became. 'Bless you beloved' was the affectionate conclusion to his letters. But as the crisis over Irish Home Rule intensified in the summer of 1914, so did the emotional outpouring. 'My darling – you are dearer to me than I can tell you', Venetia was assured while being plied with news ('which is most secret') of the latest developments. With the outbreak of war, more news ('all this is *most secret*') was daily passed on. What they really needed, Asquith suddenly realized, was 'something like a code that we could use by telegraph' to cut out postal delays. 'Do you think it is impossible to invent something of the kind?' he asked Venetia. The bright idea of the Prime Minister sending telegrams full of hot military secrets to his girlfriend in an amateur code of her own devising is surely beyond the reach of satire.

The parallels between the private lives of Asquith and Lloyd George are not exact. Whereas Asquith made Venetia Stanley his confidante for a couple of years before she ultimately decided to marry another man, Lloyd George made Frances Stevenson his mistress in a virtually bigamous lifelong relationship. In both cases, however, they found release from political tension in these dangerous liaisons with women half their age. Their sentimental anniversaries were dated by political crises – the coal strike, the Marconi scandal – and both women absorbed stresses which flowed from the heart of Government. Did nothing flow from the heart in the other direction? Can Asquith and Lloyd George have remained wholly insulated in their political judgement from their emotional entanglements?

As a peacemaker and political broker, Asquith moved with a sure instinct, rarely allowing personal feelings to divert him from the main chance. Much turned on his relations with Lloyd George, and he showed a tactful appreciation of the fact. In peacetime they had established a fund of mutual respect and good faith. In Lloyd George's later reminiscences to Frances Stevenson, the tone towards Asquith is generally cordial. Asquith's support, he would recall, had been invaluable in getting the Budget policy adopted in 1909. The Marconi affair was hardly something to look back upon with pride, but it had likewise served to bind the two men together. It was not Asquith but his lieutenant Reginald McKenna whom Lloyd George saw as his real rival and antagonist. Asquith, however, took pains to make sure that his friendship for McKenna did not compromise his good relations with Lloyd George. Hence the extraordinary episode at the end of March 1915 when Lloyd George scouted gossip about intrigue, which he attributed to McKenna, by affirming his absolute loyalty to Asquith. According to Frances Stevenson, Lloyd George 'went to have a talk with the P.M. about it, & found the old boy in tears'. According to Asquith, on the other hand, after Lloyd George had 'declared that he owed everything to me; that I had stuck to him & protected him & defended him when every man's hand was against him', it was his Chancellor whose 'eyes were wet with tears'.

March 29th 1915 was thus an unusually lachrymose day in Downing Street. Lloyd George's demonstrative nature made his behaviour seem in character; but what Asquith did not know was that his colleague had spent the previous month under considerable personal anxiety. It is likely that Frances Stevenson had an abortion, and she was certainly convalescent. She wrote appreciatively that Lloyd George 'watched and waited on me devotedly, until I cursed myself for being ill & causing him all this worry'. She knew that he faced troubling decisions as well as the strain of delivering his oratorical *tour de force*, 'Through Terror to Triumph'. There is no suggestion that he fell below his best as a result; indeed, she was assured that 'the anxiety and trouble helped him to make a great speech, for when his mind is disturbed his whole nature is upheaved and it stimulates him to greater power of expression'. Even so, his lack of composure in his interview with Asquith a few days later may have betrayed an unusually fraught emotional state; and likewise the Prime Minister shed his own (more uncharacteristic) tears in a month when Venetia Stanley was receiving two letters a day.

If Lloyd George was not incapacitated, neither was Asquith, who again managed to ease the friction over McKenna and patch things up. It was not to last, but while it lasted, the political equilibrium of the Government depended on this sort of exertion of Asquith's emollient skills. Within a couple of months, however, his equanimity was shattered by two rude shocks: privately from the engagement of Venetia Stanley, publicly from a sudden challenge to the Liberal Government. On 12 May Asquith received news of the engagement; Venetia Stanley was to marry Edwin Montagu, a member of Asquith's own Cabinet. The Prime Minister responded curtly: 'As you know well, *this* breaks my heart.' But Asquith immediately had another crisis on his hands – one threatening his political survival. Embarrassing allegations of a shell shortage in France were printed by *The Times*, and there was suspicion that the source of the leak was a Cabinet minister. Nothing was ever proved, but the usual suspects were rounded up. For once, Lloyd George was not among them; indeed, if anyone was rocking the boat on this occasion, the finger points to Winston Churchill.

At the time Asquith appeared still to be in control of events – or rather, as adroit as ever in responding to them. The man whose heart Venetia Stanley had broken on 12 May had, within a week, moved decisively to pre-empt a challenge to his position. Taking Lloyd George into his confidence, he reconstructed his administration on a broad basis, seeking to implicate the Unionists in its policies without surrendering vital posts to them. His old friend Haldane was sacrificed without apology, his young colleague Churchill demoted without explanation. As Churchill expostulated twenty years later: 'Not "all done by kindness"! Not all by rosewater! These were the convulsive struggles of a man of action and of ambition at death-grips with events.' The fall of the Liberal Government, as it turned out, was a critical stage in the decline of Asquith and the elevation of Lloyd George in his place; but Asquith's actions do not look, at first sight, like those of a man prostrated by an emotional upheaval with which he could not cope.

It is, however, after the crisis, not during it, that people often go to pieces: not while the pressure is on, but after it has been removed. The relationship with Venetia was doubtless more a symptom than a cause of Asquith's inner tensions, as his febrile dependence upon it illustrates. But its termination in May 1915 nonetheless marks a noteworthy date in political history, albeit one more clearly significant in retrospect than at the time. It points to a contrast between the confident statesman who shared his triumphs with his darling Venetia and the increasingly woebegone figure cut by Asquith thereafter – one who no longer commanded Lloyd George's confidence.

Lloyd George's later comments suggest that he did not regard the breach as predestined; and until the formation of the First Coalition there are no signs that it was impending. But within months there is a distinct change of tone in the Stevenson diary. Lloyd George may not be intriguing against the Prime Minister but his support has become perceptibly more grudging – 'D. had always upheld him most loyally, whenever it came to the point.' Other sources record his growing doubts during the summer, in particular the developing theme that 'Asquith will not face inconvenient facts'. Asquith told Lloyd George: 'There are only two men in this Cabinet who count at all, and we are those two. If we quarrel, it will mean disaster.' But Lloyd George's dissatisfaction was fed by a continual sense of the inability of the Asquithian regime to meet the peculiar demands of war. The 'wait-and-see' policy, he maintained, 'is all right in peace time, and often answers admirably, but in war it leads straight to disaster'.

As early as February 1915 he could say: 'We are conducting a war as if there was no war.' To Lloyd George, with his strong gut reactions and weak attachment to abstract principle, the needs of war could best be met by bold measures of state intervention. He was at a loss to see why many of the Liberal ministers felt qualms about this, having broached such methods themselves in peacetime. Thus in May 1916 he spoke up for compulsory enlistment, 'as I would for compulsory education, or, if you allow me, for compulsory insurance'. In all this, he claimed, he was showing himself as good a Liberal as ever. Yet conscription emerged as a characteristic Unionist demand, and by 1916 Lloyd George plainly stood apart from the other Liberal ministers. The Unionist press exempted him from many of their strictures on the Asquith Government, and the pre-war pattern of party allegiances was no longer paramount.

By 1916, Asquith could no longer draw on the bond of respect which had previously held the Liberal leaders together. We see Lloyd George waiting for the right opportunity to bring about the reconstruction of the Government. This is the story that unfolds in Frances Stevenson's transparently uncritical record. Finally, in November 1916, he is steeled to act and press the issue, and, after previous uncertainties, finds himself steady and content when the die has been cast. On this reading, Lloyd George's rise to the premiership the following month is a triumph for duty over inclination.

There is also a sub-plot. For at a personal level the real villains are Margot Asquith, with her emotional propensity to maintain a vendetta, and Reginald McKenna, who 'between them were the ruin of the late P.M.'. McKenna, installed in May 1915 as Lloyd George's successor at the Treasury, was thereafter blamed by him for virtually all the troubles of the Government. By the end of October 1916 their antagonism was reaching a climax: 'I think McKenna is the only person whom D. really detests.' Three weeks later, mere words gave way to the threat of action: 'D. literally hates him, & I do not think he will rest till he has utterly broken him.' Lloyd George saw McKenna as Asquith's malevolent *éminence grise*: disastrous alike from the point of view of the national interest, party unity, or Asquith's own career.

It was this which invested the conflict with personal over-tones otherwise lacking. When Lloyd George ultimately sent Asquith his resignation in December 1916, he wrote: 'As you yourself said on Sunday, we have acted together for ten years and never had a quarrel, although we have had many a grave difference on questions of policy.' It was not a close friendship – Lloyd George maintained that 'there is no friendship at the top' – but a partnership buoyed up by its manifest political effectiveness. Once their serious quarrel began, it engulfed the Government and the Liberal Party alike; but even as late as 1923 Lloyd George could still remark: 'The old boy and I get on well together always when mischief makers are kept out.'

After 1916 the Liberal Party fell apart: a fissure opened which within two years had grown into a fundamental disruption.

If the split had not been so equal it would not have been so damaging. But both sides had claims to Liberal legitimacy which they refused to relinquish, and neither faction could be dismissed as a mere rump. Like rival litigants, they exhausted their resources in suing for an inheritance which, in the end, had been eaten up by the costs incurred. This process was not ineluctable but it became self-reinforcing. To understand the origins of the breach between Asquith and Lloyd George it may have been helpful to dwell on contingency and personal factors; but to appreciate the consequences of the split in the Liberal Party it is necessary to analyse some of the structural constraints, in particular the party system and the electoral system.

If Lloyd George were to thrive, he needed to remake the party system, not simply to by-pass it as he was temporarily able to do in wartime. In 1915 he was proclaiming that 'party politics are gradually vanishing', and hoping that 'when the hour of reconstruction comes all will be for the State, all will be for the nation'. In this he may have been somewhat naïve, but there is no need to impugn his sincerity. If his carelessness over party considerations helped him rise, it likewise doomed him in the end. In the short term, he kept the premiership. In 1918 he appeared before a grateful electorate as the man who won the war; but his Coalition Liberal supporters were outnumbered by Conservative MPs, whose prisoner he ultimately became. Asquith at least had his independence – and much good it did him. The independent Liberals were reduced to a faithful remnant of less than thirty MPs – half the size of the Labour Party. If Asquith was now down, Lloyd George was soon out. He failed to institutionalize his own position as leader of a centre party, and when the Conservatives realized that they could do without him in 1922, his fall was immediate and, as it turned out, irreversible.

Fighting once more under Liberal colours, as he was from 1923, he now discovered that the electoral system was a deadly handicap, and it is worth considering why this was so. Lloyd George had been at the peak of his power when the Fourth Reform Act was passed in 1918, yet he did little to shape it.

As in 1832 and 1867 and 1884–5, the politics of the issue determined what happened – and what did not happen. The fact is that all proposals for electoral reform have spread the sail of principle but carried the ballast of self-interest. This applies as much to debates over Proportional Representation as over the extent of the franchise. What happened in 1918 was franchise reform, with the eventual success of moves towards a democratic suffrage; what did not happen was electoral reform, with the failure of proposals for PR.

The salience of PR at this juncture needs to be recognized, for it was by no means inevitable that the 'first-past-the-post' system would be entrenched. There were, admittedly, complex cross-currents. Flushed by memories of how they had swept the board in 1906, when they had been grossly over-represented in Parliament, the Liberals were not persuaded of the merits of PR while it lay in their power to implement it. But they had become wiser by the time the Reform Bill was under consideration. Many Conservatives now hoped to benefit – as they subsequently did – from a pattern of periodic over-representation of major parties. As a minor party, Labour might have been expected to be more favourable to PR, and there was indeed a good deal of support; but Labour was exactly the sort of minor party which could thrive without PR, since its support was so highly concentrated in certain seats.

What confused the issue, however, was the Alternative Vote – the proposal that voters should number their preferences among candidates within the existing constituencies. The Liberals liked this scheme, on the assumption that they and Labour would mutually benefit from second preferences at the Conservatives' expense. By 1917 PR had become practical politics, with a many-sided attraction to supporters in all parties; but for most Liberal and Labour MPs the Alternative Vote was seen as the fallback position, failing a fully proportional system. Thus it is not the case that PR failed to be adopted through its own incoherence or novelty or impracticality or general un-Englishness. Instead, it became fatally entwined with technical issues over the plural vote which gave the Conservatives a partisan objection to it, of the kind which Salisbury would have appreciated, because of their wish to maximize the number of business voters. And having scotched PR, which at least had some attraction for Conservatives in guaranteeing minority representation in urban areas, they then killed off the Alternative Vote which they rightly saw as a straightforward advantage to their opponents.

First-past-the-post was thus to be the rule after all. But the Alternative Vote still cast its shadow over electoral politics in the winter of 1917–18, since it was precisely then that Labour committed itself to fighting a General Election on a wide front. Why not? With the Alternative Vote there would be little to lose from three-cornered contests. As it was, Labour pressed on regardless, and did so under an expanded franchise which somewhat improved its prospects.

Household suffrage, which had been the system in the boroughs since 1867 and in the counties since 1884, had not really held Labour back. It chiefly excluded sons living at home, which was fairly classless in its effects, and it is likely that trade unionists were already heavily enfranchised. Labour MPs, like the Liberals, generally supported the adult male suffrage proposal without seeing in it a unique passport to power. But why did the Conservatives, who had consistently feared the effects of democracy, capitulate to it in 1917? The short answer is that the war had turned 'workers' into 'soldiers' with incontestable claims to be considered 'citizens'. As the new armies grew, so did the Conservative conception of the electorate. At the Speaker's Conference in 1917, therefore, a democratic settlement was possible. With a big measure agreed, female suffrage could likewise be accepted within the shadow of a measure of male suffrage that went further. The women who got the vote had not only to be over thirty years of age but also, generally speaking, to be the wives of local government electors – householders in fact. These were not, of course, the girls who had attracted publicity as munitions workers or VADs, thus casting doubt on how far the vote was seen as a reward for war service; and 'Votes for Matrons' would have been an appropriate slogan. The net effect was universal adult suffrage for men but household suffrage for women (a state of affairs which lasted until 1928).

Thus politics determined the shape of a new electoral structure in 1918 and this in turn helped shape the politics of the subsequent period. The new franchise did not in itself sweep Labour forward, but the party was now poised for a significant, though not dramatic, breakthrough. By the early 1920s it was the old voting system, not the new franchise, which more seriously affected the outcome. Polling the same level of national support as the Liberals, Labour pulled ahead in parliamentary representation under first-past-the-post. Labour thus replaced the Liberals as the parliamentary opposition. Hence, after the Conservatives had lost the 1923 election, it was Ramsay MacDonald rather than Asquith who formed a minority Government.

With the accession of a Labour Government in 1924, moreover, the Liberals lost another of their residual assets – their ministerial credibility. Asquith may have looked the part of Prime Minister but he needed more than Central Casting to send him back to Downing Street. He was still reluctant to hand over the leadership of the Liberal Party to Lloyd George, who was kept waiting until it was too late for even Celtic magic to rescue the situation. It was now hard to remember that only ten years previously the Liberal Party could look to its leaders as a focus of unity, not a source of division: difficult to credit that Asquith and Lloyd George had stood together as an impressively formidable partnership, their dissimilar qualities often mutually reinforcing – two strong men who shared '(perhaps) a slight weakness for the companionship of clever and attractive women'.

A GREAT MEDIATOR

John Bull. "I've known many Prime Ministers in my time, Sir, but never one who worked so hard for security in the face of such terrible odds."

(Punch, 5 October 1938)

5

THE BUSINESSLIKE APPROACH:

NEVILLE CHAMBERLAIN

It is pretty obvious that Joseph Chamberlain intended his son to be Prime Minister – not Neville, of course, but Austen. The boys were half-brothers; Joseph's first and second wives were cousins, members of the Kenrick family, prominent, like the Chamberlains, in the Birmingham metal trades; and both women died in childbirth leaving young children. The two sons were packed off to Rugby, but it was Austen who went on to Trinity College, Cambridge, the stable which produced three out of four Conservative leaders in the early twentieth century – Arthur Balfour, Austen Chamberlain and Stanley Baldwin – with Bonar Law as the dark horse among them. Anxiously screwing his monocle in his eye, just like father, Austen knew that he could never be more than a chip off the old block. It is thus equally true to say that he never had a chance and that he had every chance. Perhaps Joe succeeded better than he knew in making Austen into what he could never be himself. For he made him into a gentleman, which no one could accuse the old man of being, and Austen's will to power seems to have been sapped in the process. Neville, on the other hand, remained a brisk hard-headed businessman, with no Oxbridge polish, who got ahead by getting things done, winning respect rather than indulgent affection. Ultimately there was little doubt which of them was more truly his father's son.

Austen Chamberlain was the only leader of the Conservative Party in this century never to become Prime Minister. Though holding other high offices, notably as Chancellor of the Exchequer and Foreign Secretary, the indelible image is of Austen being passed over, time and again, and never making enough of a fuss about it. The last time this happened was in 1935, when his hopes of returning for a final stint at the Foreign Office were dashed; and this provoked Churchill to comment: 'Poor man, he always plays the game and never wins it.' All it needed for this remark to become the inevitable tag was for Lord Beaverbrook to appropriate the phrase from Churchill, hone it into shape, reattribute it to F.E. Smith – just the sort of thing he *would* say – and publicize it in his memoirs. Poor Austen, it is universally agreed, always played the game and always lost.

The problem in Austen's career, then, is to explain not his rise so much as his failure to rise further. The fact is that it was not push but pull that helped him up so high so quickly. Did the Border Burghs want Joe to recommend them a Liberal Unionist candidate in 1887? Why, he had just the right man ready: rising twenty-four, monocle in place, orchid in buttonhole, prepared to catch the train from Birmingham with a suitable speech in his pocket. 'I do believe,' Austen wrote home after giving it, 'these people would have been pleased with anything from father's son.' In the event, it was as Member for East Worcestershire, practically on his doorstep, that Austen entered Parliament in 1891. It was a tribute to the power of the Chamberlain name throughout the Birmingham area. Again Churchill captured the piquancy well: 'The romance of feudalism and the hereditary principle were reproduced in novel trappings around the person of a leader who had set out to abolish them both.' Joe had 'carried into the crowded streets, clacking factories and slums of Birmingham those same loyalties which had heretofore thrived only in the Highland glens'.

The Chamberlains, in short, had the temerity to form their own dynasty to rival traditional families like the Churchills or the Cecils. Moreover, the tight-knit loyalties of the clan were a lifelong bond which sustained them in adversity. Both

Austen and Neville were notably close to their father; neither of them married till over forty. 'I do not think that there was ever anything in this world more beautiful than the family life of Highbury,' Austen affirmed. Their filial loyalty remained a common benchmark for subsequent political action – 'Our Father's sons can do no otherwise' – but it was also manifested in the tenacious family ties which each nurtured, especially with their unmarried sisters, Ida and Hilda. Calling themselves 'the Click', they prided themselves on the fact that if any one of them was hit, they all hit back.

Austen's maiden speech in the Commons brought his father the rare satisfaction of congratulation from that fine old traditionalist Gladstone, with his notable susceptibility for a young man with a silver spoon in his mouth. In 1895 Joe was even speaking privately of retirement in order to 'make room for Austen who has a future before him'. What separated the generations were the qualities which usually distinguish the young from the old – vigour, vision, purpose, ambition, resilience – and in this case the old man had them and the son did not. It was Joe who continued to 'make the weather' in politics, ultimately launching his crusade for Tariff Reform in 1903 rather than remaining supine in office. It was Austen who, on his father's resignation from the Government, became Chancellor of the Exchequer at the age of only forty. But this was little more than a matter of getting someone to mind the shop – and live over it, for that matter, since 11 Downing Street was Austen's first residence away from his father's house.

Even Joe's stroke in 1906 did not make Austen his own man. Like the Kennedys in a later era, the boys were determined to get on in politics partly to gratify the unfulfilled ambitions of their father Joseph, lying paralysed as an old man in the family home. Since it was Austen who was supposed to succeed, in both senses of the word, further expectations were thrust upon him. But his role in the party remained emblematic rather than potent. He had none of his father's indomitable radicalism, but was nonetheless designated as the intransigent standard bearer of Tariff Reform. He recognized that the

Tariff Reformers looked to him 'as Father's son in a very special way', yet also that they 'do not wholly trust me as they would trust Father'. On the face of it, his position was immensely strong. The amalgamation between the two wings of the Unionist Party was an accomplished fact; Tariff Reform was now the party's official policy; Austen's credentials to succeed Balfour in 1911 were thus irreproachable. With the door open to the leadership, Austen courteously stood back and let Bonar Law stride through instead. A contested election was thereby avoided, the unity of the party was assured, and Austen's decency and loyalty and reasonableness were widely held up for admiration.

Yet after a rise which had truly been effortless, this fateful check exposed a lack of steel which could no longer be disguised. If not Mr Balfour's poodle, Austen now looked like Mr Bonar Law's doormat. In this position he loyally served for ten years, and it was only when Law resigned through ill health in 1921 that Austen at last stepped into his place as leader of the party, albeit within a Coalition Government headed by Lloyd George. Everything pointed, yet again, to the prospect of Austen becoming Prime Minister. Law was *hors de combat*; the Conservative Party dominated the Coalition and could dictate the choice; indeed Lloyd George himself at one point offered to hand over. It took all Austen's misplaced heavy-handedness to fumble such opportunities. He stuck honourably to his post while the Coalition sank beneath him. He watched stoically from the bridge while Bonar Law rose from his sickbed and commandeered the Conservative Party as a lifeboat, thus demonstrating his political survival instinct. But to Austen it merely looked like sharp practice. He was left nursing his honour while Law briefly occupied 10 Downing Street; and the leadership of the Conservative Government then fell to Baldwin, a man unsmirched by association with Lloyd George.

There was, of course, a good deal left for Austen to do after 1922. He found his way back to the Cabinet under Baldwin in 1924, and was to enjoy his finest hour as Foreign Secretary at the Locarno Conference in 1925, which brought the promise of a mutually acceptable peace among old enemies in Europe. The striking change was that his path to office in a Conservative Government now had to be eased by, of all people, his younger brother Neville, who suddenly outshone him in a new political situation. A certain amount of fence-mending all round was thus called for. Austen did his best to hide his chagrin at being superseded in a way that Father had never anticipated. Neville also behaved well and wrote in commiseration: 'I have had my time of scorching humiliation and don't need to be told what it means.' Only the Click could fully appreciate the experiences he had in mind.

In the race for high office, one obvious way to steal an advantage is to start young. This was a trick which the old governing class understood perfectly well, and new men from outside were handicapped unless they could copy it. Lloyd George got into Parliament before he was thirty, just like Gladstone; and so did Austen Chamberlain, unlike his father, who had had to wait until he was forty. It took Neville Chamberlain until he was nearly fifty to become an MP in 1918, and his swift rise thereafter is all the more remarkable. To a large extent it was due initially to luck. Most of the leadership of the Conservative Party, headed by his brother, were deeply implicated in the Lloyd George Coalition, from which they would not or could not disengage their fortunes. Bonar Law had the good luck to develop an illness which opportunely allowed him to detach himself from Lloyd George and thereby made him Prime Minister. His bad luck, of course, was to develop another illness which quickly proved fatal. Baldwin's good luck was unalloyed; he emerged at the right moment as an able lieutenant to the dying Law and benefited accordingly from an unexpected Conservative resurgence. Neville Chamberlain was lucky too in suddenly finding so much room at the top in the Conservative Party in 1922, giving rapid advancement in 1923 to a man whose career, to an unusual extent, had been made away from Westminster.

Neville Chamberlain was the man who had to do the dirty work for the family, and it left a mark upon him. If there is a name, like Rosebud, which will help unravel his life story it is surely Andros. This small island in the Bahamas was said, in the late nineteenth century, to be suitable for the cultivation of sisal as a cash crop. It was just the sort of undeveloped estate of which Joseph Chamberlain liked to speak as Colonial Secretary, expatiating on the need to encourage British investment 'for the benefit of their population and for the benefit of the greater population which is outside'. This was, of course, an uplifting sentiment, and one very close to the great man's heart; for no one knew better than he how tempting such opportunities looked to the investors concerned. The task of restoring the Chamberlain family fortunes was therefore thrust upon young Neville – 'a boy just out of his teens with no experience of the world whatever', as he later put it. He was sent out to Andros to oversee the clearing and planting of the land.

Throughout five formative years he fought against the odds to make the enterprise successful, and it taught him a lot. When the labourers went on strike for higher wages, he shipped in others from Nassau: a good lesson in labour relations. The doings of the black workers provided him with a fund of patronizing stories to retail to his sisters at home, just as munitions workers and family servants were to do in later years. Little wonder that he wrote in 1895: 'even if it turns out a failure I am not sure that I should regret the years I have spent here. The responsibility and independence have certainly called out whatever was in me and shown me that I was worth more than I thought.' It revealed him – much to Churchill's surprise when he heard the story fifty years later – as 'a hard bitten pioneer from the outer marches of the British empire!'

The wretched sisal, however, would not grow. Neville was not able to recoup his father's fortunes but instead had to tell him that all was lost. 'You and Austen have had to rely solely on my reports,' he wrote home, 'but I have been here all the time and no doubt a sharper man would have seen long ago what the ultimate result was likely to be.' In view of all that had been staked, it was a nasty moment for the Click. And yet they seem to have survived unscathed in maintaining the expense of two large houses in Birmingham and London. The mystery may be resolved by reference to Joseph Chamberlain's investments in the explosives company Kynoch's, whose booming shares benefited from burgeoning defence spending, as Radicals like Lloyd George did not fail to remark at the time of the Boer War. The Click's long-standing view was that they were much maligned by people with a poor grasp of business principles.

Back home, Mr Neville was left making his living in Birmingham while Mr Austen was making his name at Westminster. It was Neville who, for nearly twenty years, put in a full working week as managing director of a manufacturing company, arriving and leaving with such punctuality that it became legendary. It was also Neville who maintained the family tradition in municipal politics, showing his father's impatience with laissez-faire when it came to getting things done. There is little doubt that he understood local government like no other Conservative politician of his generation: experience which gave him an impregnable command of the more arcane aspects of the rating system in Cabinet arguments with Churchill in the 1920s. It was as Lord Mayor of Birmingham in December 1916 that he was suddenly thrust to national eminence. Lloyd George appointed him, sight unseen, as Director General of National Service. The Prime Minister explained his brief to the House of Commons with assurances – 'we shall not hesitate to come to Parliament and ask Parliament to release us from pledges given in other circumstances' – which were rhetorically overflowing but administratively empty.

Once more the sisal would not grow, and Chamberlain's story was much the same – he had been 'a complete stranger to the whole business from beginning to end, a child in the ways of Government departments'. His biographer Iain Macleod, with the eye of a Cabinet minister himself, saw at once what Chamberlain should have done to put Lloyd

George on the spot and to bring the realities into line with the grandiloquent prospectus he had outlined. Lacking this sort of insight, and consequently failing to grasp the nettle at the outset, Chamberlain found his position unenviable. While he himself recorded that 'it rather appeared I had no power to do any of the things that might produce any effect', his colleague Christopher Addison concluded: 'He seems not to know even now what he is going to do and does not appear to have the remotest notion as to how he is going to do it.'

Chamberlain assured his sisters, with whom he maintained a regular correspondence throughout his career, that his staff manifested complete loyalty to their beleaguered Director General. But, for whatever reason, he chose not to tell everything even to the Click. One of his abler officials tempered loyalty with the observation that he was a man whose thinking ran on tramlines – 'if his mind had been less rigid and he had been blessed with more imagination, he would never have stumbled into the mire that swallowed him up'. This image of a man trying to tackle the intractable difficulties of unknown territory like Andros with the methods which had made the Birmingham trams run on time is reinforced by the final verdict of the man who made the appointment. 'Mr Neville Chamberlain is a man of rigid competency,' Lloyd George wrote in his *War Memoirs*. 'Such men have their uses in conventional times or in conventional positions, and are indispensable for filling subordinate posts at all times. But they are lost in an emergency or in creative tasks at any time.'

If Chamberlain returned to Birmingham marked as a failure in the Prime Minister's eyes, he reciprocated with an equally unflattering opinion of Lloyd George, whose eclipse in post-war politics Neville did much to ensure, even though it was accomplished at some cost to Austen. For the iron had entered Neville's soul and, like his father before him, he determined that he would only play the game if he always won – or that, at any rate, would be his unremitting resolve. The time for 'scorching humiliation' was now past. In contrast to Austen's indolent, sophisticated, patrician airs and graces – Trinity on top and almost no Birmingham underneath – Neville was neither afraid of hard work nor too grand to acknowledge that his successes were the result of hard work.

He operated from the family's old power base of Birmingham, which he knew inside out in a way that Austen never did, and sat initially for the inner city division of Ladywood. Neville also differed from Austen in being identified less strongly with a specifically Liberal Unionist heritage. Brought up as a Unitarian, he had as little religious feeling as his father and lacked any tactical need to simulate it in an era when political Dissent had been brought to its knees (arguably its proper posture). So Neville did not attend church but did join the Carlton Club in 1922. His cultural world and moral outlook, however, was that formed by his Unitarian upbringing. He typified the way in which the awkward zealotry of Nonconformity, which had nourished Radicalism in the nineteenth century, could leave a residue of priggish respectability which, with the help of a bit of upward social mobility, fed into twentieth-century Conservatism. He remained much more a provincial businessman in politics than a traditional Conservative. This might have typecast him as a Coalitionist, but in his case personal hostility to Lloyd George, if nothing else, was sufficient to seal an uncompromising partisan allegiance. In the secularized, commercialized Conservative Party of the post-war period, he quickly emerged as an eligible leader.

It was in 1923 that Neville Chamberlain discovered the great love of his life: the Ministry of Health. Here he was in his element, overseeing the vast field of local government as a connoisseur and, above all, working on tramlines, not to mention other municipal functions. As he told Baldwin, 'the work of my present office is congenial because it follows naturally from my training'. Heartbroken, he was snatched from this demi-paradise within a matter of months to become Chancellor of the Exchequer. 'Perhaps after all I may still go back to the Ministry some day,' he wrote pluckily, 'but it will be difficult as Austen knows to get away from that beastly

Treasury.' Only fifteen months later his passion was requited. After the brief interlude of the first Labour Government in 1924, he found himself in a position to fend off Baldwin's offer of the reversion to the Treasury. 'I remain convinced that I might be a great Minister of Health but am not likely to be more than a second-rate Chancellor,' he wrote.

Moreover, he lived up to this promise. His work in reforming public health provision, extending the national insurance system, and remodelling local government and the poor law, all achieved between 1924 and 1929, constitutes a sold record of achievement. He was uniquely qualified to understand the interlocking responsibilities and demarcation disputes between administrative bodies created at different times to serve different functions. His Local Government Act of 1929 was a monument to bureaucratic rationalization, Fabian in spirit if not letter, imposing order upon chaos in a sphere where his grasp was unrivalled. When it was suggested in the Commons that he had made a slip in stating the level of central government grants under his new scheme, Chamberlain's long hours of toil paid off in enabling him to provide instant clarification. 'No, one tenth is quite right,' he explained. 'The rural district is a fifth of the urban district. Urban districts are one-half and rural districts are one-fifth of a half.' Fifteen-love, Chamberlain's service. Here, on his own ground, he knew what to do and how to get it done. Just as, thirty years previously, his father had given the Colonial Office an unprecedented new dominance in government, so Chamberlain now made the Ministry of Health into his powerhouse.

Chamberlain thus became the second man in the Government after Baldwin, fully involved in all its major decisions. Chamberlain was largely responsible for setting the Government's strategy during the General Strike of 1926 and its aftermath. His role in the negotiations with the miners is illuminated through his correspondence with his sisters. 'The miners don't think of the reorganization in precise terms of reduction of costs,' he wrote, 'they rather picture grievances, stupidities, injustices which they have personally come up against and they want to have a certainty that these things will be put right before they give up anything.' To Chamberlain's way of thinking, however, this was simply begging the question: 'They won't face up to the fact that meanwhile there is a loss and someone has got to pay for that loss.' His strong-minded reaction was in sharp contrast to what he saw as Baldwin's feeble indecision – 'His mind seemed paralysed' – so it was Chamberlain who had to stiffen the Government's resolve. The intransigence of the miners, however, evidently could not be relied upon, for the Government seems, on the eve of the strike, to have been fearful that they might be prevailed upon to accept the TUC's peace formula. Ready now for a fight, Chamberlain found the Cabinet tottering on the brink of a peaceful settlement and proposed a stern ultimatum to preclude this possibility. As it turned out, the Cabinet was saved by the refusal of the printers on the *Daily Mail* to print its leading article, which was quickly seized upon as the reason for breaking off negotiations with the TUC.

With the General Strike under way, the position of the Labour Party was uncomfortable. Ramsay MacDonald and the Labour leaders were concerned only, as Baldwin put it, to find 'an honourable way out of the position into which they have been led by their own folly'. But the Government was in no mood to help. 'The fact is that constitutional government is fighting for its life,' Chamberlain told his sister; 'if we failed it would be the Revolution, for the nominal leaders would be whirled away in an instant.' Little wonder that he was so irritated by the intervention of the Archbishop of Canterbury, muddying the waters of confrontation. All the best cards were held by the Government. The TUC's emotional sympathy for the miners was tinged with exasperation over the inflexibility of their leaders. As the unions' solidarity fragmented, the miners were left to fight on alone while the TUC threw in its hand. Throughout the long months of the ensuing coal strike, Chamberlain was at the sharp end of the conflict as the minister responsible for relief payments. The Labour Party accused the Government of starving the miners back, but was in turn accused by the miners' leaders of betraying their cause. The whole story will have unnerving echoes for anyone who lived through the miners' strike of 1984–5.

Baldwin's reputation, it must be said, does not survive an examination of these events with its benign patina unscarred. His broadcast appeal during the General Strike demanded: 'Cannot you trust me to ensure a square deal, to secure even justice between man and man?' A negative answer seems fair in view of Baldwin's subsequent conduct, and it is clear that he was as eager as anyone in his Cabinet to hit back at Labour through the Trade Disputes Act in 1927, which restricted political subscriptions by trade unions. Chamberlain was appalled at the lack of firm direction and seems to have favoured a more constructive approach. Baldwin's strength lay in his emollient public image, on the fashioning of which he bestowed his finest handiwork. He consequently feared that the effect would be spoiled by his abrasive Minister of Health, whom he chided for giving the impression in the Commons that he looked upon the Labour Party as dirt. 'The fact is that intellectually, with a few exceptions, they *are* dirt,' Chamberlain responded to his sister.

Perhaps Chamberlain deserves credit for recording such a candid comment at all. It does not seem uncharacteristic of the way that partisan differences mingled in his mind with an intellectual contempt which he was capable of displaying to friend and foe alike. It is significant that he deserted his working-class Ladywood seat in 1926, rightly fearing that it was vulnerable to Labour, and moved instead to suburban Edgbaston. When he had given his first major speech in the Town Hall he had written: '... that is the delight of a Birmingham audience; they are so extraordinarily intelligent.' But there had evidently been a sad decline in the subsequent seventeen years, and he explained his withdrawal from Ladywood on the ground that there was 'such a large mass of uneducated and credulous people, ready to be influenced by the sort of opponents I have had in the past'. Nor was the House of Commons much brighter. Challenged in the

Commons on the meaning of a clause in one of his meticulously marshalled Bills, he retorted with 'a little rhyme I used
to know when I was a child':

> Do you really wonder, Jane,
> When it seems to me so plain.

Even in the Cabinet he found that he had to correct other
ministers in the presentation of their business. The way to get
good marks from Neville was to agree with him, for he
seemed always to know best.

By 1929 Chamberlain had emerged as Baldwin's natural successor in the Conservative Party. The chain of events leading
from the second Labour Government to the 1931 crisis and
thence to the formation of a 'National' Government under
MacDonald was less favourable to Chamberlain's immediate
career prospects. He was regarded as a narrow partisan rather
than a natural coalitionist. But there were a number of com-
pensating features in the situation. He went back to the beastly
Treasury but had the satisfaction of dismantling the Free
Trade system and thus belatedly realizing his father's vision
of imperial preference. On the big issue of unemployment,
however, he was closer to the old orthodoxies of laissez-
faire, essentially pursuing a 'good-housekeeping' policy while
waiting for the natural self-righting forces of the free market
to bring back prosperity. His keen but narrow business mind
made him an appropriate executor of this strategy. By 1935
the Government could take credit for a limited but real
recovery from the depths of the world slump and, with
Baldwin's replacement of MacDonald at its head, its National
trappings were largely discarded in favour of a straightforward Conservative appeal. A better party man than either
his father or his brother, Neville Chamberlain was now poised
to succeed where they had failed.

He became Prime Minister in 1937 at the age of sixty-eight.
'Neville, you must remember you don't know anything about
foreign affairs,' Austen had recently chided him – famous last

words, perhaps, since he was to die shortly before his brother's elevation. Neville set about remedying this curious deficiency in his knowledge with his customary zeal and, like many an autodidact, soon imagined himself a polymath. The Foreign Office, presided over by the glamorous and youthful Anthony Eden, became the butt of Chamberlain's contempt. 'But really that FO!' he expostulated to his sisters. 'I am only waiting for my opportunity to stir it up with a long pole.' He did not have to wait long. His determination to show who was in charge touched Eden to the quick. When they met the Italian ambassador, they struck him as 'two cocks in true fighting posture', and he shrewdly observed that they were playing for 'the high stakes of their future destiny in the Cabinet and in the Conservative Party'. This could not go on; the Prime Minister was manifestly at odds with the responsible minister on matters central to the Government's credibility. Eden insisted on having his own way; when he could not get it, he resigned, at the beginning of 1938. In accepting his resignation Chamberlain professed that 'such differences as have arisen between us in no way concern our ultimate aim or the fundamentals of our policy'. But if the Prime Minister was at a loss to know why he had lost his Foreign Secretary, others were not so puzzled.

Eden was replaced by the initially more pliant Halifax. The conduct of foreign policy was concentrated in Downing Street so as to by-pass the Foreign Office, and a system of news management was developed, briefing journalists on the Prime Minister's own line rather than the official policy of the Government. A logical development of his personal role was the inauguration of the tradition of 'summit' meetings, with Chamberlain travelling by air for the first time in 1938 in order to engage in shuttle diplomacy with Hitler.

When Chamberlain flew to Germany for these meetings, he therefore bore a peculiar responsibility for their outcome. The very name 'Munich' carries its own pejorative charge in Anglo-American politics, and it continues to be bad form to advocate 'appeasement'. This is partly a result of a historical accident of which Chamberlain was one victim. He did not invent the policy of appeasement. To some extent it grew from the existing doctrines of the despised Foreign Office, with the aim of limiting Britain's commitments in Europe and mollifying Germany through the redress of grievances. Appeasement, as historians have come to recognize, had a lot to be said for it as a rational strategy of peaceful accommodation designed to remove the causes of friction in a constantly changing international situation. After all, who contests its basic premises? Is negotiation a worse way of making adjustments than conflict? Are not concessions the essence of any negotiation aimed at a viable compromise? Can peace ever be secured by these means if no one is prepared to pay the price for it? Are not the immediate combatants in an intractable quarrel likely to be worse judges of the general interest than an honest broker? Does not the general interest in avoiding war give a strong presumption in favour of negotiating a compromise settlement, however imperfect?

Yet this sort of reasoning, though it may suggest that appeasement has a lot to be said for it in general, throws up particular questions about Chamberlain's judgement in applying the policy, especially at Munich. As a policy of magnanimity, deliberately chosen from a position of strength which made alternative options feasible, appeasement was not only a rational strategy but an honourable course of action. But in the particular context of Munich in 1938 it cannot be denied that it also reflected Britain's relative military weakness. Chamberlain remained convinced that his critics had no conception of the restraints which circumstances had imposed upon him. He found himself in an unenviable position, unsure whether Britain could fight for the integrity of the Czechoslovak state, unsure whether Britain should.

There is ample ground for an extenuation of Chamberlain along these lines, but the arguments need to be sorted out more clearly than perhaps they were in his own mind. For there is a further sense in which appeasement can be justified – as a hard-nosed exercise in *realpolitik*, facing up to disagreeable necessities by putting the best face on a bad situation in the hope that it will improve. This sort of thinking really underlies the defence that Chamberlain was consciously buying time through his concessions at Munich. But the suggestion that he was averting war in 1938 so that Britain might be better prepared to fight later is one which relies much more on retrospective than on contemporary testimony. Such a strategy would have required a more devious and cynical figure than this self-righteous but straightforward businessman, with his principles packed alongside his umbrella. As his Chief Whip commented, Chamberlain's foreign policy was 'far simpler than those who love to discover recondite motives would suppose'.

When the concessions were yielded from weakness yet justified from morality, and paid for by others, it was symptomatic of flaws which Chamberlain was reluctant to acknowledge. He was reluctant to yield the high ground of morality to his critics. He had nothing but scorn for the League of Nations Union with its high-minded president, Professor Gilbert Murray, representing the superior wisdom of the chattering classes. He resented their glib Gladstonianism in seeing the issue as a simple matter of conscience. In a radio broadcast he deprecated the idea of going to war 'because of a quarrel in a far-away country between people of whom we know nothing'. Moreover, the Munich agreement was greeted in the press with a chorus of relief and approval, albeit one orchestrated from Downing Street. The trouble was that Chamberlain had now become the dupe of his own propaganda. He was hoodwinked into believing that he had secured a just and lasting peace – believing, no doubt, what circumstances encouraged him to believe, but investing his belief with concepts like honour and probity which made it difficult to relinquish subsequently.

In effect, he had staked his political future upon his bargain with Hitler, seeing it as the means of containing his enemies at home as well as abroad. Media manipulation reached new heights in January 1939 when Chamberlain had talks with Mussolini in Rome – a spectacular backdrop for the carefully arranged photo-opportunities. The flashy glamour of the dictators was beginning to rub off on the dowdy persona of the

Prime Minister. One of his impressionable admirers, the press baron Lord Kemsley, later told Hitler in a personal interview that he would never understand England 'unless you think of Neville Chamberlain as our Führer'.

'I ought to be good for at least one more Parliament after this to exasperate and infuriate the *Gilbert Murrays* of this world,' he wrote to his sister in March 1939 – two days before Hitler marched into Prague. This action blatantly flouted the terms of the Munich agreement, but even now Chamberlain clung to the shreds of his policy. His comment in the Commons that the end of Czechoslovakia 'may or may not have been inevitable' did not, however, inspire confidence. A significant breach opened – once more – between the Prime Minister and the Foreign Secretary. Like Salisbury, Halifax was a traditional Conservative, a pious High Churchman from an old aristocratic family, who took a pragmatic view of secular affairs; and the pragmatic fact that struck him was that the party was saddled with an albatross. Like his great seventeenth-century namesake, he trimmed. The Foreign Office had now written off appeasement, unlike Number Ten, which continued its optimistic briefing of the press behind the Foreign Secretary's back. Chamberlain's stubbornness was now leading him steadily out of his depth, making it virtually impossible for him to be rescued from his difficulties.

The businesslike approach was supposed to sort out the problems of Europe where the effete diplomacy of the old order had failed; but Chamberlain's reputation never re-covered from the deal that came unstuck. When he finally resigned from the Cabinet, discredited in his policy and within weeks of death, he looked in vain for 'any comprehension that there may be a human tragedy somewhere in the back-ground'. As long as he stayed on the tightrope he was admired for his skill, but when he fell there was no safety net of affection to catch him. He was not a lovable man. The phrases of those whom he worsted in politics have lived on to damn him from beyond the grave. His was the 'retail mind in a wholesale business', which Lloyd George deprecated from the point of view of a wholesaler who had been put out of business for good by a vindictive combination among petty retailers. Churchill, who suffered a comparable eclipse before destiny ultimately supervened, gave him credit for having been a good Lord Mayor of Birmingham – in a lean year. Even Attlee, though hardly renowned as a charismatic leader in this league, described him as a radio set tuned to Midland Regional; and to others on the Labour benches he simply looked as though he had been 'weaned on a pickle'. This is an unusually fecund harvest of mingled distaste and derision.

Chamberlain's political career ended in failure, as he could hardly fail to recognize. As Prime Minister he had dedicated himself to the preservation of peace, and war broke out instead. With the coming of the Second World War in September 1939, the whole Chamberlainite system entered a phase of terminal collapse, though it took another eight months to depose him. May 10th 1940 was not a happy day for the retail trade; the shutters came down at Birmingham Town Hall and the Midland Regional was switched off; infants cried in vain for their pickles. Once Churchill was installed as Prime Minister in his place, the Chamberlain era suddenly seemed like a bad dream. The Left was unrestrained in its denunciations, of which the tract *Guilty Men* (1940) was the *locus classicus*, giving its young co-author Michael Foot a lasting taste for polemic. Moreover, Churchill and his cronies now hijacked the Conservative Party and it subsequently distanced itself from the embarrassing legacy of appeasement and unemployment, which in retrospect were perceived as the distinguishing features of the Chamberlain years. Late in 1939, when Churchill was already back in the War Cabinet as First Lord of the Admiralty, he had invited the Prime Minister to dinner and enjoyed 'really the only intimate social conversation that I can remember with Neville Chamberlain amid all the business we did together over nearly twenty years'. This was when he heard the story of Andros.

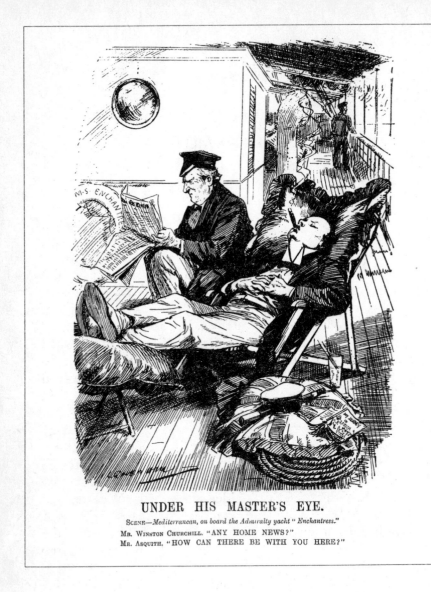

UNDER HIS MASTER'S EYE.

SCENE—*Mediterranean, on board the Admiralty yacht " Enchantress."*

MR. WINSTON CHURCHILL. "ANY HOME NEWS?"

MR. ASQUITH. "HOW CAN THERE BE WITH YOU HERE?"

6

CHURCHILL:

LOST EMPIRES

His father, whom he hardly knew, died of syphilis; his mother was a woman of easy virtue whose affairs were to cause him embarrassment; he was a victim of that peculiar upper-class form of child neglect which threw him on the mercy of servants; his education was patchy at best and if, as with Lloyd George, university was out of the question, what he lacked were academic qualifications rather than the right social background. For Winston Churchill was no ordinary deprived child any more than Lloyd George was the product of an ordinary workman's cottage; and it must be admitted that they were not noticeably overshadowed by their Oxbridge contemporaries in the cabinets of the first half of this century. Churchill was the grandson of the 7th Duke of Marlborough and, from the death of Lord Randolph Churchill in 1895 to the birth of the 9th Duke's elder son in 1897, Winston was the heir to the title. His unique record is that he might twice have become a Duke: the first time through heredity in the nineteenth century and the second time through merit in the twentieth.

Churchill's rise was as startling as that of his father. He exploited his family advantages through his own efforts, which were prodigious. Trained as a soldier, sent out to the imperial frontier, he soon put aside the sword for the pen and made his name and his fortune as a war correspondent in South Africa. By 1901 his royalties and lecture fees had given him £10,000, at a time when a labourer's wage was £1 a week. The first of his big books was naturally a two-volume *Life of Lord Randolph Churchill*, with co-operation from all the top politicians of that era and a handy advance of £8,000. Throughout his life, Churchill earned – and spent – on an heroic scale. Words dripped as profusely from his pen as the champagne flowed copiously down his throat.

Elected as a Conservative MP at twenty-five, he was, within eight years, a Liberal Cabinet minister: one who was soon second only to Lloyd George as a forceful spokesman for the Left in his new party. In the course of writing the biography of his father, he had, to his own satisfaction, reinterpreted the career of Lord Randolph as a principled essay in Tory Democracy, and drawn from its failure the lesson that an active legislative policy of social reform – populist in style and paternalist in content – was now properly the province of the Liberal Party. Moreover, he did his homework on the New Liberalism, just as he had educated himself in the Army, poring over the books which Lloyd George never read and mastering his ministerial brief with a professionalism for which Asquith had a subterranean fellow-feeling underneath his own affectation of effortless superiority. It was as Asquith's protégé that Churchill was promoted into the front rank, yet the Prime Minister could tell Venetia Stanley in 1915 that 'I regard his future with misgivings', despite a professed fondness for Churchill. 'He will never get to the top in English politics, with all his wonderful gifts,' Asquith predicted; 'to speak with the tongues of men and angels, and to spend laborious days and nights in administration, is no good, if a man does not inspire trust.'

Asquith had his own reasons for writing as he did. His Government was running into difficulties for which, rightly or wrongly, he was to hold Churchill partly responsible; and he was not, of course, on oath when he sought to amuse and divert his darling Venetia. Yet there were solid reasons explaining why Churchill was so persistently distrusted. One is that he was, in party terms, so persistently disloyal. Not merely did he cross the floor in 1904, leaving the Conservatives when they were in the doldrums and joining the Liberals when they were on the way up, but he reversed the operation twenty years later. Most of the leading members of Lloyd George's Coalition found that their association with it – however honourably maintained, as in the case of Austen Chamberlain – became a barrier to future employment. Churchill alone made the Coalition into a bridge between prosperous service in Asquith's pre-war Liberal Cabinet and Baldwin's post-war Conservative Cabinet. His name pops up in administrations of different colours over a period of a quarter of a century like that of an eighteenth-century placeman. Yet he was far from being a non-partisan executive statesman, concerned simply that His Majesty's Government should be carried on: instead, on each change of front, he took up the cudgels of his new party with the same unwearied gusto with which he had taken up the cudgels of the old. Always theatrical, his range was remarkable: one moment declaiming like Othello, 'I have done the state some service and they know't', the next moment behaving like Mr Punch ('Oh no you won't,' 'Oh yes I will'). The predictable result was bathos – plus a lot of unforgiving enemies of every political persuasion.

The verdict of history, to be sure, seems to have gone against Asquith's polished advocacy in putting the case for the prosecution. Although the jury were out for an unconscionably long time, by the summer of 1940 they had surely found for the defendant with a rare measure of unanimity and conclusiveness. Their man had indeed got to the top, and trust was pre-eminently what he now inspired. But twenty-five years had to elapse before Asquith was posthumously confounded; and it is in these years that we can gain perspectives no less valuable for being less familiar than the image unforgettably generated by Churchill's subsequent premiership. It is still worth asking why it took so very long before he could feel, as he assures us he did on the night of 10 May 1940, that he was 'walking with destiny, and that all my past life had been but a preparation for this hour and for this trial'.

★

That Churchill surmounted disabling handicaps in the 1920s is shown by his readmission to Cabinet office; it was in the 1930s that he was excluded as effectively as Lloyd George before him. In explaining this we need to understand the relation between the four salient episodes in his career during these years. Each attracted considerable attention at the time, and each has also been a source of subsequent controversy. The first is Britain's return to the Gold Standard in 1925. The second concerns Churchill's role during the General Strike and the miners' dispute of 1926. The third is the campaign which Churchill waged against measures of Indian self-government in the early 1930s. And the last, of course, is his response to the rise of Hitler in the late 1930s. It has sometimes been argued that Churchill was wrong on the Gold Standard, wrong on the General Strike, and wrong on India; and that because he was discredited in this way he was ignored when he warned about Germany, where he happened to be right. Is it so simple? Are things what they seem here? Even when he was wrong, was it for the wrong reason – or right for the right reason?

At the General Election of 1922 Churchill stood as a Liberal, albeit one who had been closely enmeshed with the Conservative Party during the Coalition period. He was defeated and did not enter Parliament for two years. During this time he was clearly moving towards the Right. The prospect of a Labour Government clarified his attitude. 'The enthronement in office of a Socialist Government,' he proclaimed, 'will be a serious national misfortune such as has usually befallen great states only on the morrow of defeat in war.' He urged the Liberals to join hands with the Conservatives in opposing it. This was his own course during its short term of office in 1924; and by the time another General Election came that October, Churchill had been adopted as a candidate by the local Conservatives for the safe seat of Epping. When the Conservatives swept to power under Baldwin, it was widely expected that Churchill would be asked to take office. In the course of an interview with the new Prime Minister, he was offered no less a position than that of Chancellor of the

Exchequer. Afterwards he professed himself astonished: 'I should have liked to have answered, "Will the bloody duck swim?" but as it was a formal and important conversation I replied, "This fulfils my ambition."'

Churchill threw himself into his work at the Treasury with characteristic energy. His father had, briefly and notoriously, served as Chancellor, and Lady Randolph had kept the robes 'in tissue paper and camphor' for forty years. The sentimental satisfaction in occupying this office was tangibly asserted when Lord Randolph's fitful efforts to cut back the service estimates were replicated by his son. Winston Churchill was responsible for reviving the 'ten-year rule' – the planning assumption that no major war was to be anticipated within that period. This made it feasible for him to pare down the defence budget. Indeed, Churchill wanted to go further, telling Baldwin in 1924 that the Admiralty 'should be made to recast all their plans and scales and standards on the basis that no naval war against a first-class Navy is likely to take place in the next twenty years'. If Britain's armaments were weak in the 1930s, this doctrine was partly responsible.

Churchill is often remembered in a highly selective way, and seldom for his economic views. Yet his Chancellorship was no anomaly in his career, and he came to it better prepared than predecessors like Lloyd George, Baldwin or even Neville Chamberlain. The big issue in British politics for thirty years after 1903 was tariffs. This was the main line of division between the Conservative and Liberal Parties. The General Elections of 1906 and 1923 were fought chiefly on this issue, giving the Conservatives their two biggest defeats, and in each case unifying and reviving the Liberal Party on the great sacrosanct principle of Free Trade. Whatever the other temperamental attractions of the Liberal Party for the young Churchill, it was in fact on the issue of Free Trade that he joined it in 1904; and it was only when Tariff Reform was effectively eliminated from the Conservative programme in 1924 that Churchill returned to the fold. His appointment signalled the party's betrayal (yet again) of its ostensible Chamberlainite commitment. Churchill's Free Trade principles, in short, amid the shifting sands of his other vicissitudes, formed a rock to which he clung.

Clinging to Free Trade, Churchill clung to its premise: the axiom of a perfectly flexible self-righting free market. The basic case for Free Trade, which Churchill had had to mug up at intervals over the past twenty years, was that an open economy enforced cheapness, and thereby efficiency, through competition. This was obviously to the advantage of those capitalists who were free to shift their capital around the world, looking for the best return. But Free Trade, so Liberals tirelessly reiterated, was also to the advantage of the working class in so far as they were all consumers. Tariffs, on the other hand, made an appeal to them in so far as they were producers for markets threatened by foreign competition. Thus the Liberal cliché, 'Hands off the people's food', was countered by the Conservative cliché, 'Tariff Reform means work for all'.

These were arguments which Churchill knew backwards, as his pre-war speeches show. He knew that there were two answers to the protectionists' case for the producer. One was simple – 'The greatest producer is the greatest consumer' – and could be applied particularly to a great export trade like cotton. The other was more complex and rested on assumptions which were seldom articulated. It was, however, seen as the knockdown argument in favour of the play of market forces because it contended that Free Trade too meant work for all – and in better jobs, with cheap bread thrown in. Employment could not, of course, be guaranteed within a particular fossilized industrial structure; instead, sunrise industries were set free to respond to the signals and incentives of the market. Tariffs, Churchill proclaimed in 1909, 'have warped and restricted the growth of the industries of the nations who have adopted them'. The efficient, competitive, dynamic enterprises which thrived under Free Trade were thus a better source of employment than the sclerotic industries which depended on protection. Free movement of capital, moreover, was beneficial to the nation not only directly, because it generated income from abroad, but also indirectly, because it stimulated British exports.

These were the ends which Free Trade purported to serve. They were highly visible – visibly present, on the whole, before the war; visibly absent afterwards, with a million unemployed. But the means were, in more senses than one, invisible. For all that this system needed by way of regulation was the operation of the Gold Standard, which guaranteed the external parity of the currency. If external prices were fixed, internal prices had to be flexible. This implied that the domestic priced level would be governed through changes in Bank rate. Nothing else was necessary. An automatic process of adjustment followed: as Bank rate rose, prices fell. No wonder that Churchill, having mastered the essential workings of this system, remained enraptured by the 'beautiful precision' with which Free Trade and the Gold Standard complemented each other – or had done, as he put it subsequently, 'not in this disastrous century but in the last'.

As Chancellor, Churchill was pressed at an early stage to put Britain back on the Gold Standard, which had been effectively suspended since 1914. The Governor of the Bank of England, Montagu Norman, was the sternest advocate of this step, just as the economist J. M. Keynes emerged as its leading critic. The Chancellor would, Norman acknowledged, meet criticism whatever he did. If he decided to return to Gold, he would be abused 'by the ignorant, the gamblers and the antiquated Industrialists', but if he refused he would be abused 'by the instructed and by posterity'. In fact what happened was almost the opposite. When Churchill announced the return to Gold in 1925 he met with little immediate criticism; the judgement of posterity, on the whole, has been that it was an error.

For going back to Gold at the pre-war parity of $4.86 meant that sterling was revalued upwards; British exports consequently cost more in foreign markets; and the difficulties of industry were increased accordingly. It became necessary to reduce domestic costs, most obviously by reducing wages; and it was a proposal to cut wages in the coal industry which led to the miners' strike in 1926. Moreover, since there was in practice no significant decrease in money wages in the late 1920s, costs were stuck at a high level; with high prices, exports were relatively low; with low output, unemployment remained high. A perverse logic spelt out the anomaly. Now the difficulties which ensued cannot simply be attributed to the Gold Standard, but this undoubtedly introduced an unhelpful new constraint into an existing problem. The gist of Keynes's criticism of Gold was that it was a rigid link between the City and Wall Street. When Churchill had to defend his decision he seized on this as a virtue, claiming that the Gold Standard would not shackle Britain to the United States; the Government, he claimed, had simply decided 'to shackle themselves to reality'. They had, in fact, adopted the view of 'the authorities' (the Treasury and the Bank of England) that only gold was a sufficiently impartial taskmaster to enforce economic virtue. In the phrase which entered their local folklore, it was 'knave-proof'.

Yet the policy with which Churchill identified himself so strongly in public was one which he had questioned with great spirit in private when it had been urged upon him by his official advisers. He saw that the interests of industry and finance did not axiomatically coincide. He accused the authorities of, as he put it, not facing 'the profound significance of what Mr Keynes calls "the paradox of unemployment amidst dearth". The Governor shows himself perfectly happy in the spectacle of Britain possessing the finest credit in the world simultaneously with a million and a quarter unemployed.' He concluded by translating the jargon into his own rhetoric: 'I would rather see Finance less proud and Industry more content.' Churchill's difficulty was that the system he had taken on trust for twenty years now seemed incapable of delivering the goods, putting all the old controversies in a different light. But in the end he could not resist the weight of expert opinion. New in office, only recently restored to the Conservative fold, not anxious to go on his travels again, and lacking any formal expertise in economics, Churchill could hardly be expected to override the formidably marshalled advice of his best officials.

His Chancellorship was therefore the final trial of the self-acting system, restored to full working order. Free Trade was kept alive; the Gold Standard was resurrected; and the authorities maintained a hands-off, arm's-length conception of their role. Their regulation of the economy thus depended on a single instrument: the rate of interest. Moreover, though its effects upon the domestic economy were widespread and diverse, Bank rate was in practice fixed according to external circumstances rather than domestic needs. For it was adjusted up or down – generally up – in response to a single overriding concern: the defence of sterling. Here was a policy which could be termed, according to taste, spare and elegant – or crude and undiscriminating. If the resolute application of laissez-faire principles had been all that was needed, this surely should have done the trick.

From a number of rueful comments which Churchill subsequently made, however, it can be gathered that he came to resent the way in which the established view had been imposed upon him. Having loyally defended it while he remained in office, he then surrendered to the evidence of his own eyes as the British economy went from bad to worse. By 1931 he was alarmed that 'something terrible is going to happen financially', and added: 'I hope we shall hang Montagu Norman if it does. I will certainly turn King's evidence against him.' Maybe he was looking for a scapegoat in the person of the Governor when the situation was actually governed by structural problems of an intractable kind. Churchill had in fact already publicly voiced his recognition that in the post-war period his own long-standing precepts were no longer tenable and that party politics were entering a new era. 'It is no longer a case of one party fighting another, nor of one set of politicians scoring off another,' he stated in 1930. 'It is the case of successive governments facing economic problems, and being judged by their success or failure in the duel.' He rightly identified the problem as one to which his whole training in pre-war party politics was fundamentally irrelevant. 'The compass has been damaged,' he said. 'The charts are out of date.'

★

Churchill's role during the General Strike left him with a highly prejudicial image in many working-class circles. The Conservative Cabinet had responded decisively to the TUC's threat of a General Strike in support of the miners by breaking off negotiations. There was a common Labour supposition that a peace party, including Baldwin, Birkenhead and the Minister of Labour, Steel-Maitland, had been overruled by a war party of which Churchill was the most prominent member. Though Churchill himself indignantly wished to repudiate this impression, it long remained widespread and even in the late 1930s was a barrier to co-operation between him and Labour. Now it is certainly true that Churchill played a notable part in organizing the Government forces. By temperament he revelled in momentous events. He could never resist the opportunity to jump in where the action was thickest. He became editor of the *British Gazette*, which presented the Government case, and its voice was naturally identified as his voice. As long as it was a question of whether the General Strike should succeed or not, Churchill saw the issue in stark terms: should constitutional government prevail? Perhaps this was too simple a view, betraying a lack of understanding of the trade-union mind. But in taking it Churchill was at one with the rest of his colleagues – Chamberlain, for example – and indeed with many people outside the Conservative Party.

Once the General Strike had been called off, after nine days, the miners were isolated. They held out through the summer and autumn of 1926, trying to maintain their existing pay and conditions. It was now that Churchill emerged as the leading advocate of conciliation within the Cabinet, while Baldwin, supposedly the man of peace, sat back in a rather detached way to watch necessity bring the miners to their knees. Whatever else he was, Churchill was not cold-blooded. His efforts to bring pressure to bear upon the coal-owners met criticism from his colleague Steel-Maitland, another of the supposed peace party. And it was Birkenhead – perhaps the least plausible of the alleged 'doves' – who upbraided Churchill most severely. 'I am not happy about your attitude,' he telegraphed. 'Why should we enable men's leaders who have done their best to ruin England to escape without the brand of failure?' Birkenhead, with his declared belief that 'the owners are entitled to victory', helped Baldwin to stiffen resistance in the Cabinet against Churchill's conciliatory initiatives. The socialist intellectual Harold Laski, an admittedly partisan witness, found when he accompanied the miners' leaders to the negotiations that Baldwin was 'a most curious mixture of the sentimental phrase and the hard act. Churchill, who was there, was bigger and more skilful in every way – he knew how to negotiate.'

Over the General Strike, as over the Gold Standard, therefore, there are good grounds for arguing that Churchill's conduct deserves more credit than it has customarily received. He was no bigoted partisan, seeing only one side of a case; but his largeness of mind was masked by his combative manner. Even on an indulgent view of these episodes, however, the question remains: why did he acquire such an unfortunate reputation with many of his contemporaries? Can it all have been bad luck and bad management of his public image?

After 1929 Churchill steadily drifted apart from the Conservative leadership. To some extent this was a result of the rise of Neville Chamberlain, whom Churchill might have rivalled for the Conservative succession. To some extent, too, it was because tariffs came back on to the agenda – exactly the issue which Churchill had hoped would go away. But chiefly the breach occurred because Churchill made himself a vocal, prominent and intransigent opponent of moves towards Indian self-government. This was a bipartisan policy which in a sense prefigured the National Government of 1931 and thus Churchill's exclusion from it. It is pretty clear that his views were sincerely held and indisputable that they brought him no personal advantage. The real charge against Churchill's campaign over India is that it betrayed lack of judgement. It seemed to offer a reactionary reflex rather than a realistic response to the rise of third-world nationalism.

Here it is more difficult to find the evidence which would

sustain a more flattering verdict. Churchill left no doubt that what he was defending was the idea of British rights in India. Time and again he appealed to the British economic interests which were at risk. He explicitly defended his policy in the context of a general recession from liberalism and justified it on the ground of a British struggle for self-preservation. In speaking against the India Bill in 1935, he sought to establish the idea 'that we are there for ever'. It is no caricature of his position, therefore, to describe it as a last-ditch assertion of Britain's imperial destiny, and it was couched in terms more redolent of Churchill's youth in the Victorian era than of the language of the mid-twentieth century. A more pragmatic Conservative, Lord Irwin (later Halifax), who had served as Viceroy for five years, gave his opinion in 1931 that the day was past 'when Winston's possessive instinct can be applied to Empires and the like. That conception of Imperialism is finished, and those who try to revive it are as those who would fly a balloon that won't hold gas.' It is all too easy to see why Churchill's sense of proportion came into question during this campaign.

In his Indian policy Churchill became the champion of the diehards. He was therefore a suspect figure in the eyes not only of the Left but of the political centre – the very constituency to which he increasingly appealed on international questions. This impaired his ability to rally an effective anti-Nazi movement. His own ideal was, as he admitted in 1937, 'narrow and limited. I want to see the British Empire preserved for a few more generations in its strength and splendour.' Yet how could this be done? In his own mind there was a direct connection between his warnings about India and his warnings about Germany, and at a superficial level the link was apparent to friend and foe alike as belligerent nostalgia. At a deeper level, however, there was surely some incoherence in his views.

A hard-nosed defence of Britain's imperial interests was a strategy of *realpolitik* which demanded a ruthless ordering of priorities. The resources were simply not available to sustain both this and an open-ended continental commitment to resist

Germany. The logic of this position was really a policy of appeasement: a cynical deal with the dictators, leaving each master race free to maintain its own hegemony within its own sphere, with no questions asked about how. This sort of thinking needed to be pursued with cold-blooded detachment, unclouded by sentiments of morality and democracy and self-determination, which could be left to perish with the League of Nations. Measured by this standard, Churchill's refusal to accept such implications can be seen as an indication of his inadequacy. It can also, of course, be seen as a measure of his decency.

Churchill's own account of these matters was published, to understandable acclaim, in his war memoirs, notably the first volume, *The Gathering Storm* (1948). These six fat volumes constitute a magnificent literary *tour de force*; what they are not, of course, is what they purport to be – a history of the Second World War and its origins. In them Churchill used his unique post-war prestige to pay off old scores. A notorious example is the entry in the index under 'Baldwin, Stanley': 'speaks for rearmament and denies its need, 140; excludes Churchill from office, 141, 156; ... confesses putting party before country, 169–70'. For nearly twenty years this account held the field, with anyone who doubted it being regarded as a sort of intellectual quisling. Now that we have the archives open, and also the necessary distance to lend disenchantment to our views, it is inevitable that Churchill's foresight and consistency in his opposition to appeasement should be queried.

One specific charge has been that some of his claims about the inadequacy of British rearmament were incorrect and that he must have known it. It is accepted that in what he said about British and German air strength, Churchill was drawing on information from various civil servants and serving officers, the most prominent being Desmond Morton, the head of the Government's Industrial Intelligence Centre. But it has sometimes been suggested that Morton had official sanction

from successive Prime Ministers for disclosing secret information to Churchill. If so, the fact that he then used it in
public to try to discredit the very ministers who had allowed
him privileged access to it seems curiously ungenerous on his
part and curiously stupid on theirs. Moreover, if Churchill
was drawing upon the same private sources as the Government – and with official permission at that – how could his
estimates honestly conflict with theirs? This difficulty has now
been cleared up by Churchill's official biographer. The fact is
that Morton had no authorization to talk to Churchill and
was thus breaking his official duty of confidence to the
Government. Like others, before and since, he was putting
his career at risk. Churchill was using leaked information,
covered by the Official Secrets Act, in pursuit of what he saw
as the public interest – which obviously did not coincide
with the view of the Government. When he disagreed with
ministerial statements glossing official information derived
from Morton, Churchill was following Morton's own
interpretation of his estimates. Of course, not all the figures
which Churchill used were correct, but the case which he
was mounting can clearly be exonerated of charges of bad
faith.

On rearmament, Churchill found his best supporters,
especially in the early 1930s, within the Conservative Party.
During 1935 and the early part of 1936 he often seemed more
concerned with securing office than organizing support for
his views. He believed that he could play a crucial role in
making rearmament a reality, and he was bitterly disappointed in March 1936 when the move to make him Minister of Defence came to nothing. Baldwin seems to have
thought that, if there were to be a war, 'we must keep
him fresh to be our war Prime Minister', which was very
considerate of him, and Chamberlain, equally concerned that
Churchill should be spared the burdens of office, was soon to
be in a position to make his own veto conclusive. Only at
this point did Churchill read the writing on the wall about
his prospects of entering a peacetime Conservative Cabinet.
He now moved with a greater sureness and consistency,

steeled by the knowledge that he was playing for high stakes, with the odds stacked against him.

Churchill's strategy was now to broaden his criticism of the Government by looking for allies on the anti-fascist Left. He suffered a further setback, to be sure, at the time of the Abdication of Edward VIII, when his wayward and romantic support of the King once more reactivated doubts about his judgement. But this episode was lived down fairly quickly. From 1936 he was involved with the work of the Anti-Nazi Council, which drew its support primarily from Jews, left-wing intellectuals, and trade unionists. He started to use a new language, seeking 'to proclaim that there are men of all classes, all sorts and conditions, all grades of human forces, from the humblest workman to the most bellicose colonel, who occupy a common ground in resisting dangers and aggressive tyranny'. The non-party movement known as 'Focus' also sought to mobilize support across the political spectrum in favour of rearmament. By the end of 1936 the great imperialist was able to tell his son Randolph: 'All the left-wing intelligentsia are coming to look to me for protection, and I will give it wholeheartedly in return for their aid in the rearmament of Britain.' Partly with this audience in mind, Churchill framed his criticisms of the Government's foreign policy in terms of a defence of the principles of the League of Nations. His remarks in a speech to sympathizers convey the tone which he had now adopted: 'Nothing could have been more admirable than the action of the Trades Union Congress ... It shows that Labour is more alive than many of the Conservatives ... We must have some Tories to show up the others ... You must get some of the Right too, or else it will look as if it were sectional ... Our policy is that we adhere to the Covenant of the League of Nations; that is our rock ... We have the means of being the spear-point of all this vast mass of opinion which guards our rights.'

Admittedly, Churchill was not very successful in his efforts. 'How is this great body of principle to be defended?' he beseeched his supporters. 'It certainly won't be defended by milksops and mugwumps and pussyfoots.' Yet this was an all too plausible description of the shadowy popular front which he now summoned to action. Churchill found it uphill work trying to convince the herbivorous supporters of the League of Nations that they would have to counter the dictators with heavier armour than typewriters. But, as he constantly reiterated to critics later, he found little to be ashamed of in his conduct in these years. The criticisms he made and the warnings he gave were in substance borne out by events, and often in detail too. The fact remains that Churchill found few open allies, even after the Munich Agreement.

It was only in the summer of 1939 that opinion turned decisively in his favour. As the international situation deteriorated, his prospects improved. The movement to bring back Churchill gathered momentum. He had not changed, but the context in which he was judged was now different. His faults turned to virtues. Was he a bad party man? Was he a blinkered patriot, set on defending this sceptered isle at all costs? Was his rhetoric high-flown and out of kilter with an up-to-date businesslike approach? Back in 1914, Churchill had concluded a speech at Bradford on the Ulster question with the words: 'Let us go forward together and put these grave matters to the proof.' It did not go down particularly well; it struck the wrong note; it was too provocative, too highly-coloured, too self-conscious. In January 1940 Churchill, now First Lord of the Admiralty, gave a speech in Manchester and had his peroration ready: 'Let us go forward together ...' This moving phrase so captured the unique mood of the hour that it was to be emblazoned on a thousand hoardings over Churchill's portrait. Where, his admirers must have wondered, does Winston find the words?

With the coming of war, the problems facing the country had, in a sense, become simpler: easier to understand, if more difficult to surmount. At the time of the General Strike Baldwin had received from his lieutenant, J.C.C. Davidson, this comment on Churchill: 'He is the sort of man, whom, if I wanted a mountain to be moved, I should send for at once. I think, however, that I should not consult him after he had moved the mountain if I wanted to know where to put it.' It may be rather anthropomorphic to suppose that the British people sent for him in 1940, and sent him away in 1945, on this reasoning. In June 1940, with the Battle of France lost, he proclaimed the start of the Battle of Britain, exhorting his fellow-countrymen to have this adjudged their finest hour, even 'if the British Empire and its Commonwealth last for 1,000 years' – an estimate which, in the manner of thousand-year Reichs, turned out to be on the high side. But if it was their finest hour, it was surely also his; and in each case there was the necessary implication, resolutely unacknowledged, that henceforward decline was inevitable. 'I have not become the King's First Minister in order to preside over the liquidation of the British Empire,' he asserted in 1942 – a vain hope if there ever was one.

In the end Churchill had to add the British Empire to his long list of lost causes. He had fought for British supremacy in South Africa; but the Boers took over. He had championed Free Trade; but tariffs ultimately came. He had pinned his hoped on the New Liberalism; but the Liberal Party collapsed. He had tried to break military stalemate in 1915; but the tragedy of Gallipoli came back to haunt him. He had supported the plan for a post-Coalition centre party; but the two-party system reasserted itself. He had restored the Gold Standard; but it failed. He had taken a stand on India; but the tide of nationalism washed over him. He had befriended Edward VIII in his hour of need; but the Abdication made him look foolish. He had spearheaded a campaign for rearmament and resistance to Hitler; but he was kept in the wilderness. Only when he reached the age of sixty-five did his luck turn; when his endowment policy matured, the pay-out exceeded all expectations and handsomely rewarded him for not quitting. It was intrinsic to his character that he never knew when he was beaten and never knew when the game was up. In 1940 this was thought admirable.

PART TWO
A NEW AGENDA

Keynes and Lloyd George try to shift Churchill (May 1929)

7

KEYNES:

ACADEMIC SCRIBBLER OR POLITICAL DABBLER?

'Practical men, who believe themselves to be quite exempt from any intellectual influences, are usually the slaves of some defunct economist,' declares the final paragraph of *The General Theory* (1936). It now seems that the author of these often-quoted words was unwittingly digging, if not his own grave, then his own posthumous heffalump trap, into which his reputation duly tumbled. In a wonderful irony of fate, Keynes himself is now mocked as the defunct economist whose slaves trod the path to ruin. 'Madmen in authority,' he maintained, 'who hear voices in the air, are distilling their frenzy from some academic scribbler of a few years back.'

Whatever the truth of the matter, John Maynard Keynes was not just an academic scribbler. It took President Reagan to put him down with the one-liner that this man Keynes didn't even have a degree in economics. Quite true. He was both more and less than a professionally trained economist. He came from an academic family in Cambridge, born to every advantage. His father was a leading administrator in the University; his mother was the first woman mayor of the City. Alfred Marshall, the leading British economist, was a family friend. The young Keynes was sent to Eton, and went on to King's College, Cambridge, to read mathematics. He gained a First Class degree in Mathematics in 1905; his position as Twelfth Wrangler made this a good but not brilliant result. As an undergraduate he was a member of the select society known as the 'Apostles', which became the core of the Bloomsbury group, a cultural coterie which included the novelists Virginia Woolf and E. M. Forster. Keynes's close friendship with the writer Lytton Strachey and the painter Duncan Grant, moreover, had a deep reinforcing bond: homosexuality.

Here, undeniably, is a fascinating topic, as is shown by the unremitting attention it has received in recent years. Roy Harrod's very fine biography of Keynes was published at a time when it was thought prudent to say nothing on such matters. For a long time, therefore, the fact that Keynes was bisexual was not widely known; but now it is in danger of becoming the sole thing that most people do know about him. Obviously, this knowledge helps to make sense of his life, but whether it helps to make sense of his work seems, on the whole, doubtful. It may be that the intense preoccupation of the young Keynes with the personal relationships of pre-1914 Bloomsbury has led to some distortion in our view of him.

Keynes's own writings are the source of some misconceptions. For many academics, the exposition of their research represents a tedious and mundane chore, often termed 'writing up' nowadays. Keynes, by contrast, neither wrote up nor wrote down (though some writing off was occasionally necessary). He was a writer whose best work deserves to enter the canon of twentieth-century literature. *The General Theory* itself, despite literary flaws in its structure, has lambent passages which make it a good read even for a high-and-dry monetarist. Above all, Keynes was an essayist of genius. The rhetoric of persuasion was one of his pre-eminent gifts and was integral to his achievement as an economist. Moreover, in his biographical essays, the spare and subtle touches with which he depicts character, and the subliminally suggestive way in which he conveys atmosphere, make his portraits unforgettable.

Literary artifice, however, has its own conventions, which can give rise to misapprehension unless they are recognized. For example, his brilliant memoir, 'My Early Beliefs', has been read as a document in ways alien to the circumstances of its composition. Written for his friends as the Munich crisis brewed, it made a profound impression upon them as they listened to its evocative account of a lost age of innocence. 'The beauty and unworldliness of it' struck Virginia Woolf, even though it made her feel 'a little flittery and stupid'. Maynard had contrived his effects with an artist's sureness of touch: it made for 'a very human satisfactory meeting'. Posthumously published, the essay has been read in cold print with a misplaced confidence in its literal veracity. Keynes's epigram, that he and fellow Apostles had 'a religion and no morals', has licensed the view that states of mind, and love, quite pre-empted political concerns.

Was he, then, a political naïf? Once he had developed distinctive views on political economy, did he, in his innocence, simply expect the world to fall at his feet in a bloodless coup for rationalism? We will understand Keynes better if we accept that he was an inveterate political animal. Like Marx, he thought that it was not enough for philosophers to understand the world: the point was to change it. Keynes saw the allure of wielding power but was himself captivated by the entrancements of exerting influence. Nor was he ignorant of government in a technical sense. He began his career, after all, as a civil servant in the India Office and threw it up only when Alfred Marshall persuaded him to return to Cambridge. During the First World War he entered the Treasury – the beginning of a lifelong love–hate relationship – and was soon entrusted with wide responsibility for the external finance of the war. As well as being an academic economist, he thus had another hat as an expert adviser, which he wore when he was called back to advise upon the Gold Standard in the 1920s.

But Keynes had also by this time acquired a third hat, as a publicist with a controversial image. He had gone to the Versailles peace conference as the official representative of the Treasury, but one who already manifested signs of unrest because of his liberal outlook. It is not altogether surprising that he resigned in June 1919, dismayed by the heavy scale of reparations demanded from Germany, and determined to expose the Treaty's shortcomings. Within a few months *The Economic Consequences of the Peace* (1919) was ready to be launched upon a tide of already expectant public opinion, which it caught with a remarkably complete measure of success. Keynes fused high moral passion with hard economic analysis, and revealed, moreover, his striking distinction as a writer. The nub of his case was that reparations implied a transfer of wealth from poverty-stricken Germany in the form of real resources, which Germany could generate only by establishing an economic domination over the rest of Europe for which no one was prepared. This was the case which the political opposition, Asquithian and Labour alike, deployed against Lloyd George. The fulsome reception accorded to the book, which made its author a household name in educated circles on both sides of the Atlantic, gave Keynes a platform of which he made full use thereafter.

After the First World War, then, Keynes divided his time between Cambridge and his house in Bloomsbury, where the cultural and business life of London, as well as politics, were open to him. He became a rich man through speculation, worth half a million pounds at the peak in 1936. (This would have to be multiplied by at least twenty in today's values.) He married the ballerina Lydia Lopokova in 1925 and they appear to have had a happy if childless marriage, sustained by a common interest in the arts, of which Keynes was a great patron. Though keeping his Fellowship at King's, Keynes did not revert to full-time academic teaching and research after the war. He never held a university chair of economics and when people called him 'Professor Keynes' he would protest that he refused to accept the indignity without the emoluments. Keynes's attitude toward economics – 'An easy subject, at which very few excel!' – was thus somewhat ambivalent. No one was less content to leave economics to the economists.

Nor could finance be left to the financiers. As early as 1922 Keynes observed that 'many conservative bankers regard it as more consonant with their cloth, and also as economizing thought, to shift public discussion off the logical on to an alleged 'moral' plane, which means a realm of thought where vested interests can be triumphant over the common good without further debate'. Far from endorsing a 'knave-proof' system of 'sound finance', therefore, he insisted that '*everything* is to be considered and weighed on its merits'.

Keynes was explicitly concerned with the proper role of the state as a matter of pragmatic political judgement rather than abstract economic doctrine. 'Perhaps the chief task of economists at this hour,' he said in a lecture in 1924, 'is to distinguish afresh the *Agenda* of government from the *Non-Agenda*, and the companion task of politics is to devise forms of government within a democracy which shall be capable of accomplishing the *Agenda*.' The terms were ones which he had borrowed from Bentham. The lecture was called 'The End of Laissez Faire'. The problem he defined was one which was to preoccupy him for the rest of his life. When he initially proposed a new agenda of government, he had little notion as to how support for it might be mobilized. But it is no accident that, set on a challenge to the knave-proof conventional wisdom, Keynes found the fate of his ideas successively entangled with the political fortunes of three rogues: Lloyd George, Oswald Mosley and Winston Churchill.

It is often said that Keynes was irresponsible. His most famous dictum – 'In the long run we are all dead' – is customarily cited in this sense. What Keynes meant when he proclaimed this in the 1920s, of course, was not that the future could be treated with feckless disregard but that it was irresponsible for policy-makers to close their eyes to the immediate impact of their actions by assuming that it would 'all come out in the wash'. He wanted them to appreciate the consequences of big decisions, not to ignore them. This is why he opposed the return to Gold. He argued that, with an inappropriately high parity for sterling, the monetary mechanism would not in fact work smoothly to deflate domestic prices but would provoke unemployment. At this stage, however, Keynes did not doubt the orthodox postulate, instilled by Marshall, that –

in the long run – a market-clearing equilibrium would be established.

When Churchill announced Britain's return to Gold in 1925, Keynes used the press to make his criticisms public. Here was a Chancellor struggling to uphold a high external parity for sterling, and condemned therefore to watch the domestic economy groan under the burden of high interest rates which caused unemployment. 'Why did he do such a silly thing?' Keynes demanded. The expectation that, in real life, domestic prices would simply adjust downwards was, he maintained, a delusion entertained by people who shut their minds to the actual process involved. 'Deflation does not reduce wages "automatically",' Keynes contended. 'It reduces them by causing unemployment.' This was 'the theory of the economic juggernaut'; and the Gold Standard, 'with its dependence on pure chance, its faith in "automatic adjustments", and its general regardlessness of social detail, is an essential emblem and idol of those who sit in the top tier of the machine'. It was thus a risky business 'to apply the principles of an economics, which was worked out on the hypothesis of laissez-faire and free competition, to a society which is rapidly abandoning these hypotheses'.

By going public in his criticisms of the Treasury – much to the annoyance of the inmates – Keynes capitalized on his reputation as a publicist. He reprinted his newspaper articles under the title *The Economic Consequences of Mr Churchill*, thus politicizing the debate and raising his own profile as critic of the Conservative Government. In the 1920s Keynes saw party politics as an obvious way to get things done. It is not a great puzzle that he should have been a member of the Liberal Party. His family background, rooted in the Dissenting tradition, was a predisposition. The primacy of the fiscal issue was a professional reinforcement; all Cambridge economists taught their pupils that protection was a despicable fallacy. The New Liberalism of the pre-war years, with its interventionist policies in social legislation and its search for an accommodation with Labour, found a ready adherent. Left Liberalism thus appealed to Keynes's conscience, his intellect and his temperament. The trouble was that the Liberal Party itself was in such poor shape. A shaky reunion was achieved in 1923, on the negative basis of resisting tariffs, but, under the benign torpor of Asquith's leadership, the party stood for nothing positive.

From 1923 Keynes was chairman of the weekly paper the *Nation* (later amalgamated with the *New Statesman*) which, under the editorship of the Cambridge economist Hubert Henderson, pressed for a more radical policy stance. They saw this as desirable in itself, as a means of reviving the party, and as a bridge to closer co-operation with Labour. This brought Keynes and Henderson into close alignment with Lloyd George, despite their old Asquithian affiliations. Among the back-biting, backward-looking sect which now surrounded Asquith, this was betrayal; but Keynes took the view, as another former critic of the Coalition put it, that 'when Lloyd George came back to the party, ideas came back to the party'.

The activities of the Liberal Summer Schools cemented this alliance with Lloyd George, and prepared the way for the work of the Liberal Industrial Inquiry, financed by Lloyd George, in which Keynes played a pivotal role. Indeed, he succeeded in stamping his ideas upon party policy and to this extent in making unemployment a major political issue. It was a problem which many Conservatives identified as a side-effect of Free Trade and which socialists could dismiss as a defect of the capitalist system. But if Tariff Reform was now ruled out, and a transition to socialism was not yet regarded as practical politics, what was to be done in the meantime? In this perspective, perhaps it is not so paradoxical that it was the Liberals, historically identified with the free market, who took the most radical line, lacking these alibis for inaction. An important part of Keynes's case for the continued role of the Liberal Party was its openness to new ideas and freedom from vested interests. He did not suppose that the Liberals could win a majority, but he undoubtedly hoped to see them in a strong enough position to influence the policy of a Government formed from the fragmented forces of the moderate Left. Lloyd George's instincts pointed the same way; he had no doctrinal commitment to sound finance; he had the personal charisma and the executive drive to spearhead a big, bold initiative. 'He can be amazing when one agrees with him,' Keynes admitted. If Keynes was the brains behind the Liberal revival, Lloyd George offered the political muscle.

When the Liberals entered the 1929 General Election with a pledge to cut the high level of unemployment to 'normal' proportions, Keynes and Henderson produced their famous pamphlet *Can Lloyd George Do It?* in support. Public works, it suggested, notably a loan-financed scheme of road-building, could stimulate a cumulative process of economic recovery. Keynes was thus identified as a prominent partisan opponent of Baldwin's Conservative Government and of the 'Treasury View' which it espoused. There were certainly other arguments against public works on the grounds of feasibility, but in 1929 the crucial objection was the Treasury View: that public expenditure necessarily diverted resources from more productive uses by private enterprise.

This proposition about 'crowding out' stimulated Keynes to find better arguments in support of his hunch that new public investment would be a healthy stimulus to the economy, not simply a waste of time and money. He had started off by maintaining that Britain was investing too much abroad at the expense of home investment, which he saw as more directly beneficial, especially to employment. Keynes did not abandon this position, awkward as it was to combine with the doctrinal purity of Free Trade, but he steadily shifted the argument towards the domestic economy itself. In the course of the election controversy, he spelt out with new clarity that the crucial point was to take up the slack in the economy by increasing investment, notably public investment. It was better, he claimed, to put resources to work in this way than to squander them unproductively in supporting men in idleness. The Conservative Government kept asking, where is the money to come from? Part of the answer was thus from savings on the dole. More important, Keynes could now claim that the wealth of the whole community could be increased by putting to work the *unemployed* resources. For an economy at less than full employment, therefore, it was a fallacy to suppose that public spending was simply at the expense of private investment, robbing Peter to pay Paul in a self-defeating circle. This was 'an argument which would be correct *if everyone were employed already*, but is only correct *on that assumption*'.

This was an argument conducted in the thick of a political controversy. It did not rely on abstruse economic theory but, as Keynes kept saying, was an appeal to common sense. It is therefore a mistake to over-intellectualize our view of his policy recommendations and our explanations of why they made little headway at this stage. The fact is that in the late 1920s Keynes used the Liberal Party to make an appeal to outside opinion and this failed for fairly straightforward political reasons. True, the Conservative Government was defeated in 1929 and the Liberal Party showed signs of a significant revival. But it was now in the position of a third party within an electoral system designed for two. Its poll of around 25 per cent did not achieve the sort of breakthrough necessary to give it decisive leverage. Polling two votes for every three by Labour, the Liberals had two MPs elected for every eleven by Labour. The result was thus a Labour Government which just lacked an overall majority but was initially confident of ruling without recourse to Lloyd George and his followers (who by now did not even include all Liberal MPs). It was thus the MacDonald Government which was left to confront economic difficulties which were already serious when it took office in 1929 and which were to snowball during the course of the next two years.

If Keynes had failed in his attempt to conquer outside opinion through party politics, he was lucky in having at least one more string to his bow. He could hardly pose as a disinterested expert, but MacDonald was more than ready to listen to his advice, if not always to heed it. Keynes was now given a chance to influence 'inside opinion' through his concurrent membership of two potentially influential bodies. One was the Committee on Finance and Industry, sitting under the chairmanship of the judge, Lord Macmillan, and including the foremost trade-union leader of the day, Ernest Bevin, with whom Keynes quickly established a rapport. The Macmillan Committee heard evidence, including that of Keynes himself, throughout 1930 before making its report in the summer of 1931. The other body which he now joined was the Economic Advisory Council, set up by MacDonald at the beginning of 1930 in the hope of opening, for the first time, a formal channel through which expert economic advice could be fed into government. Since its initial structure proved cumbersome, its work was soon devolved upon a committee of economists, of which Keynes was chairman.

With ample opportunity to make himself heard in government circles, Keynes freely propagated his views – all of them. There is a well-known jibe, in circulation from as early as 1931, that among five economists you would find six opinions, two of them held by Keynes. After all, he had advocated public works in 1929 in his pamphlet *Can Lloyd George Do It?* Yet he published an academic book, *A Treatise on Money* (1930), which stated that cheap money was the real solution. Then again, he outlined no less than seven remedies for unemployment, including both public works and cheap money, in testimony to the Macmillan Committee at the beginning of 1930. And later that year, notably in the deliberations of the EAC's committee of economists, he moved towards the option of tariffs, which was particularly shocking in someone of his upbringing.

Keynes plainly did not always say the same thing. But all these different remedies were congruent, and in fact were based upon a common analysis – that of the *Treatise*. The novelty of the *Treatise* was to repudiate the identity of investment and saving. Instead it talked of Enterprise and Thrift as different processes controlled by different people – albeit in theory brought into equilibrium by the adjusting mechanism of interest rate. With cheap money, Enterprise would be stimulated and could be relied upon to do the trick. Why, then, did Keynes urge other policies like public works in Britain at this time? Because, he contended, cheap money was not on offer so long as Bank rate had to be kept up in order to protect the high parity of sterling, as fixed under the Gold Standard.

In the Britain of 1930, therefore, the natural process of equilibration was frustrated through high interest rates, and 'second-best' expedients were necessary to take up the slack in the economy. So Keynes argued. Following his argument into the real world, where a choice of evils is usually the basis on which hard decisions have to be made, it is easy to dispose of the trivial charge of inconsistency. But could the argument have led to another conclusion? His analysis pointed to the failure of British costs, especially wages, to adjust downwards to the level demanded by the parity of sterling, with an implication, which he was reluctant to admit, that wages needed to be cut. It all depended on what was taken as given. Given the existing level of British prices, Keynes could say that interest rates were too high to run the economy at full employment. But given the level of interest rates necessary to protect sterling (so his opponents could argue), wages were surely too high and workers were simply pricing themselves out of jobs. In fact, when Keynes was pressed he had to acknowledge this as true; but it was, to his mind, quite beside the point when it came to dealing with the real world. It depended on the assumption that wage rates were flexible, which was 'not one of the alternatives between which we are in a position to choose. We are not offered it. It does not exist outside the field of pure hypothesis'.

Keynes was unusually stubborn in his resistance to wage cuts on any large scale. He thought they were unjust to particular groups of workers in export trades or in the public sector; he thought social justice demanded that other incomes should be reduced as well; he feared the risks to social stability and to political democracy. But Keynes's differences with his fellow economists were ones of degree, not of kind, on this matter. Almost all economists, including Keynes, said that relatively high labour costs constituted the problem; but they did not automatically jump to the conclusion that cutting wages was the remedy. The abstract models of economic theory, in short, did not prescribe practicable solutions. Thus, given these rigidities in the real world, Keynes was ready to outline the case for a number of unorthodox policy expedients – incomes policy, devaluation, tariffs and bounties, as well as public works – and other leading economists, notably Professor A.C. Pigou and Sir Josiah Stamp, were likewise ready to countenance some of these 'second-best' options.

Keynes therefore joined forces with others who were prepared to consider appropriate action, and in 1930 he found a champion of radical policies within the Labour Cabinet. Sir Oswald Mosley was no mere mouthpiece for Keynesian policies. He had his own ideas, and they derived in some respects from Joseph Chamberlain's vision of a strong, autarkic empire, with an unabashed appeal to nationalism and protection. Mosley played on his youth, with an appeal to ex-servicemen whom the dole queues had cheated out of the better world for which they had fought. With his dashing looks, he projected vigour. As an aristocrat in the party of the proletariat, he sought to vault over outdated class barriers. He was thus a brilliant figure, and not unaware of the fact: a class traitor who had defected from the Conservative Party and was now rapidly becoming impatient with Labour's timidity and misplaced deference towards the establishment. The sixth baronet was in awe of no one.

Keynes's support for optimistic, dynamic, radical politicians like Lloyd George and Mosley was rooted in temperamental affinities. 'We need the breath of life,' Keynes had insisted in the 1929 General Election campaign. 'There is nothing to be afraid of.' Little wonder that he later endorsed the New Deal policies of Franklin Roosevelt, with his message to the American people that they had nothing to fear but fear itself. Keynes was the quintessential exponent of 'can-do' economics. The Treasury, on the other hand, was a fund of expertise – much of it well-founded – on why things could not be done. Within MacDonald's Cabinet Mosley chafed at the administrative constraints which thwarted his big plans for an interventionist attack upon unemployment. He diagnosed the problem as one which demanded a revolution in the structure of government as well as in economic policy. In this respect his approach therefore complemented that of Keynes.

Mosley, however, like Churchill and Lloyd George, did not inspire trust. He was, on the one hand, an able executive politician: on the other, a forceful demagogue. But what he could not deliver, within the precipitate timescale set by his own ambition and a deteriorating situation, was the solid political support necessary to make sense of his position and to drive his policies through. The trouble was that although the orthodox policies did not, by this stage, look very clever, the alternatives looked too clever by half. Keynes's deficiency was not in bright ideas but in respectability, yet respectable statesmanlike figures were just the men he naturally put off. His dilemma was almost as acute as that of Groucho Marx: the support of the kind of politician who would support him was not worth having.

In 1930 Keynes pushed the committee of economists towards a programme of public works and tariffs. Neither was ideal, he argued, but both were necessary in a situation where resources of capital and labour would otherwise lie idle in Britain. The classic Free Trade case, which he had expounded with all the old Cambridge arrogance only a few years back, was that tariffs diverted employment from more efficient to less efficient forms of wealth creation. But Keynes now saw that, like the Treasury View, this beautiful principle held good only in the ideal world of flexible prices, market-clearing equilibrium, and axiomatic full employment. He questioned the assumption 'that if you throw men out of work in one direction you re-employ them in another', commenting: 'As soon as that link in the chain is broken the whole of the free trade argument breaks down.' In making this discovery, Keynes really owed a handsome posthumous apology to Joseph Chamberlain. Keynes incurred Liberal wrath by publicly questioning Free Trade in 1931. He must have expected some controversy; but what he got was not an appraisal of the relevance of tariffs to a new situation but simply a warmed-up rehash of all the old Free Trade fare. He despaired that 'the fundamentalists of free trade' had forced him 'to chew over again a lot of stale mutton, dragging me along a route I have known all about as long as I have known anything' and which was nothing but 'a peregrination of the catacombs with a guttering candle'. So much for the Liberals' receptivity to new thinking!

Free Trade still had an ideological charge in British politics which Keynes almost certainly underestimated. Thus one reason why the advice of the committee of economists was so easily shelved by the Labour Cabinet was that the divisive issue of tariffs was introduced. In a fast-changing situation, with a world slump rapidly overshadowing the problems of the British economy, the premises on which policy ought to be framed became themselves highly unstable. In an emergency situation, tariffs had become at least as important as public works in Keynes's view. He drafted an addendum to the Macmillan Report, signed by five other members including Ernest Bevin, along such lines. By the time the Report was published in the summer of 1931, however, the mounting economic crisis at home and abroad vitiated such proposals, and events rapidly overwhelmed the Labour Cabinet. The Government was caught in a mounting financial and political crisis which threatened the pound sterling on the foreign exchanges. Only when the position seemed untenable did Keynes himself opt for devaluation, though he was relieved when the new National Government found itself forced off Gold in September 1931.

'During the last 12 years I have had very little influence, if any, on policy,' Keynes told a meeting of MPs in September 1931. 'But in the role of a Cassandra, I have had a considerable success as a prophet.' He was right to the extent that the great experiment of returning to the Gold Standard, against which he had warned, had irrevocably failed. But Keynes had not spent the intervening years in lamenting the decision or in seeking its reversal through a policy of devaluation. Instead his approach had been wholly characteristic: to accept the Gold Standard as a fact of life and to make the best of a bad job. All his policy advice had therefore been framed on the assumption that, because of the Gold Standard, the British economy was subject to distortion by high interest rates. What Keynes did was to devise expedients for alleviating this condition. In his own analysis, expounded in the *Treatise on Money*, cheap money was the real path to recovery. But it was consistent with the *Treatise* to argue that, if interest rates were prevented from falling to the level appropriate to stimulate domestic production, a special case existed for other remedies. This was the justification equally for public works and for tariffs. Both of them were extraordinary measures, designed to cope with an anomaly. They were needed because, in the real world, the tendency of interest rates to restore equilibrium was thwarted by rigidities and interest rates remained stuck.

Now it is too seldom recognized that this analysis was fully compatible with orthodox economic theory. This held that there was a self-righting tendency on the part of market forces towards an equilibrium at full employment. All that Keynes had done, even in his *Treatise*, was to show that this proposition depended upon perfect flexibility of prices – including interest rates and wages – and that in its absence a position of disequilibrium existed. True, faced with persistent disequilibrium, he had been egregiously undignified in his clamour for unconventional policy expedients. But his case here was one which was accepted, albeit with becoming discretion, by such pillars of orthodoxy as Pigou, Marshall's loyal successor as professor of economics at Cambridge. Pigou did not accept the Treasury View of 1929, with its insistence that public works crowded out an equivalent amount of private enterprise, any more than Keynes did. Indeed, by 1931 it found few defenders, and the Treasury itself adroitly distanced itself from a proposition which Keynes had helped to expose as a doctrinaire fallacy, only true when resources were already at full stretch.

The argument, in short, was about policy not theory. The course of economic policy can therefore be explained largely in political terms. It was not just a Conservative Government which put Britain back on the Gold Standard but one which, in the person of its Chancellor of the Exchequer, was peculiarly committed to the axioms of the free market. Hence the reliance on Bank rate alone to regulate the economy, in the hope that by changing this one price all the millions of other prices would adjust to the discipline of the exchange rate. Keynes might dream up no fewer than seven remedies as conceivable options, but all were blocked so long as the magnificent masochism of sound finance prevailed. His own favourite remedy of public works was taken up by Lloyd George, but the Liberal Party lacked the political weight to impose its will. Likewise, Mosley's advocacy was double-edged, alienating as much support as it encouraged. Tariffs, too, as the other leg of Keynes's programme, were difficult to sell as a radical proposal since their partisan advocates were to be found in the Conservative Party – the obverse of the inconsistency which had always hobbled the Chamberlainites. So in 1931, with the advent of a Conservative-dominated Government which was disposed, through ideological prejudice, to put tariffs on the agenda, public works were, by the same token, swept aside in favour of a programme of cuts.

There was, however, a further implication of the 1931 crisis which fundamentally altered Keynes's own position. Not only was the Gold Standard itself suddenly obsolete: so too was the premise on which Keynes had previously framed all his policy advice. No longer could he lament that interest rates were kept artificially high because of Gold; and if they were not, what was the relevance of his special case for public works and for tariffs? A dutifully consistent Keynes might at this point have abandoned his advocacy of unorthodox policies, now that their intellectual rationale had collapsed, and have waited for cheap money to do the trick, as he had long insisted it could. But instead of jettisoning the policy proposals licensed by his basically orthodox theory, once the anomaly which justified them disappeared, Keynes did the opposite.

Within a couple of years he was back urging the same policies as before, having jettisoned orthodox theory. In doing so, it should be said, he could appeal to a fundamental change in external conditions. So long as Britain's difficulties were peculiar to herself, her economic disequilibrium could be blamed upon her lack of competitiveness in world trade. But now that the whole world had plunged into depression, how could it be explained? How could all countries simultaneously be uncompetitive with each other?

When Keynes produced his *Treatise on Money* his argument was in important respects fuelled by his political commitments. But in the period in which he wrote *The General Theory* it is more difficult to discern partisan motives of this kind. He broke with Mosley once his New Party displayed fascist tendencies. His breach with Lloyd George was signalled by the publication in 1933 of the portrait of 'the goat-footed bard', which Keynes had tactfully kept in his drawer since it was composed at the time of Versailles. Lloyd George's campaign for a British New Deal in 1935 was conducted without reference to Keynes, who, indeed, would not even send the Liberal Party a much-needed subscription. Nor would he join the Labour Party. In the banal English sense which equates politics with partisan commitment, Keynes in these years was 'not political'. The suggestion that he wrote *The General Theory* because he had an axe to grind in immediate policy arguments is wide of the mark.

Tactically, he would surely have had an easier time if he had stayed within the theoretical framework of the *Treatise* and justified his radicalism in policy on the expedient grounds that the real world exhibited rigidities, imperfections, jams and hitches which were not allowed for in the frictionless world of abstract theory. The notion that orthodox theory could not explain unemployment is nonsense; it explained unemployment in any one country precisely in terms of the rigidities and imperfections which prevented self-adjustment from operating as it did on the frictionless plane of hypothesis. Keynes spoke in 1934 of a gulf existing among economists, with 'those who believe that the existing economic system is, in the long run, a self-adjusting system, though with creaks and groans and jerks, and interrupted by time lags, outside interference and mistakes' on one side of it. By putting himself on the other side of the gulf, Keynes signalled a revolution in his own thinking.

It did not, however, lead him to make revolutionary new policy proposals. He remained an advocate of public expenditure, especially investment in the infrastructure, during periods of deficient demand. He still hoped to reduce unemployment in this way, without a significant cost in higher inflation, because higher demand would draw unemployed resources into productive use rather than bid up the price of such capital or labour as was already fully employed. He had not forgotten that it was crucial to transfer labour from the declining to the expanding sectors of the economy; in fact he became more conscious of the existence of bottlenecks, capable of exerting inflationary pressures, even at a time when unemployment was high elsewhere. Above all, Keynes did not, after *The General Theory*, depart from his central claim, first advanced in *Can Lloyd George Do It?* in 1929, that it ought to be possible to reduce unemployment to about 5 per cent of the labour force by raising the level of demand – but that it would be much more difficult to go beyond that point. Again, there is little evidence here that *The General Theory* was necessary in order to make out the case for political options which Keynes thought desirable and practicable. Perhaps surprisingly, the book was largely silent on policy.

The General Theory is nonetheless rightly considered Keynes's *magnum opus*. It is the book on which he lavished his care and staked his reputation with a remarkable degree of conviction. He put valued friendships at risk, as he recognized, by 'being so cocksure and putting all the driving force I know how behind arguments which for me are of painfully practical importance'. It was, as he subsequently explained, a journey of intellectual discovery, with crucial 'moments of transition which were for me personally moments of illumination', indelibly demarcating 'what I used to believe' from 'my present views'. Hence his claim in a letter of 1935 to Bernard Shaw, as one unabashed genius to another, that 'I believe myself to be writing a book on economic theory, which will largely revolutionize – not, I suppose, at once but in the course of the next ten years – the way the world thinks about economic problems.'

It was thus a highly theoretical work to which he devoted his energies from 1931 until its publication in 1936. These are, above all, the years in which he led the life of 'an academic scribbler', giving the first fruits of his labours to his lecture audiences in Cambridge. Within a surprisingly short time he had stepped outside the analytical framework of the *Treatise* and was arguing out his new theory of effective demand. He was crucially stimulated at this point by the 'Circus' of younger economists at Cambridge, especially the ideas of R.F. Kahn and J.E. Meade, suggesting a fresh approach to the problem of saving and investment. Instead of investment depending upon prior saving – the orthodox assumption – savings were seen as being generated by an initial act of investment through a process which multiplied income, output and employment.

Thus saving and investment were brought into equality by the equilibrating mechanism of changes in income or output. It followed that equilibrium might be reached while output was still below full capacity or full employment. It followed, too, that changes in output were now assigned the equilibrating task which was fulfilled under orthodox theory (including the *Treatise*) by changes in interest rate. What role, then, did interest play? Keynes proceeded to explain interest in terms of 'liquidity preference' – the premium which wealthholders exacted for tying up their resources in ways which sacrificed the liquid advantages of holding cash. *The General Theory* thus gave a wholly new account of how the economy worked – or failed to work. No longer did Keynes point to particular rigidities as the reason why the market was not working properly. He argued now that reductions in wages or interest rates, even if forthcoming, might simply be incapable of restoring full employment, which was a function of effective demand (that is, of prospective consumption plus investment).

Keynes had, of course, in the 1920s already rejected the long run as a safe guide to policy, while still believing that (in the long run) the tendency of interest rate was to bring the economy into equilibrium at full employment. Because the Gold Standard jammed the Bank rate mechanism, *in practice* the economy was regulated by high levels of unemployment. In developing the theory of effective demand in the 1930s, however, Keynes renounced the Marshallian tradition on which, as he liked to put it, he had been brought up. For he now insisted that a supposed tendency towards equilibrium was itself fallacious. It was not therefore interest rate which equilibrated the economy, but the overall level of output. And if this fluctuated, as it must in this role, then *in theory too* the economy was regulated by the level of unemployment.

The General Theory does not provide a magic toolkit, offering an infallible way to put this right, but a pair of economic spectacles through which to look at the world. Full employment, it seems, is not normal but abnormal. There is certainly no self-righting force within the economy to bring it about. The price mechanism will not clear the market in a way that leaves every willing buyer and seller satisfied. The reasons for this are not abstruse and technical but they go to the heart of Keynes's theory, which depended, as he kept saying, on a few basic, simple ideas.

The maxims which govern individual behaviour do not hold good for the community as a whole. Keynes liked to say that one man's expenditure is another man's income – a truth, however, only appreciated, if at all, in the long run. For each person can decide to spend or to save as he chooses, without any immediate consequences for his own income. Yet, for their successful accomplishment, these acts, like marriage, are essentially two-sided. Every purchase obviously requires a sale; every act of saving in the end requires an act of investment. The double-sided nature of each transaction requires these overall identities, and thus requires changes in overall prices to accommodate them – requiring in turn changes in aggregate output and total employment. Any one bargainer might beat the system, and many more will accordingly try to do so, but in aggregate it is impossible that everyone can simultaneously succeed in implementing incompatible plans. Hence the likelihood of a self-defeating scramble, either between individuals or between firms or between nations. Keynes saw this as a picture of the world in which he lived in the 1930s – a world of beggar-my-neighbour strategies which paved the way to mutual impoverishment. This constitutes, moreover, an equilibrium, in the sense that there is no tendency to disturb it – as it would have to be disturbed if it were to shift towards full employment.

Keynes ultimately became a director of the Bank of England, a peer, a confidant of the Chancellor of the Exchequer. All was forgiven – but not until the coming of the Second World War. There is, admittedly, considerable evidence that the Treasury had been educated by its protracted argument with him in the years from 1929 to 1939. Nor was this a one-way learning process. Keynes came to appreciate the hard-won pragmatic wisdom of Treasury knights like Sir Richard Hopkins, with whom he had clashed swords before the Macmillan Committee. There were shifts in Treasury policy, though of a kind, as in 1935, which can be attributed to political expediency in the face of an imminent election, rather than to a real change of heart. It was only natural that, with Neville Chamberlain as either Chancellor of the Exchequer or Prime Minister from 1931 to 1940, economic policy was framed in accordance with Conservative ideas and in terms of the Government's own constituency. The fact is that, with cheap money in force, there was a real economic recovery which cut unemployment (on the official figures) from the peak of 23 per cent at the beginning of 1933 to 10 per cent by the summer of 1937. Though the level remained stubbornly high in the depressed areas, the Government could still get comfortably re-elected with the support of the much greater number of voters who were in work. If Keynesian remedies had a political appeal, it was not one which threatened the Chamberlain regime.

Rearmament was the Trojan Horse for budget deficits. Here loan-financed public expenditure did not encounter the same sort of ideological objection as road-building, but the stimulus to the economy in the late 1930s was appreciable, and the programme was dramatically stepped up in 1939. 'It is, it seems, politically impossible for a capitalistic democracy to organize expenditure on the scale necessary to make the grand experiments which would prove my case – except in war conditions,' wrote Keynes in June 1940. By then, however, Churchill had become Prime Minister and, like it or not, now presided over a government in which the centre of gravity had tipped sharply towards the left. Keynes was one beneficiary of this political revolution. In 1940 he was invited back into the Treasury, where he served as a top-level adviser for the rest of his life. He held no official position, but he had a room, he saw the papers, he now worked closely with Sir Richard Hopkins, he was 'just Keynes'. He had what he had always wanted: influence rather than power.

A happy ending to the story may be emotionally satisfying. A macro-economic approach – designed to contain inflation by restraining demand for finite resources rather than simply to raise revenue – became the basis of the 1941 Budget in Britain. Conversely, the feasibility of maintaining full employment after the war was proclaimed in the Coalition Government's White Paper of 1944. Moreover, Keynes now emerged as an international economic statesman, who sought new means of discharging the functions of the historic Gold Standard in a post-war world. And in his spare time he invented the Arts Council.

Keynes played a large part at the Bretton Woods conference (1944), which helped to set up the International Monetary Fund and the World Bank. In contrast to his advocacy of tariffs in the conditions of the 1930s, he now reverted to

fundamentally liberal trade policies. His abilities as a negotiator were put to a supreme test at the end of the war when
American support for Britain under the lend-lease agreement
was abruptly terminated. Keynes was largely responsible for
securing a large dollar loan from the USA and Canada to tide
Britain over the transition to peace. It was an arrangement
which he recognized as at once imperfect and necessitous – a
case which he made with telling effect in the House of Lords
in December 1945. There can be little doubt that these weari-
some transatlantic negotiations taxed Keynes's strength (he
had suffered a major heart attack in 1937), and he died suddenly at Easter 1946, at the height of his powers and his fame,
just before the Order of Merit, the supreme honour, could
be conferred.

But is a happy ending historically convincing? We can now
see that acceptance of Keynesian ideas was not as swift or
complete as was once supposed. Instead this process was
halting and patchy and incremental. And what did the Keynesian revolution lead to? It is often assumed that it had its
apotheosis in 'Butskellism', the notion that there was a post-
war consensus in Treasury policy between the Conservative
Butler and Labour's Gaitskell. The salient features were, in
the first place, a policy aimed at the management of demand,
with an increasing emphasis on the management of consumer
demand; and, secondly, a reliance not only on fiscal means but
also on credit regulation. What was the Keynesian pedigree of
this approach?

On the first point, it should be noted that Keynes's concept
of effective demand was defined as *investment* plus immediately prospective consumption. He had a longstanding record
of wishing to regulate investment so as to make full use of
resources, and in *The General Theory* he accordingly suggested
'a somewhat comprehensive socialization of investment'. The
post-war nationalization measures in Britain do not, however,
fulfil his criteria of controlling the overall volume of investment, whether public or private – 'it is not the ownership of
the instruments of production which it is important for the
State to assume'. So consumer demand was only one side of

Keynes's story – and not the one which he himself chose to emphasize.

Secondly, there is the issue of *how* to regulate. According to *The General Theory*: 'The state will have to exercise a guiding influence on the propensity to consume partly through its scheme of taxation, partly by fixing the rate of interest, and partly, perhaps, in other ways.' Keynes repeatedly stressed the desirability of bringing down the rate to a low *and stable* level (in this sense 'fixing' the rate). Although Labour adopted a cheap money policy throughout the years 1945–51, under Butler the Conservatives brought monetary policy into play as well, using changes in Bank rate as well as fiscal changes in a policy of demand management. This was the policy pejoratively known as stop-go, and a credit squeeze became *the* classic way of stopping.

It is clear that this aspect of Butskellism can find no authority in *The General Theory* (nor in Keynes's other writings). Moreover, attempts to manipulate demand at a time when unemployment was way below 5 per cent similarly lack Keynes's own sanction. Perhaps it should come as no great shock that the 'Keynesian revolution' showed a highly imperfect fidelity to the classic text loosely invoked in its support. One reason is that *The General Theory* did not purport to be a handbook on economic policy. Keynes unambiguously said that his aim was to revolutionize economic theory and that it would take another book to apply this to politics. He spoke more truly than he knew when he told Shaw: 'When my new theory has been duly assimilated and mixed with politics and feelings and passion, I can't predict what the final upshot will be in its effects on action and affairs.'

PART THREE

ISMS AND WASMS

Hugh Dalton by Vicky, 1946

8

THE TUTELARY POLITICS OF
HUGH DALTON

The function of the Labour Party in its early years was to elect trade-union officials as MPs. Only after the First World War was its parliamentary representation broadened to include also a number of class traitors from the upper reaches of society. They were, not unnaturally, an odd bunch – sponge-bag-trousered philanthropists who had turned against the conventions of their own upbringing. Hugh Dalton was one who had turned with a vengeance, and it was often remarked, as he proceeded to exact this vengeance, that his hatred of the rich seemed more obvious than his love of the poor. True, it could be said that he was only the son of a clergyman and that he had attended the local school. But since his father was Canon of St George's Chapel, Windsor, and the family lived in Windsor Castle, this meant that the school was Eton, which led on to King's College, Cambridge. This was the background of Labour's most egalitarian Chancellor of the Exchequer, who claimed to impose taxation for redistributive purposes with a song in his heart.

Many Labour leaders ingenuously equated their own rise in the world with the triumph of the class from which they sprang. Their contacts with royalty often produced a peculiar thrill, recorded in memoirs with titles like *From Workman's Cottage to Windsor Castle*; and their surviving papers, moreover, often include little except the souvenirs of grand occasions. Dalton's perspective was wholly different and, starting off from Windsor Castle, he had a lifelong immunity to such sentimentality. On his father's death, he disposed of the royal keepsakes for what they would fetch, apparently to George VI's displeasure. But what Dalton did faithfully keep, in both senses, was his own diary. He was the great political diarist of his generation, just as Richard Crossman was of the next. One similarity between them was their undisguised intellectual and social assurance, such as only an expensive education could give.

Dalton was almost Shavian in his resolutely unsentimental view of party politics. Not for him the wishy-washy, squeamish pieties of reach-me-down Gladstonianism. In his youth, he later recalled, 'I had been a Tory democrat, with pictures of Joe Chamberlain on my walls in my first term at Cambridge.' As he rightly insisted in 1940: 'Whatever I have been, I have never been a Liberal.' Relishing his reputation as a tough guy, he was equally ready to defend his ends as noble and his means as necessary. The story of him entering the room, 'his eyes blazing with insincerity', was often told – too often for his own good. His moral claims were devalued by his deviousness; his Machiavellian tactics vitiated by their transparency.

Dalton claimed to have become a socialist at the end of the First World War, in which he served in Italy. After the Armistice the Labour Party seemed a promising instrument for a politically ambitious radical whose loud voice betokened his upper-crust confidence. He sized up the problem at once. 'What is chiefly needed is (1) improved organization in the constituencies, (2) an influx of brains and middle-class non-crank membership.' He was brisk and single-minded in pursuit of the main chance. His career blossomed. His emotional life, however, was stunted by an intensely private bereavement – not the death in wartime of Rupert Brooke, to which he often adverted, but that of his own little daughter Helen in 1922. Did it happen because Hugh and Ruth Dalton, that busy Fabian couple, were off fighting the Cambridge by-election? Ruth, at least, could never get this thought out of her mind. Their marriage, which was otherwise childless, became a partnership for public ends with a nightmare tragedy haunting it down the years. It seems to have made Dalton unusually dependent on public life for recompense.

Dalton's career was a quest for comradeship, especially with personable young men who would accept his patronage, in the spirit of David and Jonathan. Vulnerable even at his most cynical, he left his diary as a devastating exposure of human frailty and folly, not least his own. 'You can't talk candidly about Dalton,' one friend remarked, 'without describing him as, in a sense, a monstrous figure.' The awkward Etonian who resented not being elected to Pop; Rupert Brooke's undergraduate friend who got the cold shoulder; the professional economist who felt slighted by Maynard Keynes; the doting elder statesman whose advances were rebuffed by his young protégé, Tony Crosland – the ages of man were played out with a grotesque amalgam of bravado and pathos.

Part of Dalton's mission was to cure the Labour Party of an innate diffidence and deference against which his whole being rebelled. 'Why this Servants' Hall mentality?' he would demand. But Dalton was socially rebellious, not politically revolutionary. He applied himself steadily to giving the Labour Party a moderate, coherent and effective stance on major policy issues, especially economic issues. He maintained that 'Socialism did best when it marched in step with the rules of arithmetic'. He rose high in the party and in government, yet never quite looked like reaching the top, barring the sort of luck which came Attlee's way. Dalton believed in strong leadership but was better at depicting it than delivering it. His role was tutelary: that of the guardian and patron who aspired to educate his party, to dispel the taunt that it was unfit to govern, and to pass on a shining record of achievement to the next generation.

In the 1920s there was a sharp contrast between Dalton's patient approach and the impetuous self-dramatization of Oswald Mosley, another of Labour's upper-class recruits. This was not simply a matter of different natural abilities. When

Mosley provoked a confrontation with the Labour leadership over unemployment in 1930, Dalton maintained that he possessed 'no sense of the slow transitions of real life. Having joined the Party last week, he wants to lead it tomorrow afternoon.' Mosley's case, of course, was that the Labour Party in office was no more prepared to tackle the problem of unemployment than the Tories had been. Philip Snowden as Chancellor stood immovable in defence of Treasury orthodoxy.

Dalton, as a junior minister under Arthur Henderson at the Foreign Office, was not in the front line in this dispute. He might have been expected, as an academic economist trained at Cambridge, to have championed Keynesian alternatives. But Dalton remained professionally unpersuaded by Keynes, preferring the analysis of old colleagues at the London School of Economics, and he was politically suspicious of 'Lord Oswald', trusting instead the judgement of 'Uncle Arthur'. Thus when Mosley hinted at resignation in January 1930, Dalton could, as he wrote in his diary, 'express sympathy with him in being confronted with such a combination of stupidity and cowardice', without enlisting under this banner of revolt. Mosley's appeals to the party in the following months are likewise reported as displays of headstrong vanity. And when 'this hateful fellow, whom I have always bitterly distrusted', eventually leaves the Labour Party: 'The air seems cleaner already.' The irony was that, within a year, MacDonald and Snowden were themselves to defect, leading a National Government which appealed for a Doctor's Mandate.

Dalton was truly a Fabian in forswearing the frontal assault in favour of the tactics of permeation. Plotting and scheming to get his own way were more than means to an end: they were a delight to him in themselves. His constant watchword was never to resign, his persistent aim to instil his party with common sense and realism. The departure of the MacDonaldites in 1931 was thus an opportunity as well as an immediate setback for Labour. It was Dalton, now given his head, who encouraged a younger generation of academic economists to put their services directly at the disposal of the Labour Party. With his established position on the National Executive Committee and his own post at the London School of Economics, he was ideally placed to make this link. Hugh Gaitskell, Evan Durbin, Douglas Jay, James Meade and other members of the New Fabian Research Bureau found their ideas pillaged in Labour's policy-making process. The net result was to give Labour an agreed programme in *For Socialism and Peace* (1934) which was revised and summarized three years later as *Labour's Immediate Programme*.

This was an impressive transformation. It showed that Labour had gone to school and learnt its lesson. Every good socialist knew, as a matter of faith, that in 1931 the Labour Government had been brought down by 'a bankers' ramp', but not one in a million could have explained how. In 1932 the XYZ Club was formed in the City – anonymously so as to protect the jobs of its members, and initially depending largely upon a gaggle of financial journalists. Its historic task was to let the Labour Party into the secret of how bankers ramped. Dalton could then airily talk about 'my experts' when proposing prophylactic measures.

As well as technical understanding of the markets, the Labour Party needed a firmer grasp upon economic theory in the era of the Keynesian revolution. With some overlap of membership with Keynes's own circle, the New Fabian economists were quick to accept expansionary policies based on a new sort of macro-economic analysis. Their assent to the propositions of *The General Theory*, however, was neither automatic nor universal. Whereas Meade was fully Keynesian, and Jay a ready convert, Gaitskell and Durbin continued to stress the importance of institutional changes rather than what they regarded as short-term unemployment measures. And if a young man like Durbin could not simply be described as a Keynesian, it is not surprising that the reservations of Dalton ran deeper still. The significance of this is partly retrospective, harking back to personal lack of empathy at King's; but it is also significant in pointing ahead to tensions in the period of Dalton's Chancellorship.

In the 1930s, however, it was foreign policy which increasingly absorbed Dalton's attention. He was to the fore in bringing Labour slowly round to the acceptance of rearmament against Hitler, a cause to which he warmed with special fervour. Other Labour politicians may have felt just as strong an intellectual and moral revulsion from fascism, but none matched Dalton in simply hating Germans. In 1938 he was scheming busily behind the scenes to bring Labour into contact with other opponents of appeasement, especially the dissident Conservatives around Churchill.

Dalton became Minister of Economic Warfare in 1940. It was a post which suited him down to the ground, combining his professional expertise with his combative temperament. He took as his motto 'Belligerency at all times'. His own priorities meshed happily with those of what he liked to call 'this Churchill–Labour Government'. His current view of Churchill was just this side of idolatry; alas, the great man reciprocated with a lack of warmth that was just this side of disdain. Dalton brought in Hugh Gaitskell, then a temporary civil servant, as his *chef de cabinet*. The rising diplomat Gladwyn Jebb, who had been Dalton's private secretary during his stint as a junior minister under MacDonald, was another of the 'three sprites' on whom the minister relied and whose company he relished.

Over lunch with Gaitskell and Jebb, Dalton felt free to ponder the differences between 'intrigue' and 'diplomacy', asking: 'Should one not either be quite worldly or quite non-worldly? Is there any stopping place between?' On his own spectrum of 'monks, dons, diplomats, politicians', it was not altogether clear where he stood. Dalton might sometimes complain that his subtlety was not appreciated, but Gaitskell was ready to tell him: 'The trouble is that you are subtle one day and brutal the next.' Dalton assured another young confidant that it was not his own manner but only luck which had made Attlee leader instead of himself. 'For many years,' he claimed, 'I exercised the most tremendous control, even in the presence of the greatest fools. Only recently have I allowed myself the luxury of showing some of them – and by no means all of them even yet – what I think of them.'

It was Jebb who had oversight of the Special Operations Executive which Dalton helped persuade Churchill to establish as a means of fomenting trouble for the Nazis in continental Europe. Sabotage, black propaganda, industrial agitation, dirty tricks, cloak and dagger – this was meat and drink to Dalton, appealing to him simultaneously as social subversive, political schemer and romantic patriot. 'Set Europe ablaze,' the Prime Minister had exhorted him. This was a climax in Dalton's life, as he well recognized, rubbing shoulders with clean-limbed young men, all engaged in a common struggle where everyone was expected to do their bit. During the London blitz he readily abandoned home in favour of sleeping in the basement of his ministry, solaced by the rough male kiss of blankets.

In 1940 and 1941, in charge of economic warfare, he lectured his own party on the need to win the war before worrying about losing the peace. Now that he was a minister, he noted, 'the House at large appears as a monkey house of utterly ignorant and ill-conditioned amateurs'. Only later, as President of the Board of Trade, did he turn his attention to the problems of post-war reconstruction as politics returned to normal after the unwonted elevation of the finest hour. 'Jealousy is the foundation of public life,' he reflected in May 1942. 'Green eyes glare from every thicket at every passer-by in the political jungle.' The trick was to come out alive. Since he took the view that in an immediate post-war election 'there was no doubt that the P.M. and the Tories would sweep the board', he favoured keeping the Coalition going.

It took Dalton a long time to become persuaded otherwise, but throughout he remained true to his 'profoundly simple' guiding principle: 'Next time we had a general election, I wanted to win it.' At his age, he 'wanted either to have power or to retire and plant trees'; he was 'not interested any more in impotent gyrations in Opposition'. In the event, Labour won the 1945 election, but Dalton was wrong too in his expectation of being offered the Foreign Office, which, in a last-minute switch, went to Bevin. At the Treasury, now that he had power, Dalton faced two intractable problems. One centred on external finance and the other on domestic politics.

The Second World War had a strikingly different impact upon the British and American economies. It immensely enriched America, both absolutely and relatively. For the USA, war was the continuation of the New Deal by other means – and more effective means at that. Public spending was boosted far higher than Roosevelt had ever dreamed in peacetime, bringing a mildly inflationary boom which mopped up unemployment and raised living standards. For Britain, by contrast, it was not just a question of ceding priority to America but of facing unaccustomed national impoverishment. In a memorable metaphor, which became devalued over the years through indiscriminate reiteration, Keynes called it 'a financial Dunkirk'.

In the First World War Britain had to liquidate overseas assets to the tune of 15 per cent of her wealth, and in the Second there was a loss of 28 per cent. The cushion of foreign investments, which had served to render the long-term decline of British productive industry tolerably comfortable, had now disappeared. Everything therefore hinged upon exports. But British exports had been run into the ground as part of the war effort. The Americans had obligingly shared the strain by taking over Britain's economic commitments, while Britain mobilized manpower for military ends. As Attlee put it in 1945, 'the very fact that this was the right division of effort between ourselves and our allies leaves us, however, far worse off, when the sources of assistance dry up, than it leaves those who have been affording us the assistance'.

Within days of VJ Day, President Truman ended Lend-Lease, leaving Britain with a very large army, a very small export trade, and nothing in the kitty. She somehow had to beg, borrow or steal a living. The Government tried each in turn.

There was little real alternative to seeking a subvention from North America as the only means of avoiding not only an abrupt rundown of all external commitments but also an unparalleled degree of austerity at home. The option of simply relinquishing Great Power status looks more feasible and attractive in hindsight than it did at the time. It is easy enough now to see that Britain was ultimately weakened by her post-imperial pretensions; but these were defended after 1945 with the same bloody-minded stubbornness which had been vindicated in 1940. Keynes was to point out in February 1946 that 'it comes out in the wash that the American loan is primarily required to meet the political and military expenditure overseas'. This observation, however, coming from the architect of the loan strategy, made a case for cutting defence spending, not for doing without the loan itself. Similarly, as regards austerity, the fact that rationing helped maintain the whole population upon an adequate diet, albeit one lacking in choice and variety, does not mean that they could have subsisted on an even more exiguous basis. Luxury, like deprivation, may be a relative concept, determined by cultural as well as rational criteria. Thus there was the making of a social if not a nutritional crisis in 1949 when the ascetic Cripps, the prophet of wholemeal bread and a higher extraction rate, confronted the flatulent Bevin, an authentic working-class tribune in his attachment to white bread.

Given that American aid was necessary, it was only to he had on their own terms. Keynes was sent to Washington as a high-caste mendicant; but it is clear that he got off on the wrong foot by giving the Americans a lecture on the concept of Justice when he had been expected to get down to haggling over how to hire the money. The subsequent negotiations, however, were handled adroitly enough, and the scheme of repayments did not in the event prove onerous. Nor was the size of the advance niggardly. There was not only a loan of $3,750 million from the United States, but a remarkably generous further tranche of $1,250 million from Canada. The immediate problem, however, centred on the pledge to make sterling convertible on a fixed timetable. The British had never been confident that convertibility could be achieved so soon, but they found reasons for hoping for the best.

Because of the undertakings given in Washington, the great convertibility crisis of 1947 was in this sense a planned crisis. It was marked by a run on the pound which threatened to exhaust the remaining dollars. The Chancellor, equally exhausted, was to resign shortly afterwards over a Budget leak. If none of this was entirely accidental, the reasons for both the economic crisis and the personal débâcle need to be disentangled. How had it all gone wrong?

Keynes's calculation – or miscalculation, as it turned out – had been that the dollar drain would end once the balance of payments was back in equilibrium. Hence the size of loan needed was governed by the accumulated deficit which he forecast for the years 1946–8, namely £1,250 million (or $5,000 million). Now the aggregate of the first published figures for this period turned out to be £1,245 million, which made it look as though Keynes had scored a bullseye. Only later did an anomaly emerge. For subsequent revisions of the official figures put the actual deficit at less than half this amount, and the current account back in balance by 1948. In the crucial year of 1947 the revision is from a shock-horror deficit of £675 million, as first announced at the time, to a distinctly less newsworthy figure of £381 million. But this creates a different problem of explanation when set alongside the indubitable fact of a gold and dollar outflow of £1,024 million. Where on earth did all those dollars go?

The essential problem was that of the 'dollar gap'. Britain's imports from America ran at such a high level because there were virtually no alternative suppliers at that time for goods which were regarded as essential. Admittedly, there were two items on the import bill which consort uneasily with the image of austerity – films and tobacco. But the lifeline to Hollywood had to be maintained unless the major form of mass entertainment were simply to be shut down. Cigarette smoking, likewise, was not only a quintessential cultural symbol of the period, redolent of the spirit which had won the war while watching Bogart: it also had the additional charm for government of raising vast sums in taxation and siphoning off excess demand in the economy. The flow of

American imports, then, could not easily be staunched.

The almighty snag was that, contrary to predictions, the dollar gap did not disappear along with the overall deficit in the balance of payments. Instead it continued to gape until 1952, producing a peak deficit of $9,500 million. This came about, as we can now see, because the world economy had become lopsided, divided between hard currencies which had done very well out of the war, and soft currencies which had not. It was in the latter areas that Britain found her major export markets, with the receipts from this trade coming in non-convertible currencies. Her imports, on the other hand, came largely from countries which required payment in gold or dollars. Britain's deficit with the USA was of long standing and had never been a problem so long as it could be settled multilaterally, through trade with other countries where Britain was in surplus. What was new was the way that British exports to the sterling area were now left 'unrequited'. A surplus here could not be turned into the dollars necessary to finance Britain's imports, which were thus paid for out of the loan. Little wonder that in March 1947 Dalton warned the Cabinet of 'a looming shadow of catastrophe'.

This was the impasse which Britain faced in 1947. If Britain's current deficit explains only a third of the drain on the reserves, the rest must be accounted for by an outflow of capital. This went predominantly to the sterling area, which instead of fulfilling its historic role of squaring Britain's deficit on current account, now sucked in British capital to finance its own deficits. The net increase in British investment abroad during this period was thus broadly equal to that of the American loan – hardly the position which any of its negotiators had envisaged. Put another way, the level of capital outflow from Britain was running at about 8 per cent of net national income and was being saved at this heroic rate by a country in which bread and potatoes were rationed. The Victorian values of thrift and abstinence can hardly find a more magnificent epitome than Mr Attlee's Britain.

Such were the ironies of the position in which the Labour Government found itself. The drain on the balance of payments, coming to a peak in 1947, represented a structural imbalance beside which the losses from convertibility itself look modest. It was, however, the panic of late summer which produced the political crisis, which Dalton stumbled through with manifest weariness. The fact is that he had lost the will to go on shouldering the heavy ministerial burden which he had carried since 1940. He noted in his diary that 'one can't go on living for ever like this on pills and potions' even as he turned his thoughts towards preparing for his fourth Budget. This proved to be one too many. The careless disclosure of his measures was the occasion but hardly the full cause of his demise, as his diary serves to indicate. It was not just honour which led him to tender his resignation with an alacrity that shames more recent Cabinet ministers. Stafford Cripps took over. By 1947 Dalton's day was done – 'I am amazed how we all keep going somehow,' he had written – and he appears like a man waiting for an accident to happen to him.

The dollar gap was bridged in the short term by Marshall Aid. To some extent the convertibility crisis removed American objections to the subsequent measures of trade discrimination which became necessary. For Britain's ability to break even on her balance of payments by the end of 1948 highlighted the need to redress her trading position in dollar markets. This suggested that British goods were potentially competitive if only the parity between sterling and the dollar were adjusted. If other countries followed Britain in devaluing against the dollar, this would not really matter. The real point was to make the soft currencies harder and the hard currencies softer by means of making the leading hard currency (the dollar) dearer in terms of the leading soft currency (sterling). This was not a particularly complex argument, but it demanded a degree of economic sophistication to appreciate it. The chance to devalue from a position of strength was missed because the arguments of the experts did not speak to urgent political necessities.

The totemistic status of the currency thus put off serious debate until sterling came under pressure in the summer of 1949. Good and bad reasoning were certainly mixed up together, but in the end it was the Attlee Government's access to economic expertise which distinguished its handling of this sterling crisis from the MacDonald Government's mishandling of that of 1931. Back in the Cabinet, Dalton noted: 'How differently we ministers are reacting now!' It may have been an accident that the three young ministers (Gaitskell, Jay and Harold Wilson) who were left to decide the issue were all economists; but they spoke the same language as the official advisers and together they played a crucial role in paving he way for devaluation in September 1949. In particular, this was the making of Gaitskell, not even a Cabinet minister at the time, in revealing his grasp and determination. Moreover, the policy was vindicated in practical terms. The impact upon the gold and dollar reserves was immediately favourable, arguably too much so for Britain's own good. By the end of 1950 Gaitskell, now Chancellor himself, considered that the reserves would be 'startlingly high'. The Americans were so impressed that they promptly changed the rules on Marshall Aid and cut it off from 1 January 1951.

In domestic politics, Dalton's period as Chancellor of the Exchequer from 1945 had begun on a high note. He had long been an expert on public finance, on which he had written a textbook. He was not a Keynesian in his conception of Budget-making, and thought in terms of balancing the Government's books rather than regulating effective demand in the economy as a whole. His task was to find the money for internal reforms, and his promise to do so 'with a song in my heart' became his political signature tune. He thus made a virtue of necessity in identifying Labour as the party of high personal taxation.

There was general agreement that Labour stood for planning; there was widespread disagreement about what planning meant. There was an implicit contrast between a socialist, egalitarian approach which was directly interventionist and the sort of liberal Keynesianism which concentrated on regulating the level of demand in order to maintain full employment. This was shown in differences of attitude towards the utility of the price mechanism, and hence whether money or manpower was the best accounting unit. There were two ways of defining the problem of excess demand, presenting it as either a labour shortage, measured in manpower, or an inflationary gap, measured in money. The initiative for an overall plan had come in 1945 from James Meade, as the new head of the Economic Section of the Cabinet Office, and this was the origin of the annual *Economic Survey*s. Although the drafts were prepared in terms of national income, ministers found the alternative manpower version more intelligible, and when the *Economic Survey* was first published in 1947 this was the form it took. This device helped conceal the fact that the *Survey* year began in January whereas the Budget, which Meade regarded as 'the main instrument of carrying out the Plan', was framed for the financial year starting in April. From 1948 the *Economic Survey* published its assessment in terms of national income, and the manpower budget disappeared without trace by 1951. This betokened the shift that had taken place from physical towards budgetary planning.

Socialist planning was often concerned with micro-economic problems, on which the record was not strikingly successful. Liberal planning by contrast was essentially macroeconomic, and it was here that the Government increasingly placed the emphasis. The Treasury's crab-like scuttle towards Keynesian policies was inspired by economic constraints as much as by intellectual conviction. In Dalton's case it was virtually a deathbed conversion, for only in his fourth, final, fatal Budget of November 1947 did he explicitly relate his measures, which stepped up taxes across the board, to the problem of controlling inflation. Keynesianism was much more acceptable to the Treasury when it was a question of damping down demand through a budgetary surplus than of stimulating demand through a deficit. It was thus Dalton who piled up the surplus over which Cripps subsequently sat guard as though he owned it. Demand was now taken out of the economy by restraint on personal consumption, thus rendering many physical controls increasingly otiose. In his

1950 Budget speech Cripps repudiated the notion that planning had been abandoned, insisting now that the Budget 'can be described as the most powerful instrument for influencing economic policy which is available to government'.

This is as good a moment as any from which to date the Keynesian era in British economic policy. The paradox is that a Keynesian approach was directed chiefly to the problem of keeping the level of demand down, not up, since it was already sufficiently strong to sustain full employment without any need for a boost from Government spending. Admittedly it took some time for this point to sink in on Labour politicians whose assumptions had been formed under the influence of pre-war conditions. Cripps's fear of deflation was apparently still lively in 1949. Government policy was thus permissive in allowing expansion to take place, untroubled by a concomitant increase in the money supply.

It should be remembered that in 1951 the British economy produced more than those of France and Germany combined, even though what impresses us now, of course, is that within thirty-five years German industrial production was to be three times that of the UK and that of France nearly double. The fact is that the economic growth of the post-war years was sustained by a high level of investment, facilitated by cheap money, thus creating a cycle of cumulative prosperity by encouraging optimistic expectations. The whole process was driven by exports and investment; nearly three-quarters of the increase in production was channelled into exports. This reflected the Government's priorities, which it is tempting to summarize as those of economic virtue and electoral folly. For just as the British people apparently had little to show for winning the war except a regime of austerity, so the Labour Party discovered in due course that the reward for its responsible stewardship was, so it seemed, political oblivion.

Such a view, however, may allow insufficiently for contingency. By 1951, the incipient British *Wirtschaftswunder* had been eclipsed by events in Korea – a name fit to be inscribed on the tombstone of the Attlee Government. The effect of the Korean War was to impose upon the convalescent British economy the strains of an onerous rearmament programme, which Gaitskell's 1951 Budget sought to finance. There was talk of informal undertakings that the United States would 'pick up the check' but, as is notorious, such verbal assurances tend not to be worth the paper they are written on. The subsequent prevarications of the United States were described in a Treasury memorandum as 'more readily understandable if their purpose was to weaken the UK economy, rather than to strengthen it'. A different conspiracy theory was advanced by Aneurin Bevan, as the leading critic of rearmament: that it was part of a Russian strategy aimed at inducing the western democracies to impair their economies. Either way, the effect on the British economy was deleterious.

The planned defence expenditure for the years 1951–3 was to be doubled. There was, to be sure, one mitigation: it was impossible. The judgement that the programme was too heavy to be feasible was one reached with hindsight by Winston Churchill and with foresight by Harold Wilson. So even at its peak, rearmament fell 30 per cent below the level planned. It is probable, therefore, that it did less harm to the economy than the rise in import prices which resulted from the Korean War. Since this effect was unavoidable, there was no escape from an economic penalty, and Britain at least gained some political credit as a loyal ally of the USA.

The issues which were slugged out in the Labour Cabinet at this juncture were thus not so much economic as political, and fired by personal animosity at that. Dalton had a ringside seat, pen in hand, as usual. He had re-entered the Government, after a decent interval, as an elder statesman without ambitions of his own, taking a connoisseur's pleasure in making way for younger men, many of them, like Gaitskell, of his own choosing.

Dalton's account of the 1951 crisis, which led to the resignation from the government of Aneurin Bevan, Harold Wilson and John Freeman, has echoes from the diary of 1930. 'This is Mosley speaking!' was Dalton's foghorn whisper on

Bevan's performance at a party meeting. But Dalton was not alone in his propensity to view the new crisis through twenty-year-old spectacles. Bevan himself had accused Gaitskell of 'trying to be a second Snowden', and it was the '*wicked* Tribune attacking Hugh most outrageously, comparing him to Snowden, and his Budget to Snowden's in 1931' which stung Dalton most deeply. Maybe he identified 'Mosley speaking' a few days later because he had been perusing his old diaries; but Chuter Ede, who chaired that meeting, imprudently came out with the same comparison in winding up – without prompting from Ede diaries of the period. The main issue between the two sides in 1951 seems at times to have been whether it was a replay of 1930, with Bevan as Mosley, or a replay of 1931, with Gaitskell as Snowden. Only a party with such a rich mythology of betrayal would have been spoilt for choice in this way.

Dalton saw that the writing was on the wall for Labour. He recognized that his own high tide and that of the party broadly coincided. 'I was at my high points politically in 1940–41 and in 1945–46,' he recorded, 'but that was largely determined by events outside me, though in these events I got and took my chance.' In looking back, he also looked forward; he remained in favour of youth even when no longer young himself. He argued the case for cyclical renewal from his own experience in the 1930s, 'when the old top end of the party was blown off by MacDonald's treachery and Henderson's death', and the task of policy-making had to be taken up by Attlee and Cripps in the Commons and by Morrison and Dalton in the National Executive Committee. 'We've done all that now,' Dalton told Attlee in 1951, 'written the first chapter of the socialist story in law and administration. What next? The younger people must write the second chapter.'

Dalton hung on for the time being in the Shadow Cabinet (the Parliamentary Committee), partly so as to make life hard for his remaining contemporaries, as only he could. In November 1954 he found himself opposed to the majority line on German rearmament and opportunely dredged up a precedent from 1936-7 for members of a divided Shadow Cabinet speaking and voting as they thought fit at a party meeting. Herbert Morrison, whose longstanding service alongside Dalton had matured into a deep-seated mutual aversion, thereupon confessed that he had tried to consult the relevant minutes, only to find that they had been destroyed in the Second World War. Dalton now had his opening, the sort of chance earned by forty years of scribbling: 'I said I had a typescript, recounting the whole thing, in my hand, a bit of my next volume of Memoirs.' He knew that when the first volume had been published the previous year, Morrison's dismay – 'I didn't know the bugger kept a diary like that' – had been palpable. 'How lucky,' Dalton beamed at his colleagues, 'that, if there is no official record, I have kept an unofficial one.'

However creditable Dalton's record as the pre-war scourge of appeasement now looked, his post-war posture as the hammer of the Huns now seemed anomalous. 'The German problem is very simple,' he affirmed in 1946, 'the problem is that there are too many Germans.' Hence his rooted opposition to German rearmament in the early 1950s, when virtually his only supporters were Bevanites, with whom he was otherwise at odds. Conversely, Dalton found difficulty in communicating his feelings to his young friends on the right of the party, like Anthony Crosland, Roy Jenkins and Douglas Jay. 'I told them Germans were murderers, individuals excepted,' Dalton recorded in 1952. 'They'd killed all my friends in the First World War, etc.' Yet his vision of the German economy forging ahead did not entirely lack prescience, nor his foreboding that 'we, in our mismanaged, mixed-economy, overpopulated little island, shall become a second-rate power, with no influence and continuing "crises"'.

In 1955 he concluded that the 'Parliamentary Committee was stiff with old age pensioners', and used the announcement of his own decision to leave it on grounds of age to embarrass others into following suit. He called it Operation Avalanche, already with an eye to a chapter heading in his next volume of memoirs, and thought it went 'damned well'. It was like SOE all over again: a bold plan, clandestinely conceived by himself, to be implemented by and for his hand-picked shocktroops, none much older than Rupert Brooke had been (even though not all of them had his looks). Impotent to set Europe ablaze, Dalton showed that he could still light a firecracker under Morrison. 'Seldom has it been such fun to do one's duty,' Dalton wrote. When he dreamt of 'a Young Turk landing on the beaches of Power and Fame' in years to come, he envisaged that Jim Callaghan, Tony Crosland and Denis Healey would be 'in the van'. It was not a bad guess at the shape of the Labour Cabinet in 1976. After Operation Avalanche, with Gaitskell rather than Morrison installed as leader, and with a much younger team on the front bench, Dalton trumpeted to himself: 'I feel a little like a Creator who rested and beheld his handiwork after much hard labour and saw that it was good.'

Shadow and Substance

SHADOW AND SUBSTANCE
Morrison, Cripps, Bevin and Attlee in Churchill's shadow, by Vicky, 1950

9

ATTLEE:

THE MAKING OF THE POST-WAR CONSENSUS

It was the best of times, it was the worst of times, it was ostensibly the age of wisdom, it was arguably the age of foolishness, it was certainly the epoch of belief, it was undeniably the age of credulity, it was the season of Light, it was the season of Darkness, it was – old men will tell you – the spring of hope, it was – so others say – the winter of despair. The conflicting passions which illuminated British political life at the end of the Second World War still burn strongly. 1945, it is agreed, marks an epoch in British politics. The trite claim that an election – any election will do – is 'the most important since 1945' is one measure of how the date has established itself in folk memory. The character of the Labour Party as it reached its high tide has been the subject of widely differing claims and competitive myth-making. The agency of the Attlee Government in shaping post-war Britain is universally acknowledged, whether in celebration or reproach. At home, full employment policies, a large public sector, the Welfare State; overseas, the Atlantic alliance, the end of empire, the maintenance of Great Power pretensions – these became the political landmarks for the next thirty years. Attlee himself, instead of rivalling Bonar Law as 'the unknown prime minister', has, most improbably, become almost a cult-figure.

Politicians who get elected to government office demonstrate thereby that they possess a particular talent – that of getting elected. They are then faced with a new task, for which they may possess disconcertingly little aptitude – that of governing. Little wonder that many a well-advertised career becomes tarnished at this point, when the charismatic candidate turns out not to be a great statesman, just a great poster. Attlee, though, is unusual in posing the opposite problem. He is widely acknowledged to have *been* an effective Prime Minister without showing any obvious talent for *becoming* Prime Minister. Compared with other Labour politicians of his generation, he lacked Ernest Bevin's intuition and deep roots in the working-class movement, Herbert Morrison's organizational flair and metropolitan power base, Hugh Dalton's academic expertise and tactical cunning, Stafford Cripps's gifts of advocacy and self-projection.

Clement Attlee did not rise in the Labour Party by pretending to be other than he was. He remained a faithful product of his conventional upper-middle-class background. He regarded himself as a Victorian and took the rhetoric of imperial service which he had imbibed at Haileybury with a disconcerting literalness. As an undergraduate at University College, Oxford, he professed 'ultra-Tory' opinions and admired 'strong, ruthless rulers'. The earnest young man who became a social worker in the East End of London did not repudiate Haileybury and Oxford; he simply came to the conclusion that capitalism was a shamefully inadequate means of providing decently for his fellow beings and joined the Independent Labour Party. The straightforwardly pragmatic nature of this case at once set bounds to his radicalism and also meant that he was largely untainted by the sort of liberalism so common among middle-class recruits to the Labour Party. He volunteered for service in the trenches in the First World War, with no nonsense about serving in the ranks. Not for nothing was he known as Major Attlee between the wars. The conception of socialism which he took to 10 Downing Street remained culturally conservative. In the morning he would read *The Times*, in the afternoon he would put aside Government business for a moment while he checked the cricket scores, in the evening he would dress for dinner.

Attlee rose to become leader of the Labour Party as a result of its dogged adherence to Buggins' Law under extraordinary circumstances. It was Attlee's luck to have an East End constituency, as the legacy of his settlement work in the slums of Stepney. Attlee was therefore returned as MP for Limehouse in the electoral débâcle of 1931 – not by the princely majority he had previously enjoyed, but safely nonetheless, by 500 votes, at a time when Morrison lost Hackney South and Dalton was squeezed out in Bishop Auckland. Neither of them forgot that Attlee became Deputy Leader *faute de mieux*, with MacDonald and the old leaders now out of the party and the abler of the younger ex-ministers out of Parliament. As Deputy Leader, Attlee represented the reversionary interest when George Lansbury, the ultimate stop-gap, resigned as Leader before the General Election of 1935. As the man in possession, Attlee staved off a challenge from Morrison in the new Parliament. And so it went on.

In one important respect Attlee's conduct in these years showed the shape of things to come. Lansbury was much loved in the Labour Party; but he was a pacifist and ultimately this caused his resignation. Attlee too had accepted the characteristic ILP line of unilateral disarmament and it was not until 1934 that he declared to the Labour Party Conference that the scales had dropped from his eyes. He now advocated the official party line of backing collective security under the League of Nations with the use of force if the need arose. Perhaps the conversion of Major Attlee came readily because it was a reversion to type. His stance on foreign affairs was singularly firm thereafter and, together with Dalton and Bevin, he played a large part in giving Labour a credible defence policy. He was particularly incensed by Chamberlain's pretence that a vote against the Service estimates was a vote for no provision – 'one of those half-truths which are worse than lies'.

As Leader of the Labour Party, he became Deputy Prime Minister in the wartime Coalition, and by now he was growing into the job and stamping it with his own style. 'It is not easy to sub for the PM,' Attlee told his brother. 'It is obviously futile to try to put on Saul's armour, but I seek in a more pedestrian style to preserve a mean between dignity and dullness.' By 1945, much to Morrison's chagrin, but with the authoritative approval of Bevin, it was clear that Attlee was determined to accept office as Prime Minister if Labour had a majority. When Harold Laski, as party chairman, wrote to Attlee suggesting that he should step down, the reply showed that Attlee was now fully the master of his own style as well as his own party:

Dear Laski,
Thank you for your letter, contents of which have been noted.
C. R. Attlee.

When greatness was thrust upon him, therefore, this ostensibly ineligible little man showed himself unexpectedly but unmistakably able to take his chance. With the taste of office, Attlee's authority could no longer be ignored and his capacity for the efficient dispatch of business came into its own. He was unabashed in lecturing Churchill on his failings in government: 'Not infrequently a phrase catches your eye which gives rise to a disquisition on an interesting point only slightly connected with the subject matter.' Having stood up to him in private, Attlee showed during the 1945 election campaign that he could stand up to him in public. The great war leader's abrupt descent into bathos, with taunts about a socialist Gestapo, was met with the sort of headmasterly rebuke from which other naughty boys like Laski were still smarting. In the new Parliament, Attlee continued to abjure Saul's armour and instead played to his own strengths in establishing parity with Churchill, whose inflated rhetoric the Prime Minister mercilessly punctured. Of course, like Disraeli, he knew that a majority is the best repartee. Churchill and Attlee were rival party leaders for no less than fifteen years; this was longer than Gladstone and Disraeli, though Attlee preferred to look to his hero, Salisbury, for the appropriate lessons in containment. It was as though Attlee sensed the dramatic possibilities in confronting one stock national stereotype – gigantic, Falstaffian, heroic, absurd – with another: the quintessentially correct Englishman, eloquent only in studied understatement, but well on top of his job.

Attlee's premiership was virtually a dyarchy. 'My relationship with Ernest Bevin was the deepest of my political life,' Attlee once said. He made no move without consulting Bevin, who normally stayed behind at the end of Cabinet meetings to settle not just outstanding matters in foreign policy but the whole range of government business. Their differences of background became the basis for an impressive unity of outlook. If Bevin, with the massive prestige built up through his wartime role in the Churchill Coalition, had wished to displace Attlee, he could have done so. Instead, Bevin made Attlee the beneficiary of his own peculiarly potent doctrine of loyalty, which put the muscle of a trade-union power broker behind a set of intractable personal antipathies, notably against Morrison. But Bevin was more than a bully with a block vote; he had a creative political intuition which complemented Attlee's unimaginative grasp of executive priorities. While it lasted, it was the most effective political partnership since Asquith and Lloyd George, with the further advantage that it lasted better.

Hugh Gaitskell, as a newly elected MP, noted in 1945 that if the Government 'can last the full $4\frac{1}{2}$ years, the underlying forces working in its favour are very strong' but that 'things would be just about at their very worst' after two years. This would have read well enough in 1947, for its importance as a crisis point in the history of the Attlee Government is inescapable. It would hardly be too much to claim that up to 1947 the Government was concerned with working out the logic of the post-war settlement, at home and abroad, and fulfilling its own historic commitments; whereas after 1947 it was either at the mercy of events or struggling without respite in an effort to master them. In 1945 Labour sensed that it had a rendezvous with destiny; in 1947 it became aware that history is one damned thing after another. The process can be seen as a betrayal of ideals or an education in political realism: a tragic necessity or sheer bad luck.

When Labour came to power it did so as the legatee and guardian of an ideology forged in wartime. Its rise to power as a national party, able to mobilize broad-based popular support, was bound up with the developments of the war years. Fair shares and comradeship helped to universalize the Labour ethic beyond the sectional boundaries of trade-union solidarity. In its best pre-war elections (1929 and 1935), Labour had harvested about 8 million votes and was penned in to a share of the poll well under 40 per cent. This may look good in comparison with 1918 – or, for that matter, 1983 and 1987 – but it was clearly not enough to sustain a Government under a two-party dispensation. At the outbreak of war there was scant sign of progress, but by 1945 Labour was able to poll 12 million votes, manifesting a qualitative change in its appeal. Moreover, its rise in absolute levels of support did not stop there. The by-election record of the Attlee Government is unique in that it did not lose a single seat which Labour held in 1945. Admittedly, this achievement was protected by luck. It was fortuitous that some of Labour's worst by-election performances came in constituencies where the safety margin was ample. Even so, Labour was still moving forward in 1951, when, with a high turnout, its share of the poll exceeded that of 1945. At virtually 14 million, its vote was the highest ever recorded by a British political party, and it took the genius of the electoral system to give the Tories, who had come a creditable second, a majority in parliament.

Electorally, then, Labour stood firmly upon a peak in the years 1945–51. It had been a long march up to the top, and, as with the Grand Old Duke of York, that proved to be only half the story. Ideologically, too, Labour's strength and unity was a historical peculiarity. It is not simply that the party had always exhibited tension between an idealistic vision of socialism and the pragmatic realities of power, for it is not clear that the Labour Party can be conceived as the instrument or embodiment of 'socialism' when many arguments within the party have been attempts to appropriate this label for rival views and strategies. At any rate, in the 1940s a number of impulses could be reconciled. There was the Labourist emphasis upon incremental gains, which was usually associated with trade-unionism, bargaining for more under the present system, here and now. There was the social democratic priority for welfare legislation, which was partly a legacy from the New Liberalism, using the state to promote social justice where the market could not or would not. There was the socialist insistence on the necessity of public ownership, identifying capitalism itself as the problem, with either a Marxist appeal to the class struggle or a Fabian faith in stealthy collectivism as the means of establishing a better system. These were the main tendencies within the Labour Party, and all found some satisfaction in a common agenda.

So widespread was the acceptance of this agenda in 1945 that it overflowed the bounds of party. Most Liberals accepted most of it and some Conservatives accepted some of it, as the forward commitments of the Coalition Government make clear. This is in itself a tribute to how far Labour had already achieved an ideological ascendancy. Its own most distinctive policy was nationalization. True, the Conservatives were ready to acquiesce in limited extensions of public ownership, especially when it meant the taxpayer baling out the owners of unprofitable stock, but the debates over road haulage and, above all, steel, displayed a nakedly partisan character. Curiously, Labour had done little homework on its historic socialist plan. It seems to be true, not just poetic, that when Emmanuel Shinwell was put in charge of nationalizing coal, the only guidance that party headquarters could offer him was a pamphlet by James Griffiths, written in Welsh. The mixed economy was only retrospectively accepted as part of a consensus, with a line between the sectors that was, like the Western Front, basically the product of stalemate.

Consensus is more profitably sought elsewhere, especially in the framework within which partisan differences were subsequently defined. The commitment to 'a high and stable level of employment after the war' in the famous White Paper of 1944, issued by Churchill's Coalition Government, was fundamental. Not only was it significant in itself, but it also interlocked, tongue and groove, with a second plank of this consensus. Sir William Beveridge, rightly considered as the major architect of the Welfare State, well understood this from the outset, as can be seen from his eponymous Report back in 1942. The Beveridge Plan for social security explicitly assumed that it would be buttressed through children's allowances and a comprehensive health service (including rehabilitation). His third assumption, that full employment would be maintained, was in many ways more far-reaching – indeed, some would now say far-fetched. It should, however, be noted that the actuarial assumption made here was for an overall level of unemployment of 8.5 per cent (though Beveridge himself soon became converted to a target of 3 per cent). What it required, the Report explained, was 'not the abolition of all unemployment, but the abolition of mass unemployment and of unemployment prolonged year after year for the same individual'.

Beveridge adduced five reasons for this contention. One was that cash payments, while suitable for tiding workers over, would, in the longer term, have a demoralizing effect. Another was that it became impossible to test unemployment by an offer of work if there were no work to offer. The availability of work, moreover, actively drew in people who would otherwise lapse into debility. These three reasons were concerned with the working of a social insurance scheme. 'Fourth, and most important,' Beveridge continued, 'income security which is all that can be given by social insurance is so inadequate a provision for human happiness that to put it forward by itself as a sole or principal measure of reconstruction hardly seems worth doing.' Participation in productive employment, he suggested, was a great end in itself – reinforcing the theme that mere cash subsistence support on a dole could never be regarded as a psychologically adequate or morally civilized substitute. Finally, Beveridge pointed to the heavy cost of his Plan, warning that 'if to the necessary cost waste is added, it may become insupportable'. For unemployment simultaneously increased claims while depleting available resources.

In the 1940s few voices were raised against these principles. As so often, however, the real politics is in the detail. The principle of National Insurance may have been uncontentious, but implementation at a particular level of benefits, given post-war economic constraints, was another matter. This is where the priorities of a Labour Government mattered. It was often recalled, with scathing irony, that the fine promises of the Lloyd George Coalition had been scuppered in the wake of an economic crisis two years after the end of the war; but, under not dissimilar conditions, and whether rightly or wrongly, the Attlee Government persisted in building the Welfare State.

Moreover, the National Health Service, which was the jewel in the crown, involved a sharp departure from non-partisan agreement. Sir Henry Willink, as Churchill's Minister of Health, had shown personal good will in trying to square the circle here, but it was left to Aneurin Bevan to deliver the goods. His lightning leap into the Cabinet, with little more than a reputation as a Welsh windbag and a total lack of ministerial experience, paralleled that of Lloyd George forty years previously. The question was the same: could he match his radical rhetoric with executive ability? Nor was the answer dissimilar. No one could have been more imaginative, more adroit, or more attentive in creating the National Health Service, virtually from scratch, with little more to go on than a manifesto promise and an approving aside in the Beveridge Report.

Bevan thus determined the principles of the scheme, notably the nationalization of the hospitals, notwithstanding the organized opposition of the doctors. His struggles with the British Medical Association were tortuous and intermittently ferocious. To some extent the intransigence of its leaders can be explained by the constraints under which they were placed by the highly democratic nature of its constitution. Bevan not only gave them stick, he also offered a glimpse of carrot since his scheme, like Lloyd George's before it, meant a net increase in medical finance which, in the nature of things in a labour-intensive sector, was bound to find its way into the pockets of ordinary general practitioners.

Bevan's achievement, it should be added, was the more striking since housing also fell within his ministerial responsibilities. This was not only administratively unwieldy but also politically inept in suggesting that, as the joke went, the Government was only keeping half a Nye on housing. Bevan's record has often suffered from adverse comparison with the well-publicized efforts of his Conservative successor, Harold Macmillan, in building 300,000 houses a year at a time when shortage of materials no longer held back construction. Macmillan's formula of big talk plus small houses was a political winner. But Bevan in fact built 800,000 houses, reaching an annual figure of 280,000 in 1948, before resources were diverted elsewhere, latterly to rearmament. Moreover, it took Bevan to insist on building council houses to high standards of which owner-occupiers would have been proud, just as it took Thatcher, thirty years on, to invert his logic by selling them off.

It is a good question whether Britain could afford the Welfare State. If it represented public affluence, this was paralleled not by private squalor but by austerity in personal consumption. Even so, little would have been possible without the American Loan. The Government thus paid for its programme on tick – the tick of a time bomb, as it turned out. For the deadline on convertibility in the summer of 1947 ushered in a sterling crisis which, coming only months after a fuel crisis had brought the country to a standstill, threatened the Government's viability.

The smug claim of Emmanuel Shinwell in October 1946 had been: 'Everyone knows that there is going to be a serious crisis in the coal industry – except the Minister of Fuel and Power' (himself, of course). By February 1947, with power cuts crippling industrial output, the self-esteem of a better man than the Minister of Fuel and Power would have been bruised, though Shinwell himself hardly seems to have been affected. Admittedly, the fuel crisis could be dismissed as an Act of God, since this happened to be the most severe winter of the century, but even so, such a loss of providential sanction was unsettling. When the financial crisis broke, there were no suggestions that the Almighty was selling sterling short, but plenty that the Government might be losing its grip. Dalton was shaken at the Treasury, his confident advocacy of cheap money undermined. Attlee shivered into supine immobility. What the sterling crisis did was expose the government's nakedness. Its rhetoric of planning was not matched by a commensurate ability to control the economy. Its response was not *dirigiste* but 'deary me'.

In one sense the Government never recovered. Its pristine image was tarnished, its honeymoon period clearly ended. Yet in other ways its underlying resilience was impressive. In the summer of 1947 there had been talk of replacing Attlee with Bevin, and Stafford Cripps, despite his longstanding cordial relations with Attlee, made himself the spokesman for this view. By the time he went to confront the Prime Minister in September, the worst was already over and the projected putsch ended up as a good anecdote. Attlee simply telephoned Bevin, in Cripps's presence, to ask if he was seeking a change. 'Thought not,' said Attlee, putting down the telephone; but he now instead proposed to promote Cripps, over the heads of Morrison and Dalton, to the new position of economic supremo.

Cripps, whose reputation had been enhanced by his display of resolution throughout the crisis, thus became Number Three in the Government; and when Dalton shortly resigned as Chancellor, Cripps stood ready as his anointed successor. Cripps was like other men in that he favoured short skirts for women, but unlike them in that his reason was the saving in textile supplies. This was a sort of asceticism which stood in obvious contrast to Bevin's proletarian appetite for the good things in life. With a single-minded zeal for public ends amply sustained by his own private means, Cripps perfectly exemplified the priggish face of middle-class progressivism. Labour's road to recovery was the path of Crippsian austerity.

In foreign affairs, too, the Government drew a second wind in 1947. There had been much talk of a socialist foreign policy in 1945. Speaking at the Labour Party conference, two months before he was appointed Foreign Secretary, Bevin said: 'Left understands Left, but the Right does not.' The reference in context was to France, but his phrase was often subsequently quoted as though it applied to the Soviet Union, of which Bevin already held a well-nourished suspicion. Contrary to some conspiracy theories on the Left, it did not need right-wing Foreign Office mandarins to bamboozle Bevin about Russia as a potentially hostile power; and Russia's conduct did precious little to debamboozle him. The illusions of post-war co-operation between all the great Powers withered with the onset of the cold war. Even co-operation with the United States had its difficulties, as the breakdown of the wartime arrangements for the joint development of atomic weapons showed. At the beginning of 1947 a decision was taken to produce Britain's own atomic bomb. In effect it was a decision by Attlee and Bevin; though a handful of other ministers were directly involved, the matter was not taken to the Cabinet, nor was it reported to the House of Commons until May 1948. By that point, following the Communist takeover in Czechoslovakia and with Berlin now threatened, the international context was starker and clearer.

Bevin was an old-fashioned nationalist in many ways – true to his class once more – but his achievement in winning Labour support for his foreign policy has a wider significance. It is not just that he made the *Daily Herald* into the paper that supported our boys, he also won the assent of the Left for the Atlantic alliance. It was largely Bevin's initiative which succeeded in parlaying American sentiment into hard cash by means of Marshall Aid. He summoned the New World into action to redress the bank balance of the Old. If the Welfare State was (again) grudgingly underwritten by Uncle Sam, this certainly helped to enlighten the Labour Left about where its real friends were to be found in a divided world. Moreover, Bevin took the lead in turning his rhetoric about 'Western Union' into an effective alliance, first between the democratic states of Western Europe in March 1948, and in the course of the next year bringing others into the framework of the North Atlantic Treaty. Since NATO was Bevin's baby, it is not surprising that his supporters in the Labour Party subsequently set such store by nurturing the American alliance.

The record on which the Government went to the country in February 1950 was one which pleased its traditional supporters well enough. When the overnight results were in from the urban areas, Labour was comfortably ahead and Morrison, as party manager, went to bed well satisfied. But the broader-based support from the middle classes, whom he had courted with persistent attention, had now gone missing; and the slump in the Liberal vote was a relative advantage to the Conservatives. Once the rest of the votes were counted the next day, they revealed a revolt of the suburbs, which cut Labour's parliamentary majority down to five. 'The British people are wonderful,' Morrison commented. 'They didn't mean to chuck us out, only to give us a sharp kick in the pants. But I think they've overdone it a bit.' Behind this anthropomorphic fallacy lurked a warning to Labour that its constituency was vulnerable: not because it was lukewarm in commitment but because it was insufficient in extent.

During its second term of office, from February 1950 to October 1951, the Government was balanced on a knife edge. With its precarious majority, it needed every vote; the ambulances queued in Palace Yard as the halt, the sick and the lame were wheeled through the lobbies. The old gang who had been at the top since 1931 were on the way out. Dalton's diary mercilessly dwelt on the physical debility of a group of leading ministers who were all well into their sixties. What Attlee's Government needed was its own Doctor's Mandate. The ailing Bevin had long been accompanied by his personal physician; Morrison was unwell in 1948; Cripps went off to a Swiss sanatorium in 1949. When Attlee entered hospital in 1951, as the Korean crisis brewed, even his teeth gave trouble. 'His former dentist was too old,' Dalton observed.

Bevan and Gaitskell now emerged as the crucial figures in a new polarization of the Labour Party. From an early stage Gaitskell had been conscious of Bevan's natural ambitions, noting in 1947: 'He still leads in the race for Labour Prime Minister in 1960!' It was a view he reiterated at the beginning of 1950. With his own appointment as Chancellor, he recognized that Bevan may have felt slighted, but at this stage their relations were reasonably cordial. It was the clash over Health Service charges in the 1951 Budget which, relatively suddenly, escalated and personalized the conflict. For Gaitskell, the new boy in the Cabinet, to assert his strategy in face of Bevan's rooted opposition was a remarkable test of nerve. Gaitskell privately admitted that 'if I had realized that there were so many things which could have meant defeat, I might never have begun'. It was from this point that Left and Right in the party were mobilized against each other – perhaps in the process defined against each other – in a new way.

In response to the Korean War and American entreaties to its allies, Gaitskell championed a major rearmament programme which it proved beyond Britain's capacity to meet. The Cabinet records show that Bevan's disquiet about the programme was voiced as early as August 1950. It is thus not true, as was subsequently alleged by his opponents, that his opposition was only to the health charges imposed to pay for rearmament. Yet there is a puzzle in explaining why such allegations gained widespread currency, and why Bevanites like Harold Wilson, Richard Crossman and John Freeman also endorsed the view that it was on the narrower issue that their hero staked his reputation. The fact is that though it is now irrefutably documented that Bevan registered persistent doubts about the defence programme, he failed to stake out this as the ground on which to take his stand. The point at issue, when the chips were down, was Gaitskell's insistence that the Health Service should find £13 million in cuts, chiefly from charges on spectacles and false teeth. Such a sum was only the loose change in a Budget of £4,000 million. It was completely dwarfed by a total defence programme of £4,700 million, spread over three years, which was the ostensible beneficiary of such sacrifices. Yet the argument in fact turned upon this trivial sum. The question Bevan posed was: 'Aren't I worth £13 millions?' Everyone saw that if only this concession were made to him, the crisis could be resolved: Bevan would stay and so would the great armaments.

There was, in short, a good economic case against the rearmament programme, one which Bevan intuitively grasped more quickly than the professional economist Gaitskell, and for which he deserved more fulsome credit than Churchill's subsequent admission that Bevan 'happened to be right'. The professional politician Bevan, conversely, stumbled from one political blunder to another in handling his case, notably in failing to *make* rearmament the issue. It seemed, indeed, as though the baser as well as the more sophisticated political arts had deserted virtually every minister in the Government.

A Prime Minister who promoted Gaitskell to the Treasury in October 1950 had kept his eye for talent; but one who then put Bevan into the relatively minor office of Minister of Labour had lost his nose for trouble. To the youngest member of Attlee's Cabinet, Harold Wilson, the whole episode cried out for the skills of a political broker and fixer. He apparently tried to educate Gaitskell during a taxi ride, telling him, 'right, if you will agree to our doing so-and-so, we are not going to object when you do something else'. What with Gaitskell's intransigence, Bevan's impetuosity, Morrison's deviousness – 'not so much disloyal, as watching for a favourable opportunity to be disloyal' – and Attlee's taciturnity, the young President of the Board of Trade was practically biting through his pipe in frustration. When Wilson accompanied Bevan to see the arch-loyalist Bevin, he knew how to play his cards: 'Nye's destruction, I quietly suggested, was being supported if not indeed masterminded by Morrison. That was enough.' With Bevin now ready to activate Attlee, Wilson subsequently implied, a settlement was within reach – only to be snatched away by Bevin's death two days later. As it turned out, therefore, Wilson's own resignation, albeit talking about guns rather than false teeth, established his credentials along-side Bevan as a man of the Left.

Though the electoral impact of all of this was no doubt bad for Labour, the outcome was not actually as bad as was anticipated. Dalton gloomily brooded on how the party might split 'and our young men would be mowed down'. On Budget day the prospect was 'an early election and a heavy defeat'. He knew that John Freeman, also toying with resignation, expected to lose his Watford constituency. Five under-secretaries, headed by Jim Callaghan, similarly feared losing their seats and appealed for unity accordingly. Dalton thought 'it had taken Nye a long time to see that he'd mass-murder the Party, if he went, including nearly all his friends'. Yet when Bevan and Wilson and Freeman duly went and the election duly came, the slaughter was less gruesome than had been feared. The five under-secretaries lived to fight another day and Freeman held on to Watford.

Labour in fact polled its record vote in 1951, and it is easy to argue that it might have been returned to office had the election been postponed for a few months. Throughout 1952 Labour held a steady lead in the opinion polls; with an econ-omic improvement already in the pipeline, was there not a prospect of a social democratic tenure of power on a Scan-dinavian scale? One immediate reason for having an early election was that, with the ailing George VI about to depart on an antipodean tour, Attlee wished to spare the monarch a potential political crisis. The King (who was a Conservative) showed his gratitude by conferring the Order of Merit upon his late Prime Minister. But there were deeper reasons for the demise of the Attlee Government. 'We are all,' Dalton had written in 1950, 'stale and uninspired and uninventive.' Failure may have been averted, but success brought its own nemesis.

As Sam Watson, the Durham miners' leader, complacently assured the Labour Party conference in 1950: 'Poverty has been abolished, Hunger is unknown. The sick are tended. The old folks are cherished, our children are growing up in a land of opportunity.' The Attlee Government had thus engineered

what contemporaries saw as a fundamental and irreversible shift of wealth and power in favour of working people and their families. Since the Labour Party had now fulfilled its agreed aims, only the aims on which it could not agree remained. Richard Crossman rightly spoke in 1955 of 'how the policy differences had arisen after the death of Ernie Bevin and Cripps and the completion of Labour's mission in 1948'. The Government had eliminated a huge area of accord within the party, as enshrined in the 1945 programme, by carrying out its election promises – a hazardous procedure which most of its successors prudently avoided.

Though Attlee himself grimly held on to the party leadership, serving for the uniquely long period of twenty years, the tide was now on the turn. Dalton was admitting by 1954 that 'people were very content with the Tories. They had stolen the Socialists' clothes (full employment, welfare state, etc)' and in some moods he could 'see no reason, except crass conservatism, for voting Labour now'. This is a backhanded tribute to the fact that much of the 1945 agenda was no longer radical and contentious; it had become part of the political furniture which both major parties were now competing to rearrange rather than to replace.

Evening Standard, 6 November 1958

IO

MACMILLAN:

THE LESSONS OF THE PAST

Harold Macmillan rarely gave anything away. His voluminous memoirs can serve as a starting point, but they stand also as a monument of concealment, at once protecting and projecting the public face of a public man who took pride in his 'unflappability'. For example, they offer the reader no clue as to why, on the threshold of middle age, he was seen by a friend banging his head in despair against the wall of a train compartment. Some things could be hinted at in the memoirs – the strong influence of Macmillan's American mother, his own adolescent religious crisis. But some politically sensitive aspects of the memoirs, notably the section on Suez, can now be dismissed as (according to taste) factious, factitious or fictitious. Above all, the story of Macmillan's marriage – a theme which required, and received, particularly delicate handling during his lifetime – was laid bare only after his death. Revelation here is a gain in insight rather than a victory for prurience. For Macmillan's temperament, outlook and scale of values help to resolve many paradoxes about his career – explaining how this lonely and remote figure could put on the motley for the benefit of colleagues and public alike, with a disconcerting juxtaposition of throat-catching emotion and world-weary cynicism.

It was to his domineering, fiercely possessive, vicariously ambitious mother that Macmillan recognized a lifelong debt. Without her it is unlikely that he would have survived his

serious wounds in the First World War. She used her influence to remove him from the hands of the Army and put him into a private hospital in Belgrave Square – just as she had got him transferred into the Grenadier Guards in the first place. Macmillan commented on the circumstances of his enlistment that, though it represented 'privilege of the worst kind', nonetheless the only privilege sought was 'that of getting ourselves killed or wounded as soon as possible'. So, having pulled strings to get her son into this mess, Nellie Macmillan was simply pulling more strings to get him out again.

Nor did she stop at that. Her influence was behind Captain Macmillan's posting to Canada, at the end of the war, to serve as aide-de-camp to the Governor-General, the ninth Duke of Devonshire (nephew of the old Whig leader). Rather than return to Oxford, where his pre-war Balliol friends walked as ghosts, the young war hero spent ten months recuperating in Ottawa. If there is one word which describes this scion of a great publishing house, now picking up the threads of his severed education, it must be bookish. But at the 'permanent house-party' into which he was now catapulted there was time for more than catching up on his reading. It was here that he fell in love with the boss's daughter, Lady Dorothy Cavendish, a vigorously sensual young woman of nineteen with few intellectual interests to encumber her time. The Duke, a tolerant man who had already seen one daughter marry a brewer, consoled himself with the reflection: 'Well, books is better than beer.'

It was a marriage comfortably within the conventions of English upper-class life between the wars – perfectly conveyed in the novels of Evelyn Waugh. It can be seen as a symbolic alliance of the strenuous bourgeois ethic of the Macmillan dynasty with the luxuriant aristocratic code of the Cavendish family, who had long ago set their fortunes in stone at Chatsworth. If, as some people whispered, Nellie Macmillan had helped engineer this match – having come a long way from Spencer, Indiana – she must have felt gratified at her son's prospects. She certainly did her best for the lucky couple, making sure that the Macmillan country house, Birch Grove,

was made over to them rather than to Harold's elder brothers. Only one condition was stipulated: that she live there herself. 'This house is going to belong to the Prime Minister of England one of these days,' she told her grandchildren. In the 1920s, Harold threw himself into his work as a publisher in the mornings, moving on to the House of Commons later in the day and staying there till deep in the night. Dorothy was left with their three young children, and, of course, her mother-in-law – still pulling the strings. Was the outcome such a surprise? While Harold climbed laboriously to the top of the greasy pole, Dorothy took a lover.

Lady Dorothy Macmillan's relationship with Robert Boothby, a political colleague of her husband's, was ended only by her death forty years later. It is the sub-text of Harold Macmillan's career, involving this sensitive, reticent man in adjusting to a situation which held a continuing capacity to inflict pain. First there was the shock of revelation in 1929 – 'the Great Crash', as Boothby habitually called it. The fourth Macmillan child was in fact Boothby's. There was a crisis over whether to seek a divorce, with its implications for Harold's political career which his mother was unfailingly available to point out. The gossip at Westminster was inevitably wounding (though the newspapers were more discreet in those days). In fact, a *modus vivendi* was established, albeit one which gave Harold little more than a handful of dust. In public, appearances were kept up; in private, as Dorothy put it, 'I am faithful to Bob'. Hard cheese on Harold.

How far was the steel core of Macmillan's ambition tempered in this emotional furnace? Both his fatalism and his tenacity had a dash of bloody-mindedness, drawing upon the inner resources with which he had confronted despair. In addition, he was apparently reinforced by his religious beliefs, in a way which again requires reference to Evelyn Waugh. For when Waugh published his biography of Monsignor Ronald Knox in 1959, he printed extracts from correspondence with a young man, identified as 'C', who had evidently considered joining Knox on the spiritual aeneid that led to his reception into the Church of Rome. In fact, the 'C' of these troubled letters was, as subsequently became known, none other than the current occupant of Number Ten, then at the apogee of his worldly fame and success. Knox had initially been employed by Nellie Macmillan as tutor to her son – a role for which that stern protestant matriarch soon discerned him to be quite unsuitable. But his influence lingered on, and it was not until 1915 that Captain Macmillan decisively responded to his 'Dearest Ron' before leaving for France. 'I'm going to be rather odd,' he wrote. 'I'm not going to "Pope" until after the war (if I'm alive).' In the event, Macmillan found that a poping averted was a poping avoided; but religion continued to serve as his sheet-anchor.

There are some jarring inconsistencies, however, in the vision of him as a devout Anglo-Catholic, as the unhappy story of Sarah, the fourth Macmillan child, reveals. While an undergraduate at Oxford, she was told casually that Boothby was her father. She later encountered a drink problem – like all her three siblings – and was to commit suicide. Her difficulties, it seems, stemmed less from this revelation than from the effects of an abortion, which left her sterile. When Lady Dorothy had learned of her daughter's pregnancy – 'it will ruin your father's career' – she had insisted upon this course. In the Britain of the early 1950s, well before the Steel–Jenkins legislation, it should be noted, abortion was illegal. The teaching of the church was a major source of resistance to reform, especially in the Conservative Party. These issues raise many awkward dilemmas, but the Macmillans' ruthlessly self-seeking humbug perhaps deserves to be matched with an equally uncharitable verdict.

One formative experience in the making of the public man has always been more readily recognized and easily acknowledged: the First World War. Macmillan's decision to enlist can be called conventionally brave; but the manner in which he saw it through must be termed singularly courageous. The Army combined ludicrous absurdity – 'Officers of Field Rank on entering balloons are not expected to wear spurs' – with a deeply-moving spirit of comradeship. In the Guards Macmillan discovered a seductive compound of elegance, professionalism and *noblesse oblige*; and he lived up to this ethic in front of his men without flinching. Bravery, he reflected later, was 'a kind of concealed pride, because everybody is watching you', and it was only afterwards that he became 'absolutely terrified because there was no need to show off any more, no need to pretend'.

It will be apparent that unflappability, though not wholly out of character, was bought at a price. It was part of the public persona which Macmillan lovingly constructed in the 1940s in launching a successful political career. For it was only at this stage, when he was long past forty, that he began to rise in the profession for which he had so largely sacrificed himself and his family. His fortunes turned around in 1940 along with those of Winston Churchill, to whom Macmillan had first attached himself in the 1920s – 'it was the making of my political life, in a sense'. It was, however, a relationship which did Macmillan little good so long as Neville Chamberlain exerted an iron control over the Conservative Party. Macmillan might regard Chamberlain as 'very, very middle class and very, very narrow in view', but this was a formula which pleased the party faithful. Churchill, above all, was not a good party man; nor was the pre-war Macmillan, who almost lost the party whip when he supported the anti-Chamberlain candidate in the Oxford by-election after Munich. On 5 November 1938 the guy on the bonfire at Birch Grove was dressed in a frock-coat, black Homburg hat and rolled umbrella. Little wonder, then, that Macmillan did not hold office in the 1930s.

Why was Macmillan such a rebel? Part of the answer lies in the accident of his representing Stockton-on-Tees in Parliament. It was an unpropitious seat for an ambitious Tory, but one where a nonentity could virtually buy the nomination in the 1920s. Though Macmillan cultivated the nostalgic myth about 'dear old Stockton', he more than once considered deserting the constituency for a better prospect. But so long as he remained its MP – for twenty years up to 1945, with one short break – Macmillan championed the cause of the depressed areas against what he called 'casino capitalism'. Keynes's publisher, Macmillan was the leading Conservative advocate of the managed economy, and thus, unlike Churchill, a critic of his own Government's domestic as well as foreign policies. And yet, as he once teased a friend in the Labour Party, 'I have to remember that I am a very rich man!' His solicitude for his constituents was as much in the line of duty as the responsibility he had taken for his men on the Somme; but in 1945, it should be remembered, he was posted to a new unit in the South of England.

Until the Second World War Macmillan was a self-willed, noteworthy but unsuccessful figure in Conservative politics; thereafter, his bold and lonely stance was vindicated with satisfying completeness. The lessons he learned were ones he had special reason never to forget. On unemployment, he had spoken up for the old industrial North of England, a clever and compassionate critic who was quick to see the relevance of Keynesian recovery measures in contrast to the restrictions of Treasury orthodoxy. This was the lesson of Stockton. Over appeasement, he had again bravely dissented from the policy of his own leaders, sensing that it was folly to feed Hitler's growing appetite with abject concessions. This was the lesson of Munich. Above all, in 1940, Macmillan stood foursquare with Churchill in asserting that Britain, though pitted against overwhelming odds, should fight on alone. This was the lesson of Dunkirk.

An intensely ambitious man, he was no time-server, instead choosing to link his destiny with that of Churchill in an enormous gamble which ultimately hit the jackpot. As Macmillan later recognized, 'if I had accepted a post under Chamberlain, I would almost certainly have disappeared without trace'. The *bouleversement* of 1940 brought Macmillan into office on Churchill's coat-tails; and two years later the Prime Minister offered him an exciting but vaguely defined post as minister resident in North Africa. Macmillan clinched on it at once; it was to mark his emergence as a major British politician; it swiftly transformed his whole career. 'I enjoy wars,' he declared afterwards; 'any adventure's better than sitting in an office.'

As Churchill's crony he went on to display a new confidence, robustness and ambition. The minister resident had a direct line to the Prime Minister; he also had a free hand of an almost pro-consular kind; he had to stand up to major figures like Eisenhower and de Gaulle; and he had to exercise an iron grasp upon priorities beneath a velvet glove of the most tactful diplomacy. This was a challenge to which Macmillan rose with aplomb. With his rise, too, a developing rivalry with his near contemporary Anthony Eden became increasingly apparent. A subordinate who once watched Macmillan fall off his chair while denouncing Eden relished this spectacle of disloyalty discomfited.

It was in his wartime role, as an expatriate British minister attached to the advancing Allied armies in the Mediterranean, that Macmillan was involved in the difficulties over repatriation which have subsequently aroused so much controversy. An intertwined skein of military, logistical, legal, diplomatic and geopolitical considerations needs to be disentangled here. In his old age Macmillan was distressed by the charge that thousands of Cossacks were massacred by the Soviets as a result of his actions. The issues are both complex and confused, and the evidence both detailed and defective. But Macmillan's own role seems fairly clear. He was seeking to implement the Yalta agreement, with its provisions for reciprocal repatriation. These covered the position of British prisoners-of-war held by the Red Army as well as Russian and Yugoslav claims for the return of dissident military units which had been fighting against them. The notion that the protection of enemy combatants should have been given a higher priority than the safety of British soldiers, or allowed to compromise cordial relations with Britain's most effective allies in the fight against the Nazis, seems fanciful.

In the actual historical situation in which he was trapped, Macmillan may have been muddled over some of the legal definitions determining citizenship, but he had a clear-sighted view of the fundamental dilemma. 'To hand them over to the Russians is condemning them to slavery, torture, and probably death,' his diary recorded. 'To refuse, is deeply to offend the Russians, and incidentally to break the Yalta agreement.' There were many unfortunate people who suffered in this process and perhaps it is fair to call them victims of Yalta; but it is little less than bizarre to suggest that the minister charged with implementing this policy must have been under the influence of the KGB.

Whatever sympathies for the Left Macmillan may previously have nurtured, the Second World War cast him thereafter as a romantic reactionary patriot in the Churchillian mould. It was an image which brought him political dividends – indeed, it was the ticket on which he was to ride to Downing Street. Two crucial episodes intervened before the summit was scaled. The first was Macmillan's role as the minister who enabled the last Churchill Government to proclaim that it had built 300,000 houses a year. It was not a task which he had sought, or for which he had obvious qualifications; but, as he put it: 'I had always agreed to do anything that I had been asked by Churchill and it had up to now succeeded.' So did this – at a price.

The task was not so daunting as it seemed, since Britain plainly had the resources for construction on this scale – provided housing were given top priority. This had been Bevan's experience and predicament. The condition for success, therefore, was the Conservative Government's relegation of other priorities, notably the defence programme and industrial investment. Like Montgomery before Alamein, Macmillan was the happy beneficiary of a massive concentration of the necessary resources at the expense of rival claimants; and like Monty he made sure that his great victory did not go unnoticed by the weary British public. There were able subordinates like Ernest Marples who could be relied upon to deliver the goods. As Macmillan later declared, 'in fact, Marples made me PM: I was never heard of before housing'. But although housing precipitated Macmillan into the top tier of the Conservative leadership, he then flitted unconvincingly between successive posts: a stopgap term at

the Treasury, following an undistinguished interlude at the
Foreign Office, while at Defence, as he later admitted, 'I was
a failure.' Macmillan still lagged a stride behind younger men,
like the veteran appeaser R.A. Butler and the new Prime
Minister, Anthony Eden. The second crucial episode which
helped Macmillan get to Number Ten was thus the Suez crisis
of 1956.

It was Suez which intertwined Macmillan's fortunes with the
man who had replaced him as Foreign Secretary, Selwyn
Lloyd. Their relations form a piquant case study in loyalty.
Lloyd's origins were to be the butt of many snobbish jests in
later years. Knowing well enough that Macmillan referred to
him as 'a middle-class lawyer from Liverpool', Lloyd planned
defiantly to take this as the title for his memoirs. His father,
sprung from Welsh Wesleyan stock, had become a Liverpool
dentist – chapel-going, teetotal, Liberal. It was a textbook
story of steady, unspectacular upward social mobility and
incremental secularization, illustrated too by the family's
suburbanization, with the transfer of the dental practice from
the city to the Wirral, first as a summer adjunct, but latterly
as the main family home. Lloyd's own education, at Fettes
and Magdalene College, Cambridge, maintained the family's
trajectory of escape from the confines of Wesleyanism. But
although he became known as Peter from undergraduate days
onward – 'Selwyn' must have spelt social death at Magdalene – he exhumed his Christian name in post-war politics
and made it into a distinctive trademark. It was thought very
funny at the time when Bernard Levin in the *Spectator* hung
the Foreign Secretary's service on the Hoylake Urban District
Council round his neck. But Lloyd was no Pooterish aspirant,
with absurd social pretensions, to the inner circle of Tory
grandees. He was proud of what he was: a successful, provincial, professional man. In dismissing him (literally) in 1962
as 'a little country notary', Macmillan forgot that their mutual
hero Lloyd George had not disdained to describe himself as
'a Welsh country solicitor'.

Why had Lloyd risen so high in the Conservative Party, to which he had only finally committed himself as late as 1944? One explanation is that he had a good war behind him. He was one of the 'Tory Brigadiers' elected in 1945, at a time when this was a trump card. His main opponent on the Wirral shortlist was Sir John Smyth, VC, who gave the wrong answer to the question whether he would live in the constituency. Lloyd was transparently able to give the right answer – he had never lived anywhere else – and walked into a safe seat which he was to hold for the next thirty years. His military career had brought out the best in him: his appreciation of a firmly-ordered institutional framework for his life; his meticulous grasp of detail which made him an outstanding staff officer; his cheerful readiness to go along with a grand strategy mapped out by his superiors, combined with an anxious concern to ensure that it was implemented according to plan. Lloyd was the perfect team-player, a competent utility man who wanted to fit in but displayed no obvious ambition or capacity to take over as captain.

Looking round for talent in his new Government in 1951, Churchill offered Lloyd the post of Minister of State at the Foreign Office. The story is that he responded: 'But Sir, I think there must be some mistake, I've never been to a foreign country, I don't speak any foreign languages, I don't like foreigners.' If this reply, like Churchill's riposte – 'Young man, these all seem to me to be positive advantages' – may have been somewhat improved in the course of subsequent repetition, it nonetheless tells us much about Lloyd. Such anecdotes did not attach themselves to Eden or Macmillan, still less would either man have encouraged their propagation. Indeed Eden later warned Lloyd, if he insisted on publishing the Churchill story, not to 'overdo it to the point of making me seem half-witted in having chosen you for the job, because I was not, you know'. The fact that Eden actually wanted Lloyd as his junior minister, of course, destroys one of the compendious alibis later put forward in extenuation of Eden.

Loyal to a fault, Lloyd displayed integrity and a notable lack of vindictiveness, but his rather limited range of personal qualities showed up badly at the Foreign Office. Gauche and insensitive, he undeniably lacked the right touch on many occasions. One official's remark, 'that his teasing, leg-pulling, bullying manner was not sympathetic', was repeatedly echoed. The law, the Army, the golf club − none of these confined, conventional, male-orientated, middle-class milieus had educated him much beyond back-slapping and rib-poking. His irrepressible jokes were a specialized taste. 'Good for Nutting', a favourite tag for a fellow-minister at the Foreign Office, was relieved with similar sallies like, 'You're a deb, Sir Gladwyn Jebb.' It is not wholly surprising that the mandarins sometimes treated him with disdain, nor that Churchill once declared that he was 'that most dangerous of men − the clever fool'.

This was the statesman on whose sophisticated diplomacy, worldly wisdom, and delicate judgement it depended to finesse the British Empire out of its hapless plight over Suez in 1956. Once Nasser had nationalized the Canal, the impotence of the Eden Government was shot through with a fitful sense of frustration. There have been attempts to defend the Prime Minister on every conceivable count, from geopolitical insight (Eden alone discerned the scale of the Soviet menace) to personal foibles (Eden was not aloof and vain − he simply failed to recognize junior colleagues because he refused to wear his spectacles). The fact is that none of the ministers comes out particularly well. In particular, as Chancellor of the Exchequer, Macmillan's advice throughout the summer and autumn of 1956 was deeply flawed.

All his instincts were towards decisive action on the grand scale, with no heed for the consequences. But all his official expertise told Macmillan that Britain could not sustain such an enterprise. 'We *are* in a difficult position (particularly since we have no money),' Macmillan wrote in his diary. 'But we must have the courage to play the hand through.' It was to be Alamein without the ammunition. Macmillan's role was pivotal: as Chancellor he was formally responsible for the pound sterling; as Eisenhower's old buddy, he was informally responsible for keeping the Yanks sweet. When Macmillan advised that there would be no real difficulty if Britain mounted an invasion of Egypt, he was taken very seriously, especially by Eden.

Macmillan emerged as the ruthless exponent of *realpolitik* in a regrettably post-imperial world. 'On what "principle" can we base a "casus belli"?' he ruminated in his diary. 'How do we get from the Conference leg to the use of force?' Lloyd was characteristically straightforward in his commitment to a diplomatic resolution of the Canal crisis through the United Nations, breaking off negotiations in New York in mid-October 1956 with obvious reluctance. His fatal mistake, on being summoned back to London, was to allow Eden to browbeat him into assent for another course altogether – the plan which had now been hatched for Anglo-French military action, co-ordinated with Israel.

In executing such an operation, Eden was hamstrung by his self-image as a founding father of the United Nations. The solution adopted – secret collusion with Israel in attacking Egypt, so that Britain could pretend to intervene as peace-maker – left the Government with a tortured and implausible story. The jet-lagged Foreign Secretary was thus propelled into a wild adventure beyond his own horizon. He was bundled off within a week of his return from New York on a clandestine mission, dressed in a old mackintosh, to a villa at Sèvres, for consultation with not only the French but also the Israelis. Stumbling into a back room of the villa to meet the Israeli delegation, he quipped, 'I ought to have had a false moustache', only to be greeted by an embarrassed silence. He was to learn the hard way that the trouble caused by getting mixed up with foreigners, incapable even of appreciating the English sense of humour, was only just beginning. By going to Sèvres, Lloyd had, of course, become inextricably implicated in Eden's plan. For by now, as one Conservative MP put it, 'Eden had to prove he had a real moustache' (presumably unlike the sort lacked by his ill-starred emissary) and there could be no backing down.

If collusion was necessary to carry out the scheme, Lloyd had no qualms about defending its necessity, not least from subsequent charges that it was dishonourable to have denied it to the House of Commons. But an intractable difficulty arose from Eden's fallacious belief that the truth need never come out. That Eden continued to cover up in his memoirs in 1960 is understandable, if damaging to his subsequent reputation; that Macmillan should have done likewise in his own memoirs in 1971 is more remarkable. He claimed that he did it out of loyalty to Eden – not a trait which had been conspicuous earlier in his career. Eden's position was respected by Lloyd in later years by their co-ordinating the lines on which they would discuss the issue with historians – what might be called collusion about collusion. Left to himself, Lloyd's instinct was to avoid the persistent disingenuousness in which Eden's memoirs were clothed. This was not far from Macmillan's subsequent declaration: 'Collusion would not have been disreputable if Anthony hadn't said it wasn't true.' But in his own diary for early 1957 Macmillan wrote: 'I mislaid the volume which began somewhere about the beginning of October.' In fact this section is missing because it was destroyed, which suggests a more purposeful attempt to doctor the record, albeit one which came unstuck.

Not only did Macmillan come up with the bad advice on which the decision to invade Egypt was taken: he also came up with the good advice to call the operation off a few days later. Harold Wilson's succinct phrase – 'first in, first out' – imperishably captures Macmillan's predicament in November 1956. Yet what is striking is how his own personal responsibility for the fiasco – like Churchill's for Narvik in 1940 – did not prevent him from walking off with the premiership.

In the Narvik debate in the House of Commons, Lloyd George had advised Churchill not to 'allow himself to be converted into an air-raid shelter to keep the splinters from hitting his colleagues'. The man who desperately needed such advice in the aftermath of Suez was Butler, whose potential as an air-raid shelter Macmillan was not slow to notice or to exploit. Butler had long sensed the folly of the enterprise, but this was not what the Tory Party wished to hear, especially not from the man of Munich. 'I couldn't understand,' he complained later, 'when I had done a most wonderful job – picking up the pieces after Suez – that they then chose Harold.' It was indeed Harold Macmillan, backed to the last by Churchill, who successfully adopted the public mien necessary to outface his critics and retrieve the situation: unforgiving, unflinching, unflappable. It was a great act – and certainly did him more good than banging his head against the wall of a train compartment.

Notoriously, generals always learn the lessons of the last war. Are politicians so different? Harold Macmillan was not only the best-read Prime Minister of the twentieth century – Asquith and Churchill would be his only rivals – but also one with a pronounced relish for the hazardous game of drawing apt historical analogies, and well aware of its pitfalls. 'Max Beerbohm once said that history does not repeat itself; it is historians who repeat one another,' he reminded his Chancellor of the Exchequer in 1960, adding the caution: 'This is certainly true of the economists and professors.' Yet his own career contained within it such an evocative charge of deeply-felt experience that the outlook of the Prime Minister was crucially conditioned by perceptions ingrained during the first half of a very long life. It was as a prisoner of his past that Macmillan became Prime Minister in January 1957, and this he remained to the end, despite his intermittent signals of a wish to escape and a series of ingratiating gestures towards the future.

After Suez, Lloyd offered his resignation, which was refused. Since Eden was shortly to leave the Government in broken health, and since, as Macmillan put it, 'one head on a charger should be enough', Lloyd's position was made secure. Remarkably, for more than five years, Macmillan, with a country house of his own, made over Chequers to Lloyd, thus affirming a strong bond between them. He became Macmillan's indispensable colleague, more truly unflappable than his master, but one who recognized that it was a presidential style of government. In Aneurin Bevan's unforgettable image, his role was that of monkey to the Prime Minister's organ-grinder. Naturally Lloyd was privately irritated by 'the usual drip of denigration' in the press, especially after *The Times* had raised a rash of speculation in 1958 with a suggestion that the Prime Minister had confided to him that 'enough is enough'. But Lloyd was prepared to fall in with Macmillan's wishes, though ready on occasion to warn him that 'it is not helpful to portray the image of "Mac Winston" trying to do everything himself'.

By 1957 the sun of affluence was shining upon the British economy, combining prosperity and full employment under the benign influence of mild inflation. 'Let's be frank about it,' Macmillan told the crowd at an open-air meeting, 'most of our people have never had it so good'. He went on to warn that 'the problem of our time' was to combine full employment with the control of inflation. But the bastardized message, 'You've never had it so good,' went down as his most famous utterance, and folk myth has him stumping the country on this slogan in the 1959 General Election. If there is a poetic truth in this, it is because Macmillan projected himself with a verve which teetered on the brink of vulgarity. When Vicky, the greatest cartoonist of the period, moved to the *Evening Standard* in 1958 he produced one of his finest creations: 'Introducing: Supermac'. Of course, the socialist Vicky lived to regret it. 'This figure, Supermac, has really boomeranged on me now,' he admitted in 1960, when Macmillan's reputation stood at its peak. But it was a political, not an artistic mistake, and if its intended satire bounced off Conservative readers of the *Standard*, they were more straightforwardly affronted by another of Vicky's shafts, 'The Entertainer', which depicted Macmillan as Archie Rice, busking alongside a dole queue, chanting, 'You've never had it so good.' With a level of unemployment which oscillated around 2 per cent of the workforce, however, the political sting had been drawn.

The lesson of Stockton may now have been learned by others, but it was the borough's illustrious former MP who most obviously took it to heart. Hence his differences in 1957–

8 with the Chancellor of the Exchequer, Peter Thorneycroft, whose plans for 'some swingeing cuts in the Welfare State expenditure' soon had the Prime Minister alarmed. It was a complete contrast of styles. 'He shouts at one (with a cockney accent) as if we were a public meeting,' Macmillan noted in his diary. But he was prepared to lose all his Treasury ministers – Nigel Birch and Enoch Powell were solid with Thorneycroft – rather than yield to demands for deflation. It is characteristic that Macmillan should have publicly discounted the resignations in January 1958 as 'little local difficulties'; characteristic that this should have been passed off as a spontaneous throwaway remark; and characteristic that the sally should later turn out to have been meticulously prepared for the occasion. Not for the last time, ruthless calculation wore the mask of nonchalance.

So much for Thorneycroft, who had to await the advent of Thatcher for his full rehabilitation, in face of Macmillan's subsequent amnesia about 'that man who looked like an English butler, with the nice Italian wife – I forget his name ...' Derrick Heathcoat Amory was a more amenable successor, whom the Prime Minister would seek to inoculate against the wiles of the Treasury – 'What is wrong with inflation, Derry?' – while rekindling the memory of Stockton. In retrospect Macmillan considered the great consumer boom of 1958–60 'slightly overheated', but at the time of the 1959 General Election, with a Conservative majority of 100 under his belt, he is not recorded as entertaining such curmudgeonly doubts. By 1960, however, the pace had told upon Amory, as Macmillan's diary reveals: 'a sweet man – a really charming character. But he is tired and overdone.' He had to go. Once more Macmillan sought a Chancellor whom he could bully and cajole, and in Selwyn Lloyd he thought he had found a lasting replacement.

Lloyd knew not only that Macmillan had been looking for 'someone with original ideas' as his Chancellor, but also that he himself did not fit the bill. 'I told him he was wrong if he expected any originality,' Lloyd recorded. 'I had v. orthodox ideas about taxation and public expenditure, and knew nothing about the City.' There was, however, more to it than that. Lloyd's early career was rooted not in Conservatism but in Lloyd George Liberalism, and it was only after Lloyd George's serious bid for power had failed that the young Selwyn Lloyd drifted towards the Conservatives. At Cambridge in the 1920s, it was Lloyd's Liberal activities which were the making of his prominence in the Union and which led to his adoption as a parliamentary candidate in the 1929 General Election. He campaigned fervently but unavailingly for the expansionist policies in Lloyd George's manifesto, *We Can Conquer Unemployment*, and counted its rejection by the electorate as a lifelong disappointment, along with the failure to establish a centre party in the 1930s.

The record of Harold Macmillan as an early pioneer of Keynesian measures has long been appreciated, and the resonance of 'Stockton' in understanding his outlook as Prime Minister has become a cliché. Is it Macmillan's past alone which helps explain the new interventionist thrust in Treasury policy in the early 1960s? Should Lloyd's surprising record as a reforming Chancellor, proclaiming an annual growth target of 4 per cent and establishing the National Economic Development Council, be viewed as the belated triumph of Lloyd George, thirty years on? There are, to be sure, one or two snags in such a scenario, not least the possibilities of bathos in envisaging a hypothetical encounter between grimly deflationist Treasury knights and a Chancellor whose eyes would mist over at the evocative mention of 'Hoylake'. Nonetheless, in Lloyd Macmillan truly found a Chancellor after his own heart.

Nobody was more loyal in implementing unpopular policies like the pay pause, but Lloyd was to discover that, under this regime, loyalty was a one-way street. Macmillan, who had declined to make Lloyd the scapegoat for the failure of Suez, eventually rewarded him by instead making him the scapegoat for the incipient failure of the Government's economic policy. How far, or far ahead, this was planned is not clear – certainly it was not clear to Lloyd at the time. As late as March 1962, his diary details an intimate discussion with

Macmillan about a possible reconstruction of the Government. The Night of the Long Knives in July, when Macmillan sacked a third of his Cabinet, was to be the result. Four months earlier Lloyd's diary had recorded the scenario thus: 'I said, "What about myself?" He said, "You would have to stay on if PM." I said I was not sure I wanted this.' Macmillan had offered a further assurance: that he would not write his memoirs. Never a man to renege in anything but spades, he was to reserve his longest knife for Lloyd four months later and eventually completed his memoirs in six fat volumes.

There are signs that Macmillan felt some remorse over the whole business in the abattoir – pangs to which even organ-grinders are not wholly immune. As it turned out, it was worse than disloyalty: it was, as Macmillan came to realize, 'a great error'. Above all, it impaired the public image of unflappability, and offered a sudden revealing glimpse of a man who had for some time privately admitted that he was 'beginning (at last) to feel old and depressed'. Sanguinary if no longer sanguine, he struggled on to the moors in time for the Glorious Twelfth, despite his infirmities, and reported back that 'I hope to still be able to see – and kill – a few grouse ...'

In becoming Prime Minister after Suez, in preference to the old appeaser Butler, Macmillan was a clear beneficiary of the lesson of Munich and the lesson of Dunkirk, which recruited him support among Tory right-wingers. If Suez had failed, it was because it had been not misconceived but merely mismanaged; the Americans were to blame; and the British lion, though looking a bit mangy as a result, simply needed time to recuperate and another Churchill to supply the appropriate roar. No surrender! It has long seemed a paradox that Macmillan's premiership was nonetheless a crucial period of adjustment to Britain's diminished world role, witnessing a reconciliation with the USA, the dismemberment of the British Empire in Africa, and an attempted rapprochement with the European Community. Does this not suggest that

Macmillan had in fact moved (albeit stealthily) beyond the rhetoric of his supporters and discerned (albeit circumspectly) a coherent vision of a less grandiose but more viable future for his country? This is surely the issue that will finally determine Macmillan's place in history.

The evidence now available, notably his private diary, suggests that we should be wary of exaggerating any such shift in outlook. For Macmillan, it seems, was not just manipulating the stereotyped imagery of Munich for his own ulterior purposes: he fully accepted it himself. The best way he could make sense of the situation in Lebanon was: 'after Austria – the Sudeten Germans. Poland (in this case Iraq) will be the next to go ...' Nasser seems to have stalked the pages of the diary like an over-promoted understudy for Hitler. During the Cuban missile crisis in 1962, there was inevitably a smell of Munich in the air. Foreign policy, on this reading, continually presented the same, simplistic, existential choice, enacted against the same tatty scenery, with the same stylized theatrical props for the role of British Prime Minister – either an umbrella or a big cigar. More significant than the imagery was a stubbornly atavistic view of the world and Britain's place in it. Adenauer's remark, that Britain was 'like a rich man, who has lost all his money but does not realize it', captures this well. When, in 1962, Acheson said that Britain 'has lost an empire and has not yet found a role', Macmillan's immediate private reaction was that Acheson was 'always a conceited ass'. The notion that the emperor had no clothes, as seemed devastatingly obvious to these foreigners, was somehow regarded as capable of refutation by shutting one's eyes and thinking of Winston Churchill.

Macmillan once confessed that he may have 'played the cards above their face value' in his communications with Kennedy over Cuba; but this was hardly the sole occasion when he sought to conjure a foreign policy out of the nostalgic shreds of his own rhetoric. The 'special relationship' was peculiarly susceptible to this treatment, with a high point at Nassau in December 1962, when Macmillan pulled out all the stops – the Great War and the pity of war, his own experiences on the Somme – in the course of trying to get his hands on a few Polaris submarines. Macmillan's determination to retain a British nuclear deterrent was a paramount objective, to which he was prepared to sacrifice almost anything else. To Kennedy, wondering how to humour an old man whom he rather liked, it appeared as 'a political necessity but a piece of military foolishness'.

The real reason for an independent nuclear bomb was mistrust of the Americans, yet the British were now embarrassingly dependent upon the same untrustworthy Americans to supply them with the weapon system necessary to make it effective. By 1962 Macmillan's credibility thus hinged on the technical feasibility of the Skybolt rocket, which the Americans had previously promised him but which McNamara, as Defence Secretary, now described as 'proven to be a pile of junk'. Only Polaris would do instead – that was Macmillan's desperate plea to Kennedy at Nassau. But if the Americans' reluctant agreement to supply Polaris was a great tribute to the unique bonds of the special relationship, the point was not, of course, lost upon de Gaulle.

Macmillan seems to have remained confident that, at their meeting at Rambouillet, he had placated the General over the terms on which Britain proposed to enter the Common Market. Whether he had offered the French a measure of nuclear co-operation, or merely tantalized them with elliptical hints (in French, without an interpreter), remains disputable. What is clear is that Macmillan thought that he could develop his two big schemes simultaneously, without requiring the island race to confront that drastic reappraisal of priorities unhappily demanded of those in reduced circumstances. 'I only hope that nothing I have done at Rambouillet or Nassau has increased your difficulties,' he wrote to Heath, his negotiator in Brussels. Maybe nothing could have stopped de Gaulle uttering his famous monosyllable a few weeks later, but he was certainly given good grounds for depicting Britain's commitment to Europe as lukewarm, condescending and half-hearted.

Nor was Macmillan emotionally ready to make more than

a limited tactical disengagement from Britain's imperial past. 'I bring you greetings from the Old Country,' he would say on his Commonwealth tours. Even in South Africa, the language was the same and it evoked the same old-fashioned loyalties – 'to the old country – "home" they called it'. Apartheid, of course, was a regrettable mistake, but chiefly because the South Africans had elevated it into a doctrinal issue. 'If they didn't make an ideology of it,' Macmillan confided, 'they would almost certainly succeed in getting the results they seek with a minimum of concession.' He wrote after visiting Durban, where South Africans of British stock flew their Union Jacks to greet him: 'It is those people I care about.' Hence his surprisingly strong feelings against the exclusion of South Africa from the Commonwealth in 1961, for all his famous warnings of a 'wind of change' the previous year. Hence, too, his bitter reproaches to Canada for breaking ranks with the 'Whites' at this juncture. Without that, he noted in his diary, 'we could have got through – though we might have failed at the next Conference'. Here speaks the authentic Macmillan: overplaying his hand again, shamelessly employing a bit of bluff in the hope of squeaking through, optimistically supposing that he might be able to take the next trick, but uneasily aware that he might, after all, be playing a losing game.

How, then, should Macmillan's premiership now be viewed? One valuable insight has been to stress Macmillan's ambiguity, which still seems central – and finally impenetrable. Despite his romantic air and his youthful radicalism, which suggest parallels with the maverick Toryism of Disraeli or Churchill, there is also a case to be made for setting Macmillan in another tradition – that of Salisbury's pragmatic Conservative statecraft, with its tough-minded cynicism about the affairs of this imperfect world unashamedly licensed by deep Christian convictions. Macmillan's religious beliefs were manifestly a great personal solace to him, faced with the distressing and prolonged crisis in his marriage. But there was also a surprisingly strong public resonance, with his reiterated view that a secular belief in decency was simply not enough.

Admittedly, his magnificent rebuke to Adenauer (in 1959 of all years), 'that I was not thinking of elections but of our duty to God and mankind', must have been hard to swallow. But there was surely self-reference in the commendation of Quintin Hogg (Lord Hailsham) which Macmillan once inscribed in his diary: 'He belongs *both* to this strange modern age of space and science *and* to the great past – of classical learning and Christian life.'

When Macmillan wrote this, in October 1963, he was recovering from emergency surgery, necessitating (as he thought) his resignation from office. Not all his colleagues, it must be said, were disposed to take an eirenic view of the great Christian statesman, still tenaciously exercising power from his hospital bed over the choice of his successor. When Home was chosen instead of Butler, allegations that Macmillan had manipulated the advice given to the Queen were soon raised, notably by Iain Macleod, who, along with Enoch Powell, refused to serve in the new Cabinet. Macmillan's active role in the crisis is well documented, confirming the impression that he never considered Butler a suitable successor. But it now appears that Macmillan's initial scenario of promoting Hailsham was abandoned only at a late stage in favour of the Trollopean twist in the plot which converted the 14th Earl of Home from confidant to candidate. More baffling is the list of Cabinet ministers' alleged preferences, compiled by the Lord Chancellor and used to deadly effect by Macmillan, which represents Macleod as a declared supporter of Home, not of Butler. It is very difficult to make sense of this; but, whatever the confusion generated by the episode, the fact remains that the old convalescent managed to get his way, with Home if not Hailsham to keep out Butler.

By the time he left office, Macmillan's standing had undeniably slipped. He may have made a misjudgement in thinking that his prostate operation demanded his immediate withdrawal – even while still in hospital he began brooding on how he might have carried on and overcome his critics ('at least temporarily'). It was not, of course, the Profumo affair that summer which had caused his downfall, though his handling of it did him no good. Macmillan recognized this in blaming the popular press, which had so recently lauded him as Supermac, for now depicting him as 'old, incompetent, worn out'. But the swing in public mood and perception in 1963, though unfairly exaggerated, was not without substance. After the humiliating failure of the Common Market negotiations at the beginning of the year, Macmillan's administration palpably lacked a strategy. 'All our policies at home and abroad are in ruins,' he wrote in his diary, adding, with a sub-Churchillian conditioned reflex, 'except our courage and determination.' In the end, the dogged virtues of Dunkirk were not enough. In retirement, he saw Britain's extrication from its position east of Suez as 'the most disastrous thing that has happened in twenty years' – practically since the time of Munich. Almost his final intervention in public life, as the nonagenarian Earl of Stockton, was an elegiac lament over the miners' strike in 1984: 'They beat the Kaiser's army and they beat Hitler's army. They never gave in.' It was one of the lessons which the old man had never forgotten.

Wilson, Bevan, Foot and Mikado on the left. Morrison, Attlee, Gaitskell, Dalton, Shinwell on the right (by Vicky, July 1951)

II

BEVAN VERSUS GAITSKELL:
SPLITTING THE DIFFERENCE

As old-fashioned artisans, historians have sometimes made a
good thing out of implying that the mystery of their craft
is arcane because archival. With the attenuation of private
correspondence, however, they are now haunted by a spectre
of technological redundancy. 'Political crisis seems to mean
chatting on the telephone and doing nothing,' Richard Crossman recorded in his diary in 1955. The telephone has become
the characteristic medium for urgent and confidential communication, and letters have increasingly become a formality,
used for deliberate record. Increasingly, what survives in the
archives is what was meant to survive. Hence the indis-
pensability of private diaries in reconstructing developments
at certain levels of recent political history. Crossman's own
diary was a natural extension of his role as he understood it.
He had not only a political fascination with the pursuit of
power but an intellectual fascination with the analysis of the
process in which he was involved, first as an opposition
backbencher, later as a Cabinet minister. For he remained
incorrigibly attached to his habits and training as an Oxford
don and a journalist, without ever forgetting that it was as an
intellectual *in politics* that he had a peculiar usefulness. He saw,
he knew, because he was there. His diary, especially the 1,000
pages of his backbench diary, thus gives a unique insight into
Labour Party politics in the transition from Attlee to Wilson.
   It is obvious, of course, that the diarist is not immune from

the effects of hindsight, ignorance, partiality, bias and self-justification. In Crossman's case these distortions are not disabling. He was singularly free from self-deception, and his candour often punctured his own pretensions. He usually wanted to learn rather than to cover up. He had a good opinion of himself; but his was not the smooth, imperturbable vanity consonant with concealment, but a rough, thrusting arrogance that made for exposure. Perhaps it helped that, almost to the eve of his appointment to the Cabinet, he saw himself as 'first a political journalist and only secondarily a parliamentary politician'. He had none of the tactful, discreet, dissimulating ways of the political time-server. He could never resist blowing the gaff, and was happiest making the news, finding the news, telling the news. The chronic factionalism of Labour politics in the 1950s gave him a good long-running story.

Between them, Aneurin Bevan and Hugh Gaitskell not only dominated the party: they threatened to destroy it as a serious contender for power. In fighting for its soul, they fought each other to a standstill. Two dissimilar but magnetic figures, they repelled each other and attracted eponymous bands of supporters who vilified each other more effectively than either hurt the Tories. It was commonly seen at the time as a simple clash between Left and Right, not least because this perspective flattered the self-image of many active participants. The fact is that the conflict was on three related but not identical levels: Bevanites versus Gaitskellites, Left versus Right, and fundamentalists versus revisionists. Indeed the simplistic conflation of these categories is the reason for some prevalent misconceptions about what happened and about the nature of the Labour Party.

It can truly be said that Aneurin Bevan's life was the stuff of which legends are made. The chief myth-maker was his lieutenant, Michael Foot, ultimately leader of the Labour Party himself. His noble biography not only chronicled Bevan's life with clarity and verve; it explicated his political philosophy with understanding and insight and used high literary gifts to convey the sense of the man and the rich complexity of his personality. Warts and all? Yes and no: for the portrait came not from a judge but from an advocate of rare single-mindedness who did not conceal Bevan's warts but wanted us to admire them, as Bevan's warts. Foot's Bevan is an immensely attractive, iconoclastic figure, standing in a long and bookish tradition of British radicalism, with a Marxist turn of phrase, to be sure, but essentially a great parliamentarian and, above all, the untrammelled voice of the backbenches – Nye in the looking-glass, in short.

Yet there is also a strong case for seeing Bevan as a much more faithful product of his environment, not just the South Wales coalfield and the miners' union, but also the Central Labour College, where his Marxism was imbibed. 'I know all its faults, all its dangers,' he used to say of the Labour Party. 'But it is the party that we have taught millions of working people to look to and regard as their own. We can't undo what we have done.' The party leadership was, in his view, the obstruction to radical policies. The way to remove this obstacle was to make a left-wing appeal to the ordinary party workers, who in this respect represented workers at large. The class struggle and public ownership were to remain fundamental tenets of his political doctrine, and his pursuit of power was deadly serious. This is illustrated by Bevan's response to the 1944 White Paper which pledged the wartime Coalition Government to maintain a high and stable level of employment. Bevan called it 'an impracticable proposition. Indeed, I will go so far as to say that if the implications of the White Paper are sound, there is no longer any justification for this Party existing at all.'

The essential role of the Labour Party – the task for which it had been called into being by the proletariat – was to reorganize the economic basis of society in the interests of all (since the bourgeoisie could hardly be expected to participate in this process). 'Nobody believes in public ownership for its own sake,' Bevan explained. 'This party did not come into existence demanding Socialism, demanding the State ownership of property, simply because there was some special merit in it.' It was the only means of escaping the necessary evils of capitalism and of achieving prosperity for all. 'If private enterprise can deliver all these goods, there will not be any argument for Socialism and no reason for it.'

As long as Bevan held to this analysis, he was a potent threat to capitalists, like Lord Beaverbrook, whose champagne he had no compunction in appropriating as a first instalment of the social revolution. The 'Bollinger Bolshevik' had so much sparkle because he was buoyed up by the wave of the future. In 1945 both he and the class he represented had their golden opportunity. Bevan became one of the outstanding successes of the Attlee Government. For the working class he later reserved a more jaundiced verdict: 'History gave them their chance – and they didn't take it.' As he recognized, the trouble was that Labour was trying to change a society moulded by a capitalist psychology. 'We know that unless the workers can divest themselves of that psychology, we shall fail,' he said in 1949. By then he was betraying new anxieties about the course of politics, and in April 1951 his ministerial career came to an acrimonious end – for ever.

It proved to be the first of many maladroit episodes in which Bevan simultaneously infuriated his enemies and baffled his friends. Freed from the discipline of office, Bevan pursued a fitful and disaffected course in opposition to the party leadership. His charismatic force meant that he quickly attracted followers, though some of them, like Crossman, were driven to distraction by his instability of purpose. Crossman had no suspicion of any lack of ambition, noting in January 1952: 'I think Nye is almost exclusively concerned to be Leader of the Party rather than to formulate left-wing policy.' More than once, Attlee is recorded as thinking of Bevan as his successor. 'Nye had the leadership on a plate,' he told Crossman in March 1955. 'I always wanted him to have it. But you know, he wants to be two things simultaneously, a rebel and an official leader, and you can't be both.'

Gaitskell's perspective, by contrast, was essentially min-isterial. His background of educational privilege at Winchester and academic excellence at New College, Oxford, fitted him more obviously for his pre-war career as a don and his wartime service as a high-flying civil servant than for being a Labour politician. Entering Parliament in 1945, he spent little more than a year as a backbencher before Attlee singled him out for advancement. The seeds of Gaitskell's caution about the development of Labour Party policy were sown early. His pessimistic forecast of the result of the 1950 General Election scooped the pool in the ministerial sweepstake. His vision of socialism did not postulate a seething mass of oppressed workers, poised to seize the state as their instrument. Perceiving the voters as essentially moderate, he was tempted to appeal to them over the heads of the party activists – tempted also to see the trade-union leadership as the best proxy for the real working class.

Gaitskell saw the Labour Party as the agent of responsible government, from which he considered the parrot cries of the Left as remote as the power-seeking opportunism of the Tories. Nor did loss of office in 1951 change his outlook. He preferred to behave as a leader in an alternative Government rather than as a frondeur indulging in the joys of opposition. Even Attlee rather shocked him at this stage by being 'not as honest as he should be in Opposition, regarding it as quite reasonable to take a line which he knows he would not take in Government'. This was an austere standard, set by a man who despised the harlotry of politics and instead offered responsibility without power. No wonder the Left found him less fun than Nye Bevan.

Some early encounters between the two men were at informal ministerial dinners organized by Cripps, a mutually admired friend. There was a clash of styles as much as of substance: Bevan eloquent and passionate, Gaitskell dry and dialectical. Asked by one of his friends why he was risking 'a rift between yourself and one of the really considerable men of the Government', Bevan replied: 'Considerable? But he's nothing, nothing, nothing!' A solemn view should not, perhaps, be taken of the spontaneous invective of a man who was capable of good-humouredly calling one Labour MP 'a pimp' and saying to another, 'Shut up, bonehead.' For if Gaitskell had simply been 'nothing', Bevan would have been spared much subsequent difficulty.

That Bevan did not so radically misjudge his rival is suggested by a familiar remark, which continues to be misconstrued. Angered by the imperturbable Attlee in 1954, Bevan sarcastically commented: 'I know that the right kind of leader for the Labour Party is a desiccated calculating machine.' That the epithet should have stuck to Gaitskell was most implausible, as Bevan well saw: 'For one thing Hugh is not desiccated – he's highly emotional.' Gaitskell's stubborn sense of principle was not calculating. His public oratory had an undertow of emotion all the more thrilling in its unexpectedness. Even in his private life, his exuberant partygoing embraced a recklessness which was seen in his affair with the fashionable hostess Anne Fleming; and 'machine' is simply not the right word for a man with the reputation of cuckolding the creator of James Bond.

The portrait of Bevan in the Crossman diary is graphic evidence both of his immense potential as a leader and of his fatal disqualifications. It was Bevan's self-indulgence which made him an impossible colleague, whether in a Cabinet or a cabal. His whims made him unpredictable and his self-centredness made him unreliable when mundane norms of consistency, responsibility and loyalty were at stake. 'What a past master Nye is at rationalizing his own convenience,' Crossman observed about an incident in which he had revealed his support for Winston Churchill instead of his own follower Barbara Castle. Bevan felt an affinity with Churchill and perhaps hoped for an analogous vindication in ignoring all the ordinary rules of political advancement.

Crossman warned Bevan early in 1955 that he must play in with the team if he was ever to have a chance of becoming leader. 'I'm not sure I really want to be under these conditions,' Bevan said, 'I'm not a proletarian or an intellectual. I am an aristocrat, with a real distaste for that kind of politics.' Crossman was depressed to find him still playing with the same notion – 'it meant really nothing' – in his years of eclipse:

'The worst of Gaitskell is that he isn't a patrician but a bourgeois.' But by then it was just another rationalization, a romantic gloss on his own failings. Moreover, even when he had accepted a supporting role under Gaitskell's leadership, Bevan continued to pain his admirers by his tergiversations. 'He's like a great big jelly, which has to be pulled back into shape about once every three months,' Crossman wrote. 'Not a very good look-out for a future Foreign Secretary.'

How far, then, did the Bevanite movement manifest a principled challenge by a coherent Left? The division in Parliament, Crossman claimed in July 1952, 'was quite grotesquely obvious to anyone looking down from the Gallery. It really does look like two parties.' Bevan himself had earlier been ready to consider an actual breach – 'Yes, it would mean setting up a separate Socialist Party organization. Yes, it would mean fights in every constituency.' This was, however, second best to his declared strategy of 1951, which was 'to capture the constituency parties and so put a squeeze on the Parliamentary Party. If Members knew that they would not be renominated because they were anti-Bevanite, things would move.' This struck Crossman at the time as 'impracticable and, if the mere idea of it gets out, insanely dangerous'. One reason for the impracticability of the strategy, of course, was Bevan's own lack of Leninist rigour in implementing it. Crossman observed him in Coventry some two years afterwards, wreaking his magic in support of a non-Bevanite colleague. 'Since Nye has been telling us that we ought to get rid of the anti-Bevanites and see that they are not adopted, I pointed this out to him afterwards. But he is a wonderful man. He really is too nice and generous to carry out the things he tells us to do.'

There was some truth in the official line under Attlee that no real ideological division existed and that personal animosities were the root of the trouble. Thus at a party meeting in October 1952 Attlee 'repeated that there were no serious differences of policy and that attempts to talk about a Right and Left of the Party were misleading'. A few weeks later, when Bevan returned to the front bench, Crossman was inclined to agree, marvelling at an abrupt reconciliation which 'couldn't have happened if there had been real fundamental issues of policy dividing the two sides'. And he conceded now that 'between Nye and Hugh Gaitskell there are really only differences of emphasis, temperament and will as regards domestic policy'. Such amity did not prevent Crossman from subsequently reverting to a justification of the Bevanite challenge to Morrison in policy terms – 'the policies Herbert stands for are so revolting to the constituencies that they vote even for me'. Nonetheless, he remained constantly aware of the large extent to which the names Left and Right covered not only ideological factionalism but atavistic tribalism within the Labour Party.

'What a mysterious thing "the Left" is,' Crossman reflected in 1951. 'Why is this person Left and that person Right? What binds the Group together?' It included leaders like Bevan and Wilson with 'virtually nothing in common'; and followers 'who, as far as I can see, have no coherent political attitude'. Wilson subsequently went further, in describing the Bevanites as 'always in high good humour, enjoying each others' company', rather than acting as 'a party within a party'. When they denounced the Gaitskellites as cliquish, they knew whereof they spoke. Hence some of the confusion during the years that followed, with Right and Left conscientiously embattled in defence of their principles – though why, they could sometimes hardly say. 'One of the things we object to most strongly is the blind loyalty of the Right,' Crossman acknowledged, 'but really the left of the Party shows that kind of loyalty just as strongly. It only confirms my contention that in British politics loyalty to people and not ideas is universally regarded as the prime quality.' He later added a temperamental dimension to this analysis: 'The definition of the Left is a group of people who will never be happy unless they can convince themselves that they are about to be betrayed by their leaders.' The other irony which did not escape him was the dissonance between the rhetoric of concern for the party and the actual damage inflicted. He commented in 1954 that 'what we think to be our efforts to save the soul of the Party are certainly helping it to disintegrate as fast as possible'. It was much the same seven years later, with most of the inner Left group 'only concerned to be anti-Gaitskell and openly saying that they are not prepared for unity if it strengthens him . . .'

If Bevanite and Gaitskellite allegiances cannot easily be collapsed into a simple Left–Right stereotype, neither can the division between fundamentalist and revisionist views of socialism. Morrison's charge against the Bevanite group was that 'it creates the assumption that only some Members of Parliament are good Socialists', and he added, to loud applause from his own supporters, 'I resent that.' He was well justified, according to his lights, in invoking in support the 1945 programme, with its nationalization measures, in the implementation of which he had played so significant a part. Both he and his critics were agreed in taking this as the relevant benchmark. In a rather curious way, the fundamentalists, seeing the essence of socialism as the substitution of public for private ownership of the means of production, had come to look with reverence upon the Morrisonian public corporation as the word made flesh. Hence the best socialists were those who demanded the longest shopping list for further nationalization.

There might be plenty of Bevanites; the real flop was the attempt to invent Bevanism. What, after all, did it amount to, beyond a strident call for more nationalization coupled with a hankering after fewer armaments? Certainly the Bevanites lost the battle of the books. Bevan's own eagerly awaited tract, *In Place of Fear* (1952), had some fine rhetorical passages but little coherent analysis. Whereas fundamentalists shared with the Morrisonian Old Right a view of what socialism was about (and disagreed over what to do next), the revisionists offered a different analysis of the problem facing Labour and accordingly suggested different remedies, notably in Anthony Crosland's book *The Future of Socialism* (1956). As Crosland put it: 'Many liberal-minded people ... have now concluded that "Keynes-plus-modified-capitalism-plus-

Welfare-State" works perfectly well.' Though he himself was not endorsing this as a sufficient political creed, he worked on the premise of making the mixed economy the means of promoting social justice. And in practice, though Bevan might balk at the 'fresh thinking' of revisionism, he accepted the mixed economy.

Just as Crosland was the intellectual champion of revisionism, so Crossman was often regarded as the spokesman for fundamentalism. He brought this on himself, after Labour's defeat in 1959, by taking a public stand on his professed belief that public ownership was necessary since capitalism was doomed, and that if he did not believe this to be so, he would prefer to reconstruct the Liberal Party as the real alternative to Toryism. But this was not a consistent view. For Crossman, despite his emotional investment in the Left, was one of those awkward people who could not seem to grasp that the salvation of the economy, not to mention the realization of fraternity, lay in nationalizing the sugar and cement industries. Indeed, back in the summer of 1952, he is to be found writing: 'We are drifting into the worst economic crisis since the war and nobody really pretends that nationalization or denationalization are any help whatsoever in such a situation.' He remained acutely aware that there were no simple answers here, least of all for the Left. After the 1955 General Election he wrote of the Labour Party, in terms which echo Crosland, as 'ideologically disintegrated by the fact that Keynesian welfare capitalism is proving, for the time being, quite an adequate substitute for socialism'.

One measure of the problem was lack of electoral appeal. 'If you give people a bourgeois sense of security, the type of working-class movement we had forty years ago will no longer appeal to them,' Crossman observed in 1953. 'The younger people don't feel the same significance in the slogans; on the other hand, the older people won't give up the slogans or the organization.' The British class structure, as Gaitskell sought to explain to the visiting Russian leaders in 1956, was undergoing fundamental change: 'Our trouble was that prosperity had made too many workers vote Tory!' Crossman agreed. Assured in Moscow that 'workers are always interested in progress', he retorted: 'Are they? Our workers in Coventry certainly are not. They are interested in getting the highest wage for the smallest amount of work.' Bevanite that he was, Crossman can hardly be accused of harbouring inflated illusions about the capacity of the working class as bearers of an ethic of social redemption. He was not unsympathetic to the sort of psephological analysis which underpinned revisionism, for example Gaitskell's claim in 1958 that 'working-class people are week by week becoming less working-class, less class-conscious and more allergic to such old appeals as trade union solidarity or class loyalty'. As Gaitskell put it a few months later, 'the kind of emotions and behaviour which held the Party together in the past were all based on class. Yet, since the war, progress has all been such as to weaken the sense of class loyalty upon which the Labour Party is based.'

Crossman noted a TUC view of Butler's economic policies in 1954, that 'the decontrol suits trade unions pretty well, since we can revert to our old function'. The election slogan 'Conservative Freedom Works' touched the right spot in 1955. It showed, in ways that adumbrated Thatcherism, that Conservative freedom worked wonders for their working-class support, at least among the strong bargainers who could cash in on it. Yet Crossman saw that the 'selfish, egotistical Budget' which the Tories introduced in the run-up to the next General Election in 1959 was offensive in ignoring the plight of old age pensioners, the unemployed, the sick and disabled – 'the submerged fifth of the community, who are on the edge of destitution'. There were still people who *never* had it good. Labour's traditional rhetoric as the party of the poor had subsumed trade unionists as a special case of maldistribution and social injustice. But now it was apparent that their experience was pulling them in opposite directions as the old working class fragmented. Labour leaders were finding that the affluent workers were doing very nicely thank you, whereas the poor – marginal, under-privileged, inarticulate and forgotten – the poor they had always with them.

The Gaitskellite emphasis on reappraising Labour's appeal spoke to this problem, and Crossman, as the least sectarian of Bevanites, was able to admit this. It was not a personal attraction, although the two men went back a long way together. Having outshone Gaitskell at Winchester, Crossman noted that 'if you were at school with somebody who seemed innocuous and insignificant throughout your school life and who since then has been an ascending backroom boy, it is difficult to believe in his greatness'. There was also a distinctive intellectual and temperamental gulf between them, as illustrated by their attitudes towards the 1956 Suez crisis. Crossman readily admitted that 'I'm not the sort of moralist who can believe that an action such as Eden and Mollet planned would not be justified by complete success.' He had perceptively entered his objection to Gaitskell as, 'most serious of all, someone who takes a moralizing and reactionary attitude, which is in my opinion almost instinctively wrong on every subject outside economics'. Crossman not only had positive reasons for being a socialist in ultimately asserting a class analysis; he also had negative reasons in that he was left cold by Gaitskell's social-democratic insistence on conscience rather than class as the key to radical politics.

Gaitskell, by contrast, made Suez into the stuff of his own politics of conscience – once he had discerned which side was in the wrong. We now know from his diary that he had warned Eden 'that, while, of course, there were certain circumstances in which force would be appropriate, it had to be in self-defence'. It is indicative of the continuing obfuscation surrounding the Suez episode that this passage was quoted by Gaitskell's official biographer as 'force would be appropriate [only] in self-defence', and by Eden's official biographer merely as 'force would be appropriate in self-defence', which undoubtedly gives a different impression. Hence the subsequent charges about who misled whom and about Gaitskell's alleged trimming. His diary unfortunately contains some later interpolations which make clear its sense better than they make clear when it was actually written. What is quite clear is that it was Gaitskell who first struck an endlessly resonant note in the Commons when he said in August 1956: 'It is all very familiar. It is exactly the same that we encountered from Mussolini and Hitler in those years before the war.' But having got uncomfortably hot under the collar about Nasser, Gaitskell positively boiled over with indignation three months later when Eden unilaterally sent in the troops. With unwonted passion, and with Bevan's backing – but without heed to the electoral consequences – Gaitskell denounced the Government. 'And what's so wonderful, Dick,' he told a dismayed Crossman, 'is that we are morally in the right.'

Whatever else it did, Suez helped to consolidate an incipient Bevan–Gaitskell axis in the Labour Party. Crossman's work on old age pensions was his own contribution to the policy review. He saw that such efforts as Gaitskell's Fabian pamphlet on nationalization in 1956 were 'making people think that the Labour Party is a party to be taken seriously, that it is thinking, that it is beginning to get a policy and that there can be such a thing as a second stage of socialism'. It was also clear to him that in this endeavour 'Gaitskell and his friends are playing the major role, since no one else has anything positive to propose'. As he saw it, his own associates, Bevan and Wilson, had failed to take the necessary initiatives: 'The fact is that Nye and Harold are not interested in rethinking policy at all.' In Crossman's eyes, this contrast showed the glimmer of promise in Gaitskell's leadership, and marked the fundamental reason for Bevan to throw his weight behind it.

With Gaitskell installed as Attlee's successor, Bevan grudgingly deferred to the claims of a leader some eight years his junior. By 1957 he was ready to affront the tender consciences of his own followers over nuclear disarmament. He told the Labour Party conference at Brighton that its proposed resolution would 'send a Foreign Secretary, whoever he may be, naked into the conference chamber', and, in an unforgettable thrust, called such a response 'an emotional spasm'.

Crossman was well pleased that 'on two really critical issues – nationalization and the H-Bomb – the two big leaders, Gaitskell and Bevan, have strengthened their position with the electorate at large by curbing the Party extremists and asserting their authority over them in defiance of their dogma. After all, the two most important emotions of the Labour Party are a doctrinaire faith in nationalization, without knowing what it means, and a doctrinaire faith in pacifism, without facing its consequences.'

No one could have suspected how short both their lives were to be; at his death in 1960 Bevan was still younger than Macmillan had been when he became Prime Minister. If the Brighton conference of 1957 was arguably the end of Bevanism, it is also arguable that Bevan lived just long enough to see the end of Gaitskellism too. Following Labour's third electoral defeat in a row in 1959, Gaitskell was rebuffed in his bid to rewrite Clause 4 of the Labour Party constitution, enshrining the necessity of public ownership. Bevan might complain that Labour's election manifesto in 1959 was not socialism, only 'pre-1914 Liberalism brought up to date', but that did not mean that Labour was ready for the sort of historic break with its past that the SPD made that year at Bad Godesburg. The outcome was almost wholly negative, with a rebuff for revisionism as much as for socialism. The real triumph was that of old-fashioned Labourism, and at the end of their lives both Bevan and Gaitskell made their terms with it.

If the Labour Party had genuinely been converted to social democracy under Gaitskell, its subsequent recidivism would be almost inexplicable. Rather, the real historical problem is to account for the nature of Gaitskellite ascendancy in the party in the first place. For it is surely a fallacy to explain it merely by reference to the ideas which Gaitskell upheld, giving an intellectual answer to an institutional question. As Crossman noted in 1952, what the Labour Party 'really can't abide is thrashing out Socialist policy among themselves. It is this solidarity which keeps the Party invincible against splits and almost impregnable to clear thinking.' Within the National Executive Committee (NEC), he found 'the MPs stertorous and somnolent with tiredness and the trade union-ists stertorous and somnolent as usual'. Truly can it be said that it was in their hands that the business of policy formation and the challenge of rising to new issues reposed. The party conference seemed hardly more promising, even in Crossman's hour of triumph at Brighton in 1957 over national superannuation. He observed the party's 'fear and suspicion of ideas and the intellectuals who produce them. Just as intel-lectuals are potential traitors, so the new ideas they put forward are always by nature assumed to be anti-socialist, until you can show that they are not.'

What had transformed Gaitskell's position in the party in the early 1950s was the development of links between himself, as a middle-class intellectual and parliamentarian, and the leadership of the right-wing trade unions, notably Bevin's successor as secretary-general of the transport workers' union, Arthur Deakin. The key phase in Gaitskell's rise dated from the 1952 Morecambe conference and the anti-communist speech which he delivered at Stalybridge shortly afterwards. After this, Foot commented in his life of Bevan, Deakin 'knew he had found his man', and Foot subsequently refers to 'the Gaitskellites or the Deakinites, which ever they properly be designated'. This points to an important truth. For Deakin was plainly no revisionist social democrat but the archetypal union boss with the biggest block vote in the business. He had a stolid conception of Labourism which drew upon trade-unionist norms of solidarity. Through these spectacles, the activities of the Left looked merely factious. He berated the Bevanites at Morecambe 'for their disregard of those prin-ciples and loyalties to which Our Movement has held so strongly throughout the whole course of its existence'.

Deakin's influence in the Labour party, though more dis-creetly advertised, was like strong drink: it reached parts which other brands could not reach, and the effect was shat-tering. In 1951 Gaitskell had noted in his diary: 'Jim Griffiths is the obvious successor for Attlee and Morrison.' When he resumed his diary, after a break of three years, however, we find Griffiths 'regarded at any rate for the moment as more or less finished', and a couple of months later Gaitskell dispassionately recorded an ex-minister as reckoning it 'highly probable that I would be leader of the Party before long'. So it turned out. Attlee hung on as leader until 1955, simultaneously ensuring that Bevan had enough rope to hang himself and that Morrison would be too old to succeed.

If Crossman appreciated the intellectual attraction of a revisionist approach, and often acknowledged the political expediency of Gaitskellite leadership, he could nonetheless never see the point of the Labour Right. Yet, undeniably, it was the Deakinite Old Right which called the shots. At the Morecambe conference in 1952, Crossman's impression was that 'the Executive was scared of what the Conference might do and that Right and Left were seeking to preserve unity and respectability but were terrified that some individual delegates from the floor would cause Arthur Deakin to blow off and then the whole thing would catch alight'. It was a standard piece of Labour ritual in these years that, whenever Michael Foot attacked Deakin in *Tribune*, the TUC General Council should deliver a letter of protest during the next meeting of the NEC. 'This has now become a ceremonial, rather like Black Rod entering the House of Commons from the House of Lords,' Crossman observed. Hence Bevan's standard speech 'about the Labour Party being hopeless, dominated by four trade union leaders, etc.'. He had in mind, of course, the transport workers (TGWU), the engineers (AEU), the miners (NUM) and the municipal workers (NUGMW), which together controlled over half of the block vote in the Conference. As George Brown, full of sherry and faith in the TGWU, put it in 1955: 'It's our Party, not yours.' Crossman had recently been apprised of the inwardness of this situation when receiving unwonted support from Fred Lee. 'If the T & G think they're going to dictate Parliamentary policy,' Lee had expostulated, 'it's time the AEU told them to get out ...'

Crossman once asked the current chairman of the TUC why intellectuals of the Attlee generation were accepted by trade-union leaders, whereas the generation of Crossman and Foot was bitterly resented. The answer was brilliantly simple, and helps to explain also the changed regard in which Foot was to be held later – 'They've been in the Movement all their lives.' Time the healer. Until the best part of their lives had slipped away, however, the Bevanites remained the prime target of trade-union hostility. Their position on the NEC was protected by the Chinese walls of the party constitution as amended in 1937, creating a constituency section where the writ of the block vote did not run; with a sweep of six Bevanites out of seven at Morecambe in 1952, the Left took charge here. Even so, the unions still possessed the ultimate deterrent, even if they never actually used it. For when it looked as though the elections to the constituency section might come unstuck in 1956, Sam Watson of the NUM was undismayed. 'If that happens,' he said, 'the trade unions will change the Constitution back, making all members of the Executive elected by the whole Conference.'

In view of the Bevanites' power base in the constituency section, there was a rough-and-ready logic in the situation. Roy Jenkins told Crossman in 1953 that 'just because the Bevanites were so strong, Gaitskell was more and more forced to rely on forces such as Arthur Deakin, which made him further to the right than he would naturally be'. Crossman reckoned that Gaitskell must have got half the constituency votes in the 1954 election for the party treasurership, but, by the same token, so must Bevan. With the whole conference voting for this post, these totals were dwarfed by the block votes of the big unions. In the early 1950s this meant sewing up the vote for the right-wing leadership. The trade-union members of the NEC were accordingly reluctant to admit television into the conference, and, above all, opposed to the televising of voting. 'What they meant, of course,' Crossman explained, 'was the disclosure to the public that, though practically the whole Conference votes one way, by show of hands, the block vote, when it is taken, usually shows 4 million to 2 million. It was immensely funny listening to the trade unionists showing their terror that anyone should see what really goes on.' In this era it was the Labour Right which had a wholesome suspicion of the media. By the time the Left had inherited this in later years, it had also, and perhaps not coincidentally, inherited the block votes.

With such support Gaitskell was carried to the treasurership – a crucial step towards the leadership. Crossman warned Gaitskell at the time 'that he seemed to be playing the role of merely being a stooge for big forces outside'. This was a fear echoed later in the year by the Bevanite George Wigg, who apparently believed 'that the moment Gaitskell obtains the leadership he will revert to type and become the stooge of the big trade unions'. There were adequate grounds for such fears on the Left. In the days of its power, the Right ruled with a rod of iron, hinted at in Morrison's informal rebuke to Crossman in 1952: 'You know, Dick, we shan't be able to tolerate much longer the sort of organized opposition that you're running.' Admittedly, the Left entered into this game with one eye on the attractions of martyrdom. By 1954 Crossman had the measure of Bevan on this score: 'When Nye talks about renewed attempts to expel us from the party, he means that we must do things which might get us expelled.'

Even so, the ferocity of the Right, with Gaitskell in the van, was a remarkable spectacle. He evidently thought it squeamish, even disloyal, to refuse to do the 'dirty work' of his Deakinite backers. With his trade-union allies behind him, he took the lead in moves to withdraw the Labour whip from Bevan in March 1955, and even to propose his expulsion from the party. When Gaitskell assured Crossman at this time that there were 'extraordinary parallels between Nye and Adolf Hitler', Crossman was reduced to pointing out Bevan's commitment to parliamentary liberty. 'Oh,' Gaitskell said, 'there are minor differences but what's striking is the resemblance.' In this confrontation, as Gaitskell admitted afterwards, 'nobody has come out of it very well, as compared with the position at the start.' Throughout this period the Left perceived itself as a persecuted minority with the weight of the party apparatus poised to crush its legitimate dissent. In 1958 it was the proposal to establish a new propaganda network, Victory for Socialism, which provoked the immediate displeasure of the NEC. 'At once the trade unionists there clicked back into the intolerance which had marked their behaviour throughout the whole Bevanite crisis,' wrote Crossman.

Gaitskell's leadership, therefore, far from signalling the party's conversion to revisionism, was sustained by the old-fashioned power-broking methods of the trade unions. When Gaitskell broached the big issue over Clause 4 of the party constitution in 1959, challenging the fundamentalist commitment to public ownership, he found his social democratic prognosis was brushed aside by the unions. Little wonder that Gaitskell confided that they now lacked 'a really formidable figure, like Deakin, to give a lead on policy'. As Crossman saw it, Gaitskell perished by the rules on which he had formerly thrived. 'Everybody knows that the trade unions are now bitterly against what they call the right-wing intellectuals,' he noted at the end of 1959. He was himself opposed to Gaitskell's tactics here. Toying with revisionism was one thing, but proposing to tamper with Clause 4 itself, indelibly inscribed on the tablets of stone which Sidney Webb had brought down from the mountain in 1918, affronted Crossman's own tribal instincts. Inside the fat Bevanite, however, there was a thin intellectual who could not resist noting that 'of course it's true that the antis, led by Michael Foot, are completely antediluvian'.

'We were wrong (*all* of us),' wrote Anthony Crosland to Gaitskell, 'to go for *doctrine*; we should have gone for *power*.' Bringing the issue out into the open had exposed the hollowness of the Gaitskellites' position, and it was only now that they discovered their tongues in denouncing the irresponsibility of the block vote system. 'Ironical to remember that Gaitskell got his leadership because he was shoved into it by the trade union leaders,' Crossman commented in May 1960. Within the NEC, the left-wing constituency members

could now safely leave the running to the trade-union representatives. 'Very soon it was clear that not one single trade
unionist present was in favour of amending Clause 4,' Crossman noted. This ostensible conversion to socialism among
such dogged slaves of precedent and convention was only so
remarkable if one cardinal fact were overlooked: that Clause
4 had always been in the rule book.

The situation was turned around for Gaitskell in 1960–61
because doctrine was made subservient to power. Challenged
by the campaign for unilateral nuclear disarmament, Gaitskell
backed down on Clause 4 and put his authority on the line at
the 1960 Scarborough conference on the defence issue. When
the NEC's policy was defeated, Gaitskell gave his stirring call
to 'fight and fight and fight again to save the party we love'.
As chairman of the party in 1960, Crossman took his stand
on the principle of 'upholding the authority of the Conference
and accepting its decisions as instructions'. There were many
ironies here. He naturally found it hard to take Jim Callaghan's
complaints that the Gaitskellites had been 'defeated by dubious
methods, and that it was a scandal that unions had made up
their minds before they arrived at Conference. All this from
Jim, who has been living on such Conference methods for
thirty years!' Conversely, it was Crossman himself who had
concluded back in 1956 that the party conference was 'wholly
unrepresentative of public opinion'. Crossman, like Wilson,
nonetheless determined that, fissured and flawed as it was, this
was the rock on which to build.

It was true, of course, that at Scarborough Gaitskell won
the argument even though he lost the vote. Moreover, the
margin by which he went down was narrower than expected
because uncommitted support, especially from the constituency parties, swung towards him on the day. Gaitskell
was now able to appeal to outside public opinion in a way that
legitimized his political position and enhanced his personal
authority. But what turned his moral victory of 1960 into his
actual conference triumph at Blackpool in 1961 was the fact
that the big unions rallied to him. Three out of the big six
unions changed sides. This was the support which revisionism

could not reach. The fact that the block vote could be brought into line on defence can be attributed to familiarity with the issue, loyalty to the leadership, anti-communism and, not least, a lot of business in smoke-filled rooms. Gaitskell's personal authority was restored but his revisionist crusade was over. When the Common Market became a major issue in 1962, Gaitskell's uncharacteristically ambivalent, fence-sitting attitude created no difficulties with the party conference but brought a new chill in his relations with his younger pro-European followers.

The end of the story is ambiguous because Gaitskell's death in January 1963 came out of the blue. It was a stunning blow to his friends, at a moment when Labour was beginning to look electable. Conversely, the accession of Wilson as leader brought new hope to his old Bevanite comrades. 'I ran into Michael Foot,' Crossman noted in February 1963. 'He, too, had this wonderful sense that the incredible has happened and that all kinds of things which had been impossible before Gaitskell's illness are now possible again.' The trouble with Gaitskell, they were agreed, had been that 'he was making the Party into the Gaitskell Party, forcing it to suppress its nature and strait-jacketing it under his leadership'. Crossman welcomed the fact that it was free to be itself again. 'Maybe in certain ways it is a silly and demagogic self, a sentimental self,' he allowed, 'but as a Party it's personality that we have had for a long time, a personality which Gaitskell disliked and manoeuvred for his own purposes.' Hence Crossman's judgement, at the time of the party conference in October 1963, when Wilson famously linked socialism with science, that he 'had provided the revision of Socialism and its application to modern times which Gaitskell and Crosland had tried and completely failed to do. Harold had achieved it.' With one bound Jack was free – or so, for the moment, it was possible to believe.

Denis Healey and Michael Foot at the time of the 1983 General Election (*Observer*)

12

THE DECAY OF LABOURISM
AND THE DEMISE OF THE SDP

Lack of leadership is an elusive theme. Whether it is a fair description of the way in which the social-democratic consensus broke down in the 1960s and 1970s – and could not be reconstituted in the 1980s – is a moot point. There is no shortage of structural explanations for why Labourism was undermined: the economic dilemmas in reconciling full employment with free collective bargaining, the sociological vulnerability associated with a significantly transformed class structure, the political obstacles against adaptation entrenched in the Labour Party's own constitution. These were serious problems which help explain why the forward march of Labour was halted in this period. Yet they indicate the nature of the challenge; they did not in themselves determine the necessary outcome. What actually happened was to some extent the result of contingency, and in that sense of will and skill and luck. The way that events unfolded presented various options and opportunities for leadership, notably to six men: Harold Wilson, James Callaghan, Denis Healey, Roy Jenkins, David Owen and David Steel. How well did they measure up? Might any of them have succeeded, and why did all of them fail, in the task of remaking the social-democratic Left?

The leadership of the Labour Party fell into Wilson's lap in 1963. When Gaitskell died unexpectedly, his following on the Right of the party was divided between the rival claims of George Brown and James Callaghan, and the Left congratulated itself on an uncovenanted triumph. The fact is, however, that all Wilson's instincts were centrist, and he was so successful, for a time, in staking out the middle ground because he took advantage of the multi-dimensional factionalism of the Labour Party. He was neither Left nor Right but a Bevanite revisionist. Socially, too, he fell outside the traditional stereotypes: neither a Bevinesque robust proletarian nor a Crippsian conscience-stricken toff. In fact he was the first major leader to represent the new ruling class – an upwardly mobile Oxbridge meritocracy recruited through provincial grammar schools – which was to take over during the next twenty-five years, producing Heath as well as Healey, Jenkins as well as Thatcher.

Wilson claimed to follow in Attlee's footsteps as leader, puffing away at his pipe while giving top priority to pragmatism and party unity. Already in the 1950s he had, like Crossman, settled for working with Gaitskell, on the general principle that politics is like rowing – 'the ideal solution is to get the boat along as quickly as possible without turning it over'. The doctrinal authority for such a view would have to be the conservative philosopher Michael Oakeshott rather than any socialist ideologue; and ultimately Wilson's pipemanship left him looking more like Baldwin than Attlee. But if his non-doctrinal outlook had led Wilson to co-operate with the revisionists in the 1950s, it also justified him in breaking with Gaitskell in 1960–61. Wilson was ready to swallow the dogmatic affirmation of Clause 4 in the confidence that it would be tempered by pragmatic application. Why upset the faithful by questioning the realism of the sermon on the mount? 'What Hugh Gaitskell never recognized,' Wilson concluded, 'was that from the Party's earliest days, a great number of converts had joined Labour because they believed that socialism was a way of making a reality of Christian principles in everyday life.' The road from Huddersfield Congregational Church to Downing Street was paved with composited resolutions.

Three crises illuminate Wilson's style and priorities. The first was the great sterling crisis of 1966, which called into question the compatibility of Labour's commitment to economic growth with an exchange rate set since 1949 at $2.80. The fact that Wilson had been involved in the last devaluation made him determined to defend the pound at its existing parity, a decision which probably did more than anything else to set the constraints under which his first Government laboured. In this he had the full backing of Callaghan as Chancellor, and on significantly similar reasoning. 'The Conservatives would have crucified us,' Callaghan subsequently explained. In conniving at the way that the parity of sterling was politicized, Wilson showed brilliant short-term tactical flair. He played the game of confidence with zest, finessing setbacks in the currency markets into a widely disseminated conspiracy myth about 'the gnomes of Zürich'. His patriotic stand was good party politics, which temporarily squared the circle by permitting growth in consumption at home while staving off mounting difficulties over the balance of payments. The result was Wilson's great electoral triumph of March 1966, turning a precarious parliamentary position into a majority of 100, thus pulling off his own confidence trick with the electorate in style to match Macmillan at his best.

Wilson's position, however, was rapidly revealed as less strong than it appeared, partly for external economic reasons, partly for internal political reasons. The looming choice was immediately obvious to Crossman, albeit as a minister who made no claims to economic expertise. 'The only way to prevent deflation is of course devaluation, which Wilson irrevocably opposes,' Crossman recorded in April 1966. 'So if he leaves things as they are, it looks as though we shall be driven into deflation and into a wage freeze at the same time.' But he also noted one of the reasons why an outcome which nobody really wanted was made more likely: 'Harold is obsessed by the feeling that the Common Marketeers, led by Michael Stewart, Roy Jenkins and Tony Crosland, are ganging up against him.' Wilson's fitful suspicion about Europe paled in comparison with his full-blown paranoia about his Cabinet colleagues.

Since entry to the European Community would require a

devaluation of sterling, its desirability – or undesirability in Wilson's view – was given further extraneous reinforcement. Hence, when the issue was forced by a run on the pound in July 1966, the alignment within the Cabinet became skewed by the identification of the Right as in favour of the Common Market and of the Left against it. Crossman found support at this juncture from Barbara Castle, who noted: 'We must state our intention to do everything necessary to put the balance of payments right, but that we are not going to try to defend the pound.' Tony Benn, too, though not yet a fully-paid-up member of the Left, was brought in. 'So the numbers had been mounting up all that day,' Crossman recorded (18 July). 'We had Roy, Tony Crosland, Tony Benn, Barbara Castle and myself all firmly committed to opposing a new package of cuts except as a preparation for floating off the pound.' As Brown had said to Castle, 'You are left-wing and I am supposed to be right-wing,' but on the big issues they were now united.

On the face of it, this was a sufficiently formidable combination to swing the Cabinet. Admittedly, Brown's own volatility ('he had drunk enough to be voluble, though not offensive') was not helpful in reaching a settlement. But he saw the real difficulty more clearly than anyone else – that he could not win because the Prime Minister's own authority was now at stake. He therefore challenged Castle's optimistic arithmetic about the Cabinet. 'No, this involves his leadership,' Brown told her. 'Do you want me as Leader, Barbara?' The answer was inevitably, and emphatically, No. Hence the Prime Minister could still win. 'And you will side with him,' Brown predicted to Castle, in a shaft of insight born of defeatist frustration.

The fact that deflationary measures were needed whether or not Britain devalued had hitherto been used as an argument for first deciding on the strategy of which they were to form part. But Wilson now pounced. If a decision *either way* on the exchange rate was premised on a deflationary package, this was a reason for giving top priority to the shape of the package. 'I'm not adamant against devaluation,' he blandly

assured Crossman, 'but we shall have to get the pound sta-
bilized first so that we can float from strength not from
weakness.' (Castle might have recalled her earlier comment,
'Can you see us devaluing when we *are* strong?') The Cabinet
was thus cajoled into following the Prime Minister's
programme, now larded with minor concessions to his critics
and promises of further concessions, especially the latter. 'If
we got through this crisis, we would have to work out a
strategy; and if the level of unemployment was to rise mark-
edly above 2 per cent (480,000), then he would consider
devaluation,' Crossman recorded. 'This was an assurance he
gave across the table to George Brown.' Brown was effectively isolated, in a conspiracy in which his own conduct
played a notable part; and having thrown down the gauntlet
of resignation, he then picked it up again. With the big
economic issue settled, in favour of a package to defend
the pound, Wilson set about mending his political fences,
confiding to Castle over a drink: 'You've been taken for a
ride by the Europeans, who only want to devalue to get us
in.' Though, on the spot, Castle at once denied this, a couple
of weeks later Crossman noted that, 'deeply influenced by
Harold's story', she was 'shaken by this and will take far
greater care in future'.

In a superbly judged exercise in dissimulation, Wilson had
succeeded in shifting the argument on to ground of his own
choosing and had called in his political debts in order to
reassert his mastery. Callaghan loyally renewed his subscription, year by year, to the conspiracy theory of history. Even
in his memoirs the story of his tenure at the Treasury turned
on recurrent emergency measures to counter misleading
reports in the *Observer* which were forever upsetting sterling.
The outcome, when Britain was forced to devalue after all in
November 1967, was thus fitted into an interpretation which
made the economic arguments subservient to the political
presentation. 'The man in the street,' Callaghan opined, 'felt
let down because he had been led to believe that if devaluation
took place, it would be a consequence of the Labour
Government's incompetence.' On this showing, perhaps the

man in the street may have been not very wide of the mark.

A second revealing crisis was that over reform of trade-union law in 1969. The Government's proposals here were the brainchild of Barbara Castle; she paid tribute to Bevan's *In Place of Fear* by calling her White Paper *In Place of Strife*; and her most loyal ally throughout was the Prime Minister. But the old Bevanites were joined by old Gaitskellites like Michael Stewart, Denis Healey and, above all, Roy Jenkins, now Chancellor. If one fracture line in the party had been healed, however, it was only at the price of reopening another. Now it was the trade-union vested interest which proved immovable against change, and in James Callaghan they found a fitting champion. Discredited at the Treasury in 1967, as Home Secretary Callaghan seized his chance to rebuild his position, not least within the Labour movement. Though in retrospect he complimented Castle on 'an exercise in brink-manship' which proved 'a brilliant success' in securing a commitment to voluntary reform from the TUC, the fact was that his clearly signalled opposition to *In Place of Strife* served to undermine the Cabinet's negotiating position. There was little doubt whom Stewart had in mind when he passed a note to Castle in Cabinet: '. . . anyone who lets you down at this stage is a prize shit'.

Once more, Wilson's leadership was at stake; once more, he had to live by his wits; once more, he survived. Callaghan's cause was that of old-fashioned Labourism; his challenge was overt, but that made it easier to foil. In a potential leadership struggle, Jenkins might have seemed a bigger threat. But his impeccable social democratic credentials aroused suspicion among party loyalists who zealously protected the status quo; and Jenkins personally was pledged to support Castle. Wilson was characteristically adroit in bluffing out the position almost to the last, seeking to bargain real concessions from the TUC even when he and Castle were virtually isolated in the Cabinet. Jenkins stuck to the letter of his agreement to support Castle but privately told her, as she noted, 'with that evasive look he has been developing lately, that I would have gathered that he no longer thought that the fight was worth the cost.

I replied that, yes, I have noticed it.' When the chips were down, Labour got the worst of both worlds in first acknowledging the need for reform and then backing down. Faced with the new axis of resistance forged between the TUC and the parliamentary Left, the Government was forced to withdraw proposals which, fifteen years later, trade-unionists would have gladly embraced as their salvation. Even Callaghan had to admit that the agreement reached with the TUC proved a dead letter because 'the unions failed to take heed' once the threat of legislation was withdrawn. One immediate effect was to cement Callaghan's own relations with the trade unions.

A third crisis confronted Wilson after he lost the 1970 General Election. Although in office he had come round to supporting an application to join the European Community, in opposition it all looked very different. Anti-Europeanism served as a populist cry which fuelled the Left's rise within the Labour Party. Whereas Jenkins resigned as deputy leader rather than renege on British membership, even though the conduct of negotiations was now in the hands of Heath's Conservative Government, Wilson adopted an uncomfortable posture on the fence. The charge against Wilson is plainly that his conduct was dishonourable; that in opposition he repudiated terms for membership which he would have had to accept if still in office; that he played party politics with a great national issue; and that his acceptance of continued membership once he returned as Prime Minister clinches the case on inconsistency. Yet, given the state of the Labour Party, and given Wilson's determination to stay on as leader, the net results of his strategy were paradoxical. His was a policy of appeasement which appeared to capitulate to the Left, but in fact bought time to fight later on more favourable ground; having betrayed the pro-Market Right in 1970–71 by refusing to support entry, Wilson went on to betray the anti-Market Left in 1974–5 by throwing his Government's support behind the campaign for an affirmative vote in the referendum on Britain's membership. The result was that a Labour Government, buttressed more firmly by public opinion than

Heath had ever been, was now unambiguously committed to the European Community. Could an honourable strategy have achieved as much?

It is not surprising that Labour loyalists like Denis Healey ultimately came to doubt whether more was possible. Healey was unambiguously a figure on Labour's right wing, and, as a young MP for a Leeds constituency in the 1950s, he was naturally drawn into Hugh Gaitskell's circle. By the time he wrote his memoirs, however, Healey's view of Gaitskell was tinged with scepticism 'whether the fierce puritanism of his intellectual convictions would have enabled him to run a Labour Government for long, without imposing intolerable strains on so anarchic a Labour movement'. As Wilson's Defence Secretary, Healey was the guardian of the Gaitskellite tradition in foreign policy. He was a reluctant convert to the abandonment of Britain's posture East of Suez; nonetheless the decision to withdraw, once taken, was implemented expeditiously so as to save money where Britain could no longer save face. Healey looked beyond the 'illusions of grandeur about our post-imperial role in Asia and Africa' which he discerned in Wilson. Though deeply affected by his own wartime experiences, notably as a beachmaster at Anzio, Healey did not lose sight of his essentially civilian role in making the defence establishment accountable. He was intellectually capable of responding to the challenges posed by defence strategies in face of a shifting balance of power and a rapidly evolving nuclear technology.

Over the British nuclear deterrent, Healey's approach can be termed either brutally pragmatic or woefully disingenuous; but, either way, it did him no good in the long run. Labour had no commitment to continuing the Polaris programme – rather the reverse – and Healey discovered in 1964 that the two hulls already laid down could have been converted into hunter-killer submarines at no extra cost. This news, however, was withheld from the Cabinet. 'Wilson wanted to justify continuing the Polaris programme on the grounds that it was "past the point of no return". I did not demur.' In a period of leapfrogging technological rivalry between the superpowers, however, the recurrent problem was still that of staving off British nuclear obsolescence by trying to cadge American weapons on the cheap. In the 1970s Polaris was eventually updated with Chevaline – a commitment inherited from the Heath Government which Healey came to regret not having scuppered when he became Chancellor in 1974. More than anyone else, he was responsible, by commission and omission, for the maintenance of 'a British bomb'. And it was this which became the dominant emotive symbol in the subsequent political controversy over defence, which might more pertinently have been focused on the clear issue of British membership of NATO. If Healey's career was ultimately stalled by the rise of unilateralism in the Labour Party, he can truly be said to have been hoist with his own petard.

The view of Wilson's first premiership (1964–70) as presented in Healey's memoirs in 1989 cannot be thought flattering. Wilson, it is said, lacked political principle and sense of direction, yawing between 'a capacity for self-delusion which made Walter Mitty appear unimaginative' and a propensity for paranoia which discerned conspiracy on every side. Yet Wilson's personal attributes are not represented as fundamentally disabling in a man who went on to lead the party into another decade. Indeed, the same characteristics are seen as functional in the context of Labour's fissiparous inconsistency over the Common Market in 1971. Healey commends Wilson's 'great courage' at this juncture in seeing that the Leader's 'overriding duty' was to secure party unity, 'fully aware of the ignoble role' which was demanded of him. Hence Wilson's feeling remark: 'I've been wading in shit for three months to allow others to indulge their consciences.' This, it is suggested, is the final measure of what the Labour Party owed to Harold Wilson – the Ordure of Merit.

Given advance warning of Wilson's impending resignation in 1976, Callaghan emerged as the candidate least likely to antagonize any major section of the party. He was ineradicably set in a deep-rooted tradition of Labourism: at once the greatest loyalist and the greatest disloyalist in the party. Reared amid desperate poverty, he rose to hold the four greatest offices of state. His memoirs endearingly evoke the air of an earlier generation of autobiographies by Labour leaders. ('My father had taken me aboard the *Victoria and Albert* when I was a toddler, but I did not suppose it ever crossed his mind that one day his son would be invited to return as the Prime Minister of the United Kingdom.') Elected as MP for Cardiff South in 1945, after a pre-war stint as a trade-union official, he served as a junior minister at Transport and at the Admiralty. Like George Brown, his competitor as the right-wing standard-bearer in the 1963 leadership election, Callaghan was a Gaitskellite who could claim authentic working-class trade-unionist roots. It was by rediscovering these in 1969 – digging them up and passing them for admiration from hand to horny hand – that Callaghan re-established his political credentials after his failure at the Treasury. The journalist Peter Jenkins dubbed him The Keeper of the Cloth Cap.

Wilson's departure in fact opened the era of clarification in Labour politics. His heritage of manipulative Labourism now faced a double challenge. On the left, the idiom of Marxism acquired a new cachet and a new militancy, neatly symbolized in the self-proclaimed conversion of the technocratic Bevanite Tony Benn. Conversely, on the right of the party there was a more self-conscious adoption of the language of social democracy. A good definition of social-democratic politics (and one cited by Healey) is that of the philosopher Lesjek Kolakowski: 'an obstinate will to erode by inches the conditions which produce avoidable suffering, oppression, hunger, wars, racial and national hatred, insatiable greed and vindictive envy'. Yet in the Labour Party most arguments had traditionally been conducted as a contest for the copyright on 'socialism' and by commending one's own side as better socialists than one's opponents. Hence in the 1950s Gaitskell and Crosland, though manifestly social democrats, were lured into tortuous attempts to redefine socialism so that revisionists too could claim to be good socialists. It may be an example of the British genius for seizing on an opprobrious epithet as a defiant self-appellation – the Old Contemptible syndrome. If the *Daily Express* called them socialists, who were the Gaitskellites to flinch from the description?

The fact is, however, that as an intellectual tradition social democracy had long constituted the main rival to socialism within the Labour Party. It is surely a gratuitous confusion to define socialism except in antithesis to capitalism. Socialists need capitalism like dogs need lamp-posts – that is, not primarily for illumination. The central socialist insight concerns the ownership of the means of production by a particular class under capitalism, and this gives rise to a consequent proposal for common ownership as the fundamental means of changing the system. Obviously there has been much in the Labour Party's policy, outlook and rhetoric – especially the latter – which has been consistent with socialist objectives. But historically the party has given priority to the persistent piecemeal tinkering of social democracy.

Equality has thus been more directly aimed at within a mixed economy, with welfare and fiscal measures supplying the means and social justice defining the ends. The trade unions, with their sectional interests in Labourism, generally went along with the social democrats so long as the system seemed to be working. Only when their claims became heavier than the existing mixed economy could conceivably bear were these demands dressed up in the borrowed clothes of socialism (a disguise easily penetrated despite the mediaspeak about 'militant unions'). This analysis is largely uncontentious. A Marxist, whether in the tradition of Lenin or Trotsky, would simply say that the onset of British economic decline marked the end of reformist attempts to prop up capitalism by buying off its natural antagonists. Thus we have an explanation for two phases in the Labour Party's recent history, answering at once both questions: What used to make the Right run? What then made the Left Trot?

In practice, three views could be taken about the Labour Party in this period, each with some verisimilitude. One was to accept its historic role as a class party, represented through the trade unions: to acknowledge its vested interests but to maintain that they were the right vested interests. With the rise of a more militant Left, such arguments became increasingly explicit. If this was hard-nosed and mechanistic, another view was soft-hearted and romantic: to glory in the party's peculiar, populist, radical heritage, albeit one so often corrupted by the machinations of the leadership. The old Bevanite Left took this line, eloquently conveyed by Michael Foot. A further position was more critical: to identify the developing structural weaknesses of a party ostensibly devoted to the cause of the disadvantaged but, in the literal sense, constitutionally incapable of resisting the entrenched sectionalism of the trade unions. This became the social democratic critique, first inside the Labour Party and subsequently outside.

Healey's outlook was compounded from aspects of all these views, as befitted his self-declared position as an 'eclectic pragmatist'. He was manifestly a cosmopolitan figure – well-travelled and multilingual – who could see perfectly well that 'the continental parties have adjusted much better to social and political change than the Labour Party', which remained 'still the most conservative party in the world'. Its constitution, he maintained, 'must be the weirdest in the world', vesting the block vote in the hands of a small number of power-brokers. Hence the Labour Party's inability to adapt to the sort of social changes which it had helped promote. 'The trade unions were now emerging,' Healey wrote of 1970, 'as an obstacle both to the election of a Labour Government and to its success once it was in power.' These difficulties intensified during the 1970s, especially during the period of Labour Government from 1974 to 1979 when Healey was Chancellor of the Exchequer.

Passed over as leader in 1976, Healey made pact of mutual support with Callaghan and together they dominated the Government. There is ground for a sympathetic defence of his record, faced with pressing external difficulties for which the conventional Treasury policies offered an inadequate remedy. Showing understandable irritation with self-styled Keynesians ('who had usually read no more of Keynes than most Marxists had read of Marx'), Healey later made no bones about saying, 'I abandoned Keynesianism in 1975.' To call him a convert to 'the monetarist mumbo-jumbo', however, has never been more than a polemical taunt, though one to which he laid himself open by publishing the Treasury's monetary targets, albeit in a spirit of weary cynicism.

In fact, his strategy was to obviate the necessity for the restrictionist measures of monetarism by relying on the trade unions to fulfil their side of a bargain with their own Government. In Healey's view, they did not. Callaghan likewise has claimed: 'I cannot be accused of failing to recognize that an incomes policy is a wasting asset, but I can be faulted for not finding a viable alternative before its credibility expired.' After two years of creditable success, the policy notoriously collapsed during the 'Winter of Discontent' in 1978–9, when the unions set out to break the Government's declared norm for pay settlements of 5 per cent. Healey was subsequently prepared to acknowledge 'hubris' in aiming at an anti-inflationary norm that proved too ambitious. Where did this crucial figure come from? Callaghan recalls mentioning it at a Cabinet meeting in December 1977, but, 'because no formal proposal was before the cabinet, there was no discussion of my 5 per cent suggestion and Ministers probably assumed I was thinking aloud – as indeed I was'. In the Prime Minister's New Year broadcast from Chequers, however, 'the 5 per cent idea hardened and popped out when the interviewer tempted me to outline my hopes for the coming year'.

Having popped out, it would not pop in again. Indeed, it became the basis for a disastrous confrontation between the Government and the trade unions. Callaghan later called it 'the latest demonstration of a truth we have all uttered to the effect that the fortunes of the unions and the Labour Party cannot be separated'. Healey more forthrightly apportioned the real blame for the Winter of Discontent and Labour's subsequent loss of power. 'The shambles was of course a triumph for Mrs Thatcher,' he wrote. 'The cowardice and irresponsibility of some union leaders in abdicating responsibility at this time guaranteed her election; it left them with no grounds for complaining about her subsequent actions against them.'

Yet his memoirs explain that 'the Labour Party's financial and constitutional links with the unions made it difficult for us to draw too much attention to their role in our defeat'. He calls Callaghan 'the best of Britain's post-war prime ministers after Attlee' but points out that he 'belonged to the generation of Labour leaders which had come to depend on the trade union block vote for protection against extremism in the constituencies'. Callaghan may have made this his stock-in-trade; but his position was one implicitly adopted by many old Gaitskellites who were more chary of admitting it. Behind a paper-thin screen of social-democratic theorizing, Gaitskell's leadership had relied on the block votes of the right-wing unions in the context of the Cold War. As these conditions passed, the hollowness of the social democrats' position was progressively exposed. When a number of them left the Labour Party to found the Social Democratic Party (SDP) in 1981, the taunt was that they were machine politicians whose machine had broken down. But was the main difference between them and Healey that he obstinately refused to acknowledge that the machine had broken down?

Roy Jenkins and Tony Crosland were the two most faithful Gaitskellites of the younger generation. Already by the late 1960s their paths had perceptibly diverged and their personal relations perceptibly cooled, partly as a result of a harder streak of ambition which each detected in the other. Crosland belatedly adopted the strategy he had once urged on Gaitskell: to go for power, not doctrine. In every crisis, it now seemed, he was tempted to draw back from confrontation by arguing that the issue was not worth a fight. He latterly found a faithful disciple in Roy Hattersley, who likewise opted for keeping his head down rather than sticking his neck out. Even had Crosland lived longer (his tragically early death came in 1977), it is likely that he would still have ended his days inside the Labour Party.

Jenkins, by contrast, had left the Cabinet in 1976, if not under a cloud, at least under a misapprehension. He was beginning to look like a busted flush with a brilliant career behind him. To be sure, he had been a great Home Secretary – back in the 1960s. He had been a successful Chancellor of the Exchequer: no mean feat, given the underlying state of the British economy. But was it so difficult to look better than the two Chancellors (Callaghan and Barber) between whom he was sandwiched? Jenkins, long identified as a Marketeer, had taken his stand on Britain's entry to the European Community in the early 1970s, fighting an unholy alliance between the Left and xenophobic populism. His resignation from the deputy leadership in 1972 appeared to be a conclusive setback; only in retrospect did it also look prescient. The deselected Labour MP Dick Taverne, fighting for his political life at Lincoln, privately appealed for Jenkins's support, suggesting that he 'could then lead a split away and form a new social democratic party'. Jenkins may have regretted not doing so; but delay served him well in making out his case.

Jenkins's relatively poor showing in the leadership election of 1976 sealed his fate in the Labour Party and fuelled a growing mutual antipathy. He was fortunate at this point to have the opportunity of a well-paid sabbatical away from British politics, with a four-year term as President of the European Commission in Brussels, in a high-flying ambience of avion taxis and astronomically expensive dinners – usually 'agreeable', sometimes 'highly agreeable' – at Comme Chez Soi. The diary he kept in exile traces the path he trod. If disenchantment with the Labour Party had marked Jenkins's departure for Brussels, his prospective return, when his term expired at the end of 1980, was not augured by any mellowness towards the new Conservative Government. Rather abruptly, from the summer of 1979, the diary introduces a new theme. It was to Bruno Kreisky, the Austrian Chancellor, that Jenkins 'disclosed a little of my thought about the re-orientation of British politics'. It was an appropriately cosmopolitan social-democratic context for such discussion. More piquantly, before his televised Dimbleby lecture in November

1979, when Jenkins aired his centrist thoughts, he received good advice from Sir Ian Gilmour, then one of Thatcher's ministers, who considered the draft 'too right-wing, and in particular objected to my using the phrase "the social market economy"!' It was Gilmour, too, who predicted that a new party might conceivably find it easier to achieve quick success than to advance slowly.

When the urbane biographer of Asquith undertook the Dimbleby lecture, he was clearly prompted by his historical studies in broaching his theme. He pointed to the way that the Labour Party had 'achieved a remarkable feat in breaking through the defences of the system to replace the Liberal Party'. He was among the first to popularize the measurable decline in the electoral hold of the two-party model over the previous thirty years. He banged home the point: 'The Labour party in 1951 polled 40 per cent of the total electorate, including those who stayed at home, and it just lost. In October 1974 it polled 28 per cent and it just won.' The sharpening polarization of the Labour and Conservative Parties was thus accompanied by a shrinking of their islands of support, as social class became a less adequate guide to political allegiance. The inference was put rather tentatively: 'the possibility that a break-out *might* now succeed'.

The chances could not realistically have been put higher. 'If history is any guide,' wrote one historian at the time, 'the prospects for a breakaway party are, of course, appallingly bad.' It took no great insight to predict as much when the SDP was launched, and with hindsight its failure can be given the gloss of inevitability. 'I was not surprised by the consequences of that unhappy experiment,' Healey concludes, 'right-wing breakaways from left-wing parties have never come to anything.' This confident proposition, of course, imports undeclared postulates about the meaning of left and right, and their unchanging relevance to a static class structure and a given role for trade unions – postulates which, in other compartments of Healey's eclectic mind, had long since been discarded. The real trouble with historical precedents is that they hold good only so long as things go on in the same old way. But now and again things do change, in quite remarkable and unpredicted ways, which only start looking inevitable in retrospect. It was easy to see, therefore, that the social democrats might simply be sending up the old cry of wolf. But the last time that the boy cried wolf, the wolf really came, and tore him limb from limb. Sensible people, however, were too shrewd to be taken in by his feverish appeals – they knew, of course, that something was eating the boy but suspected that it was thwarted exhibitionism.

It can be said, then, that Jenkins's decision to back his hunch in the Dimbleby lecture was at most foolhardy rather than simply foolish. Anticipating the charge that his was 'an unashamed plea for the strengthening of the political centre', Jenkins simply retorted: 'Why not?' Coupled with the break-out strategy, this identified him with the notion of a centre party. He knew what he wanted; and he foresaw one side of the SDP fairly accurately in surmising that 'such a development could bring into political commitment the energies of many people of talent and goodwill who, though perhaps active in many other voluntary ways, are at present alienated from the business of government, whether national or local, by the sterility and formalism of much of the political game'. But there was another side to the SDP, as it subsequently took shape, consisting of social democrats who, in 1979, saw no advantage in leaving Labour for a putative centre party. Shirley Williams spoke for many when she said it would have 'no roots, no principles, no philosophy and no values'.

By 1979 the crisis of Labourism had unmistakably arrived. The theme of the crusade for accountability which Tony Benn now launched was the intolerability of the Labour Party proclaiming one set of objectives in opposition and acting on different priorities in government. This discrepancy, he maintained, had become vexatious and self-defeating, sapping credibility and morale. With much of this social democrats could agree. Generally speaking, they found much to commend in the Labour Governments of the years, say, 1967–70 and 1975–8. But these were, of course, precisely the years of betrayal according to the orthodoxy of the paranoid Left.

So any notion of the Labour Party learning the lesson of consistency by building upon its record here, and promising more of the same, was bound to come to grief after the defeat of the Callaghan Government in 1979. The only terms on which the consistency could now be achieved were those offered by the Left. The old inconsistent answer of Wilsonian Labourism was that captured by David Owen's seminal concept of 'fudging and mudging'.

Healey, the most formidable figure on the social democratic wing of the party, showed that he accepted much of this analysis; but he was frankly unprepared to draw radical inferences from it, because he too remained rooted in so many of the conventional assumptions of Labourism. No doubt there were personal as well as intellectual reasons for his stance, so that 'any thought of leaving was ruled out by my sense of loyalty to my friends in Leeds'. Temperamentally, too, the 'inertia and indifference' which had stopped him throwing in his lot with Jenkins and Crosland in student politics in 1940, when they had led a breakaway from the Communist-led Labour Club, now came into play on a bigger stage. Healey had so many reasons to stay in the Labour Party that the issue was truly overdetermined. He still hoped against hope that, if only he kept his head down, a bit of opportunistic tinkering with the old machine could stick things together again. Hence his circumspect refusal to take a stand against the constitutional proposals put forward in 1980 – 'The fight I was being asked to lead would have had no prospect of victory' – and his continual calculation on the likelihood of this or that union delegation delivering its block vote, by hook failing crook, by accident failing design. This was fudging and mudging of a high order. Healey's tactics were not only inglorious but unsuccessful; they left him roundly defeated for the leadership on Callaghan's retirement.

The division between those social democrats who were if necessary prepared to break with the Labour Party and those who were determined to stay at all costs was in the end cultural as much as ideological. Roy Jenkins, as the son of a union official on the South Wales coalfield, had gilt-edged credentials in the historic working-class movement but was too fastidious to trade on them. Instead his persona was not what he had been but what he had become – a meritocratic intellectual for whom Oxford had opened the doors to a cosmopolitan life which he manifestly enjoyed while persistently proclaiming the gilt-edged politics of 'conscience and reform'. 'Claret' was the pejorative code-word for all this. Shirley Williams was another rootless intellectual; she had spent her teens as an evacuee in the USA and later sat in Parliament until 1979 for the new town of Stevenage, the epitome of the socially mobile environment where the SDP was to flourish. As against this, Labour maintained a traditional identity in parts of provincial England, as well as in Scotland and Wales, which held the loyalty of some younger politicians who were well able to discern the party's defects. Thus Roy Hattersley, with the same social democratic principles on his lips, had his heart elsewhere. He was an accomplished essayist who disclosed an imaginative world somewhat down-market from that of Alan Bennett: a time-warp where Mr Attlee was always Prime Minister, Yorkshire were always playing at home, and aspiring artisans queued for improving books at the public library. In the end Labour was to be saved not on its merits, which were shallow, but by its roots, which were deep; and, in particular, by Scotland, where the SDP never looked plausible.

The precariousness of Jenkins's initiative in 1979 is tellingly brought out in his diary. He made little impression on the 'Gang of Three', with David Owen hostile, Bill Rodgers initially unpersuaded, and Shirley Williams uncertain. When Jenkins followed the Dimbleby lecture with a widely-reported Press Gallery speech in June 1980, he privately wondered if it had been 'a major tactical error. It took me to a ledge on the cliff-face from which it was going to be very difficult to get up or down.' But the Gang of Three did not rise to the bait; in a statement published in the *Guardian* in August they reaffirmed that 'we will not support a Centre

Party for it would lack roots and a coherent philosophy'. In this desperate situation, however, Jenkins was saved by forces beyond his control – indeed, at that time, beyond anyone's control – namely, the Labour Party itself. Week by week, its collective behaviour gratuitously made out Jenkins's case for him and recruited him an army to lead. 'I now feel much easier about the political situation and whatever it may hold,' he recorded in October 1980; and there was better news to come in November, when Foot was elected leader. With an unwonted rush of blood to the head – 'I cannot pretend that I was other than elated' – the President of the Commission prepared to pack his bags. After 'my last avion taxi back to Brussels', after the farewell visit to Comme Chez Soi, the exile found his return to British politics more agreeable than he had feared.

'If you remain in a beleaguered citadel you must necessarily look for a relieving force,' Jenkins had argued in the Dimbleby lecture, with reference to the deteriorating position of the social democrats in the Labour Party. Otherwise, stalemate or surrender were the only possibilities. But the only source from which a relieving force could come was 'the power and money of the trade union leadership, increasingly irritated by the intransigence of the left'. He dismissed such a development as unhealthy, because it would make Labour 'more and not less of a trade union party'. Only with the Labour Party's Wembley conference in January 1981, establishing the unions as the masters of Labour's new electoral college, was Jenkins's analysis vindicated: his vision turned into a nightmare for the social democrats.

By now the Gang of Three had come together with Jenkins to make a Gang of Four and had effectively decided that a new party must be created; but a strong section of the Manifesto Group, led by Roy Hattersley, were still committed, as they put it, to continuing the fight within the Labour movement – or, as their critics said, to accepting defeat. It was on the issue of trade-union control of the party that the split came at Wembley. 'One member, one vote' had belatedly become the social democrats' cry, which was to be upon their lips as they rehearsed a noble death. There was only one possible hitch at this stage – suppose, by some fluke, they carried the day? It was all right on the night, of course. The deals which stitched up the block votes in order to produce a crushing victory for the Left now looked like an object lesson in cynicism and showed the shape of things to come.

If this result was fit for Saturday night, the Limehouse Declaration was perfect for Sunday morning (25 January 1981). 'The calamitous outcome of the Labour Party Wembley Conference demands a new start in British politics,' it declared. 'A handful of trade union leaders can now dictate the choice of a future Prime Minister.' There was admittedly one inconsistency in the position of these old Gaitskellites, which it needed time to obviate. For, if they were questioned on their own record in the Labour Party, did it not emerge that they had relied upon these very methods themselves? How had Gaitskell turned defeat into victory over unilateralism in 1960–61, except by squaring the union bosses? The Campaign for Democratic Socialism, with William Rodgers as full-time organizer, could never have been vindicated without assuring itself of trade-union support. Moreover, Shirley Williams sat for years on the NEC, and was thereby able to conduct her long rearguard action, precisely because the block votes had been sewn up, conference by conference, in order to put her there.

The most graphic demonstration of this system in action, however, was to come in the contest for deputy leader between Tony Benn and Denis Healey. The voting at the October 1981 conference, with a million votes labelled TGWU flopping to and fro at the whim of the power brokers, showed the price at which the Left could be stopped. If Healey was eventually declared the winner in the new electoral college, it was only by a decimal place of nothing in particular. The elections for the NEC at the 1982 conference were to prove even more wonderful. Were 600,000 NUPE votes mislaid? Hardly surprising, with so many vicariously regimented members to account for. Had the NUR really failed to deliver its mandated vote to the NUM candidate because the NUM had renounced a longstanding reciprocal agreement to back an NUR candidate? Did the outcome look like a swing to the Left, or a rebuff to the Right, or simply an affront to any decent sense of political integrity? When the deals that had been stitched up in private came unstitched in public, the system was widely indicted as a democratic veneer upon trade-union vote-jobbing.

The Limehouse Declaration – originally drafted by Jenkins – proclaimed 'the need for a realignment of British politics' while dismissing 'the politics of an inert centre'. This was a nice ploy against those who quoted back the Gang of Three's rejection of centrism, but it could not disguise the fact that they had in fact changed their tune. Since, in the meanwhile, they had also turned their coats, this acknowledged the fact that some elementary tune/coat correlation is *de rigueur* in politics. Jenkins might endorse the call 'for more, not less, radical change in our society, but with a greater stability of direction'. The SDP was nonetheless a centre party *faute de mieux*. It was essentially Jenkins's strategy which prevailed.

When he was elected leader of the SDP in July 1982 this marked a major accomplishment in political rehabilitation. In one of his historical essays Jenkins identified persistent ambition as the crucial ingredient in the achievement of supreme power in British politics. In 1979–82 he confounded those who had written him off by showing that he was a man who made his own luck. It was not, in fact, at all lucky that the first by-election after the launch of the SDP cropped up in Warrington, nor, when Shirley Williams hesitated, was it an obvious blessing to find the candidature on offer. It required decisive action to seize hold of a disintegrating situation, and dogged professionalism to hang on until the prospects ripened. Old Smoothiechops was on a hiding to nothing, as his former comrades in the Labour Party gleefully pointed out. The impact of the Warrington result in July 1981, when Jenkins narrowly lost but showed for the first time that it was possible to rip open the soft underbelly of the Labour vote, was thus a milestone in the SDP's advance.

Back in 1958 Crossman had observed that Labour's constituency was 'growing squashier and squashier and less and
less solid, so that one fine day a sudden landslide could take a
whole section of it off us'. If this comment benefited from
foresight as an adumbration of what was now happening, later
comments have often suffered from hindsight. To convey a
contemporary perspective, authentic albeit sympathetic, I can
only offer an assessment which I published in October 1981:

> Liberals and Social Democrats, standing together, seem to have
> tapped a reservoir of popular support which has been quietly
> welling up for a long time. The immediate conditions of their
> present success can hardly be expected to last. Thatcherism may
> soon be buried, and the Labour Party may have no stomach for
> the strenuous regime prescribed by Benn. But the deep wounds
> inflicted by the Thatcher Experiment will not heal quickly, and the
> reassertion of old-fashioned trade-union control over the Labour
> Party is merely a recipe for the sort of immobilism which led to
> the present frustrations. Moreover, there are subterranean springs
> which cannot be dammed – changes in the political sociology of
> modern Britain which leave the Labour Party's power base looking
> like an anachronistic anomaly. The working alliance with the
> Liberals might never materialize and the SDP could well fail in its
> mould-breaking enterprise. Historical inertia may prove an all too
> stubborn antagonist. But it is by no means obvious that things can
> go on as they are in British politics.

David Steel ended up with the ambivalent distinction of being
the last leader of the historic Liberal Party. But, for a moment
at the beginning of the 1980s, Steel found himself in a pivotal
position in seeking to remould British politics. It is for the
strategy of the Alliance between the Liberals and the SDP
that he will be remembered – and judged. One reason why
it looked so promising in its early days was because one party
was led by a man who was quintessentially a liberal and the
other by a man who was fundamentally a social democrat.
Roy Jenkins, of course, was the liberal and David Steel the
social democrat. Observations like this never did Steel any
good in the eyes of Liberal purists, making their toes curl up

in their sandals. Though no one fought harder to keep the party going, for Steel this was never an end in itself: he wanted to see the party going places. And for this he needed allies. He could readily cite statements testifying to his vision, going all the way back to his days in student politics at Edinburgh University. 'The emergence of a social democratic party may well come from a union of the Liberal Party and the Labour Right,' he had said in 1960.

Elected to Parliament in 1965 as 'the boy David', Steel soon made his mark. His Abortion Bill brought an early contact with Jenkins at the Home Office. The notion of a realignment on the left, put forward by Jo Grimond as Liberal leader in the 1960s, found an ardent young supporter. When Jeremy Thorpe, as Grimond's successor, fell prey to scandal, the upshot was to make Steel party leader at the age of thirty-eight in 1976. In his twelve years in the post he drove his flock like a Border sheepdog, not without some snapping at the stragglers, in the direction he desired. He made them face compromise in a pact with the Labour Government and he succeeded in holding the line at the 1979 General Election. Above all, he responded imaginatively to Jenkins's initiative for a new party, and to the split in the Labour ranks which gave it a constituency. Instead of strangling the social democrats at birth, as the Liberal MP Cyril Smith recommended, Steel decided to 'smother them in kindness and assume a putative alliance'.

It may not be true that Jenkins was dissuaded from joining the Liberal Party by Steel, but plainly the two men were working together from Brussels days onwards to create a new opening on the centre-left. The Alliance was thus peculiarly the fruit of their efforts. From the start of his leadership, Steel had been educating his party 'to be an altogether tougher and more determined force' rather than 'just a nice debating society'. Just as this son of the manse had put his life savings on a bet that he would win the by-election which first returned him to Parliament, so he now revealed an extraordinary capacity to play for high stakes. 'The road I intend us to travel may be a bumpy one,' he warned, 'and I recognize therefore the risk that in the course of it we may lose some of the passengers, but I don't mind so long as we arrive at the end of it reasonably intact and ready to achieve our goals.' This was what he told the Liberal Assembly at Llandudno in 1976, and he was able to quote it back to the Assembly when it returned to Llandudno in 1981. By then the political landscape had been changed by the unveiling of the Alliance, a conception undoubtedly forged under the steady and intense ambition of two men who knew their own minds.

It was the Alliance which offered the Liberal Party a prospect of promotion from the periphery of British politics to a central role; equally, it was the Alliance which made the SDP more than a transiently interesting splinter group. The proverbial alternatives – hanging together or hanging separately – were sharply posed. Thus the electoral system constituted the tactical imperative on which the Alliance was founded. Dedicated to electoral reform, it was numbly aware that reform could be achieved only by working within the constraints of the unreformed system. Logically, perhaps, those in each party who were keenest to preserve their distinct identities in the long run ought meanwhile to have been readiest for any sacrifices to keep the Alliance together in the short run until the system could be changed. At a number of levels, however, the Jenkins–Steel strategy encountered a formidable opponent, and one who offered a strikingly different sort of leadership.

David Owen's family background was almost pure Tafia. Great-grandfather Morgan was a Congregational minister who spent some time in America. Great-grandfather Llewellyn was a prosperous grocer – the sort of self-made Liberal businessman who hobnobbed with Lloyd George. His son started as a Methodist minister but ended up as a parson in the Church of Wales. The Owens, meanwhile, were shipowners in Penarth; grandfather Owen became a sea captain; father a doctor in Ynysybwl, until he moved, not inappropriately, to Plymouth. English public school and Cambridge turned young David into the forceful public man who became a national figure as a stop-gap Foreign Secretary following Crosland's death in 1977. The youngest appointment since Eden, he matched him in his dashing looks and the vanity of his further ambitions.

From early schooldays – 'I was good at games, all games, but a bad loser. If I didn't win, I'd sulk' – to the heady eminence of the Foreign Office, it was the same story: 'I wanted to be in the driver's seat, and take full responsibility for the direction in which we would go.' He maintained a vivid recollection of the lesson he read, as a fourteen-year-old, at his grandfather's memorial service: 'Put on the whole armour of God, and stand against the wiles of the devil.' In his career he was rarely spared from the obligation to apply this maxim. Disillusioned with Crosland's equivocation over the Common Market, disappointed with Hattersley's refusal to back Jenkins in resigning as deputy leader, Owen vainly enjoined Healey to put on his armour in 1980.

Owen found his only allies, therefore, in the Gang of Four. But, he recalled, especially on relations with the Liberals, 'I found myself becoming increasingly a minority voice and then somewhat inhibited by a collective decision of the four of us.' First, Rodgers let him down by talking of an equal division of seats under the terms of an electoral alliance. Then Jenkins kept him in the dark about his real vision of the Liberals. When Rodgers and Williams started talking informally to Steel, things began to go 'critically wrong' so far as Owen was concerned. At its Llandudno conference in 1981, the Liberal Party was swept off its feet at a fringe meeting addressed by Williams, Jenkins and Steel. When it came to settling the terms of an electoral pact, Owen realized that he must himself stand against the wiles of the devil – alone, if necessary.

What Owen could not accept was that the Alliance was founded not only upon a tactical imperative but upon an ideological affinity. His attitude to the Liberals was an amalgam of distrust and disdain, and he regarded joint selection of candidates as the thin end of the wedge – or rather the fudge. To be sure, there were irreconcilable purists on the Liberal side too. It was plausible to think of the Liberals as essentially a cranks' party, whereas the SDP was a prigs' party. Yet these stereotypes seldom survived face-to-face encounters in the constituencies, when both sides came together to talk and work with each other. Indeed, the difficulty became that of finding a convincing answer to the question of what really distinguished them. The cause of such friction as arose was not mainly philosophical but territorial, when it came to allocating constituencies between the two wings of the Alliance.

This proved an intractable business, reflecting a real difference in the nature of the parties. The Liberal Party was old and established and particularist. It had fought the good fight over the years and had carved out its niche in British politics; or rather it had carved out hundreds of little niches up and down the country, each one the product of its own sweat and self-sacrifice. And while this patient, painful, unglamorous groundwork was being done, the people who later called themselves SDP were either trying to undo it or else professing that politics was a dirty game. When the Little Red Hen, who had much the same experience, was asked at the end of the day to share the fruit of her labours, she made the memorable reply: 'Oh no, I shall eat it myself.'

The SDP was founded with the possibility of the Alliance already in view. Most of its members signed up to work not against the Liberals but with them in a common endeavour. The structure of the party was centralized, built around a national plan of campaign. Above all, the SDP started with no electoral capital, unless one counts the local following of the couple of dozen Labour MPs who defected to it. In entering negotiation with the Liberals over the allocation of parliamentary constituencies, therefore, the SDP found that its weakness was its strength – it had no vested interests – and it could establish a structure capable of settling a rational scheme of priorities. But it also found that its strength was its weakness, since the Liberal negotiators could not guarantee to deliver the goods. Parity was a fine principle; but the costs to the SDP were mainly the opportunity costs of renouncing dreams; those to the Liberals were often the actual costs of giving up something tangible. The SDP simply wanted a *quid pro quo*; the Liberals simply asked, whose quid?

Owen regarded the final allocation as a gross affront, and could quote a Liberal boast that they 'stitched up the SDP, make no mistake about it'. In Owen's view, 'the SDP stitched itself up'. In the winter of 1981–82, he recalled, 'we were trying to agree an allocation not even based on the balance of power at Westminster, where the SDP had twenty-eight MPs and the Liberals twelve'. Yet no conceivable arrangement could have followed these proportions. The Liberals had won their seats, and could confidently expect more from their own efforts. What the SDP brought to the Alliance was the prospect of capturing new ground. Could Owen really have imagined that an old firm like the Liberals would have made over most of their hard-earned assets in a takeover financed on junk bonds?

Repeatedly, Owen showed little understanding about what made the Alliance tick. Instead he chose, on a number of levels, to present the anti-liberal face of the SDP. This was a consistent stance, elaborated with passion and hard-hitting skill in communication. From the time of Suez onward, he said later, 'I never identified with the liberal – with a small "l" – establishment.' His was a populism which responded with telling readiness to the appeal of resurgent British nationalism, abhorring 'the "haul down the flag" philosophy, the belief that we're all just European now'. The difference in style and outlook between him and Jenkins was always apparent. Owen was the more effective in presenting a clear-cut image to the public, and he was aided in raising his profile by the course of events.

The very logo of the SDP, using red, white and blue, was envisaged by Owen as countering 'the Tory Party's belief that they exclusively could conduct their operations under the aegis of the Union Jack'. It was hardly surprising, therefore, that during the Falklands War in 1982 Owen should have missed no opportunity to wrap himself in those remnants of the flag which were not already draping Thatcher. It seemed to him 'a test of how the British lion should behave when somebody really twisted its tail'. Not for nothing was an independent nuclear capacity the Owenite test issue, transposing subtle arguments about deterrence, weapons systems, resources and alliances in a changing world, into a brute display of a virility symbol. 'To retreat from the view that Britain should be a nuclear weapon state,' he declared, 'is to retreat from the view that Britain has an influence which is greater than our economic strength.' The seeds of Owen's subsequent breach with the Liberals are thus not hard to find – and not just in the small print of policy statements.

The window of opportunity, which opened unexpectedly wide for the Alliance, was to close with equally unexpected swiftness. Just as events conspired in its favour during the twelve months from October 1980, so they conspired against it in the following year. An intelligent Labour politician like Healey could well appreciate the potential fragility of the two-party system in 1981–2, as his memoirs show. He writes of Benn that 'when he came close to capturing the Party machine, he came close to destroying the Labour Party as a force in twentieth-century politics'. If Benn had been elected deputy leader in 1981 instead of himself, Healey asserts, 'I do not believe the Labour Party could have recovered.' And since the outcome of that contest was so unpredictably close, and determined in such a bizarre fashion, the survival of the *ancien régime* in British politics must surely have been less than predestined. Moreover, far from lending comfort to the Tories, the Alliance was at this stage rightly seen by them as the only effective threat to their position. As Healey admits, it was the Falklands which restored the fortunes of the Thatcher Government, causing 'a collapse in support for the Alliance, which never recovered'.

This is much the same moral as Steel drew; the tide in the affairs of men had not been taken at the flood, and the rest of the story is, for all its vicissitudes, 'bound in shallows and in miseries'. For the Alliance's performance in the 1983 election, though formidable by third-party standards, fell short of a breakthrough. A poll of 25.4 per cent nationally was only 2 per cent short of Labour, but it returned only twenty-three

MPs to Labour's 209. Even if the Falklands factor accounted for only a 5 per cent swing from the Alliance to the Conservatives, the shape of a very different result can be discerned – one with Labour in third place and the Alliance challenging the Government. Jenkins read the writing on the wall, for himself if not for the SDP, and handed over to Owen. The logic of a merger with the Liberals was now implacably resisted by the new leader. It was a veto which Steel accepted after this General Election, with unfortunate consequences, but challenged after the next, with consequences that proved appalling.

These events repeated a cycle – the first time as tragedy, the second time as farce – from which the Alliance could not escape. Perhaps what needs explaining is not so much the failure of the breakthrough strategy, once the Falklands had robbed the Alliance of the necessary momentum, but the refusal of the SDP to lie down and die during the 1983 Parliament. Labour's refusal to respond to its electoral lessons with a reappraisal of strategy that was more than cosmetic kept the door open for a third party. The SDP's greatest by-election victory was actually achieved in February 1987 at Greenwich, for the first time capturing a safe Labour seat and briefly recapturing the hopes of its founders. Only a month before the General Election of June 1987 one national opinion poll (Gallup) showed the Alliance ahead of Labour. But the final result put the Alliance almost as far behind Labour as it, in turn, was behind the Conservatives (23/32/43 per cent). The stresses between Steel and Owen, which had been hinted at during the campaign, were now resolved – into a full-scale blazing row about whether to merge the two parties. Yet again the ambivalent fact that the appeal of the SDP rested upon its immediate merits turned sour the moment its image soured. Opinion polls recorded a catastrophic drop in support, with no sociological lagging or dampening effect, and the Alliance's challenge to the two-party system evaporated into thin air. Easy come, easy go.

Social democrats might well ask, was it all worth it? Those who stayed in the Labour Party could point, in the end, to its re-emergence as an electable alternative to Thatcherism. But a humiliating price had been exacted. Healey knew this better than anyone, from the time he was narrowly elected as Michael Foot's deputy at the end of 1981. 'I felt myself compelled to agree with Michael in public on all issues at all times,' he admits in his memoirs. It was hardly a happy position; and a less robust and pragmatic man might have found it unbearable. On the defence issue, which came back to haunt him, Healey was not, of course, convinced by any of the versions of official Labour Party policy which emerged in these years, but contented himself during the General Election of 1983 with a 'feeble statement of my real views' on a radio phone-in programme. His excuse that Labour did not nail itself to an explicitly unilateralist policy until after the 1983 election cuts both ways; on his role in fighting the 1987 election on a defence policy to which he was, therefore, unambiguously opposed, his memoirs were to remain discreetly silent. The old Gaitskellite had evidently resolved not to fight and not to fight and not to fight again to save the party he loved.

Healey has written percipiently of the contradictions of politics, as a necessary but flawed process, in which moral uprightness is not a sufficient guarantee of constructive achievements. Stating these precepts, of course, is one thing and applying them is another. Politics, Healey argues, means accepting the 'constraints and disciplines' of party, and entails 'acquiescing in policies you dislike until you can persuade your party to change them. It will often bring defeat – and sometimes personal humiliation.' This begins to sound like his own bid for the Ordure of Merit.

It is undeniable that, by 1990, Labour had accepted a range of policies – on Europe, on defence, on the trade unions, on one-member-one-vote – which, back in 1981, would have been unthinkable. They would, at any rate, have been unthinkable for Labour, though their thrust was actually not so different from what the SDP originally stood for, however embarrassing this came to seem on both sides. It could be argued that Labour had belatedly adopted through bitter experience much the same posture which the SDP had adopted a decade previously through intelligence and fore-sight. In the world at large, moreover, a rigorously socialist analysis, founded on the class struggle and public ownership, was now looking very tatty; whereas the relevance of a liberal analysis, seeking to extend social democracy only on the essential basis of political freedom, had been vindicated by experience, much of it painful. In the battle of institutions, the Alliance had lost all ends up; in the battle of ideas it had won hands down.

Margaret Thatcher with Norman Tebbit at her heels (© *The Times*, 13 May 1987)

13

THATCHERISM:

THE REMAKING OF THE CONSERVATIVE PARTY

If Gladstone had the distinction of becoming Prime Minister four times, it was partly because his governments never retained a majority in successive Parliaments. In the thirty years after the Second Reform Act, the swing of the pendulum became the rule, so much so that the traditionalist Salisbury was disconcerted when his Government was nonetheless returned in the 1900 General Election. In the twentieth century, the Liberal Government won three elections in a row before the First World War (in 1906 under Campbell-Bannerman and twice in 1910 under Asquith). The Conservatives matched this record after the Second World War (in 1951 under Churchill, in 1955 under Eden and in 1959 under Macmillan). This was a unique example of a one-way pendulum which, in four successive General Elections after 1945, moved towards the Conservatives. Wilson sometimes mistakenly claimed to have equalled Gladstone's achievement in serving four times as Prime Minister. The fact is that he served twice but was twice re-elected during his tenure, each time as the result of a snap election intended to convert a knife-edge result into a working majority – a policy which yielded handsome returns in 1966 but barely broke even in October 1974. Margaret Thatcher only served as Prime Minister once, but her eleven and a half years at Number Ten comfortably surpassed Asquith's record, and in winning three successive General Elections she did enough to make the great Lord Salisbury turn in his grave.

Thatcher's accession signalled the end of what has been called 'the Keynesian social democratic consensus', which had prevailed since the end of the Second World War. It is generally agreed that this consensus had three main planks. The first was the commitment to 'a high and stable level of employment after the war', as proclaimed by Churchill's Coalition Government in 1944. In practice this meant that demand management on Keynesian lines was the basis of Treasury policy. The second was the Welfare State, as created by the legislation of Attlee's Labour Government in the 1940s. Not only did this extend and reinforce a social security system based on state-subsidized insurance but, through the National Health Service, it aimed to provide free medical care for the whole population, financed from general taxation. The third feature was a mixed economy, in which there was a large role for state intervention. Together these policies formed a stable and interlocking triangle and, despite modifications and changes of emphasis, the framework of consensus was broadly accepted by both parties for about thirty years.

There were, however, dissident voices within the Conservative Party, of which one was unmistakably distinctive, undeniably insistent – and arguably prescient. The fact that the post-war liberal consensus was ultimately undermined – pronounced morally unsound, declared politically bankrupt – inevitably raises queries about the supposed failure of Enoch Powell's political career. Being a Powellite in the early 1970s never remotely attained the cachet of being a Thatcherite in the early 1980s; but the parable of Enoch the Parliamentary Leper, with which liberals comforted each other in the 1960s, has subsequently been challenged by the story of Enoch the Baptist. He was not that light; but the notion that Enoch was sent to bear witness of that light makes a suggestive opening to the Thatcherite gospel.

Of course, things are not so simple. In fact, making Powell *easy* to understand does violence to the very nature of a man who did everything the hard way. His early education at home – Harmsworth's Encyclopaedia at the age of four – reads like a lower-middle-class simulacrum of that inflicted on John Stuart Mill, and produced the same result in inculcating not only lifelong habits of intellectual application but also professions of filial gratitude for the experience. The undergraduate at Trinity College, Cambridge, poring over his classical texts, was almost wholly unsocialized: 'I literally worked from half past five in the morning until half past nine at night behind a sported oak, except when I went out to lectures.' The Master's wife found her invitation to dinner declined by the young man from Wolverhampton, who politely informed her that he would be too busy working.

Such were the methods which gained Powell the Craven Scholarship in 1931, the Chancellor's Classical Medal, the Browne Medal and the Porson Prize in 1932, First Class Honours in the Classical Tripos in 1933, a Fellowship at Trinity in 1934, and the Chair of Greek at Sydney University in 1937. The outbreak of the Second World War put paid to all that: the professor resigned, flew home, joined up as a private, and gave his classical library to Trinity. Yet Powell's facility in scaling the academic rungs stood him in good stead as he discovered in the Army another ladder for his relentless ascent: to lance-corporal, to second lieutenant, to captain on the General Staff by 1940; to major, to lieutenant-colonel by 1942; to full colonel and to brigadier by 1944. We can see the same unforgiving drive to succeed, the same mastery of arcane detail, the same rigorous perfectionism, the same scorn for comfort, the same intolerance of human frailty and indifference to what others thought of him. He ended the war in India, a mad dog of an Englishman who went out in the midday sun in full-dress uniform, having risen early in the morning to draft unavailing recommendations on how to perpetuate the British Raj. This was the remarkable young man who put himself at the disposal of the Conservative Party on his demobilization in 1946.

The Conservative Research Department in those days regarded itself as a cut above the party hacks housed around the corner in Smith Square. One might expect that the effortless superiority evinced by the clever young chaps in Old Queen Street would have suited Powell perfectly (except for the lack of effort, of course), and he certainly found congenial colleagues when he was put, three to a room, alongside Reginald Maudling and Iain Macleod. Here was the nursery of statesmen for the Conservative Cabinets of the 1960s. Yet Powell already stood apart from these easy-going men, deplorably tainted with pragmatism and suspiciously tinctured with liberalism, with their irritating knack of always finding an easy berth. On his own hard road to Westminster, with nineteen rejections behind him, Powell was ultimately adopted as Conservative candidate in the 1950 General Election for his native Wolverhampton.

The story that Powell was planning to reconquer India with ten divisions, which Rab Butler later liked to retail, may be a canard; but the centrality of the Empire to Powell's thinking is unmistakable. He did not assuage his regrets over the loss of Britain's imperial role by looking towards Europe, still less by swathing the Commonwealth in residual shreds of nostalgia. Instead he made a bitter, tough-minded, inward-looking reassessment of the new situation that had been created. It is worth observing the stance taken by Powell on issues which appear, perhaps, more significant in retrospect that they did at the time. For he was a lonely if eloquent opponent not only of the Labour Government's British Nationality Act of 1948, which superseded allegiance to the Crown as the legal basis of British citizenship, but also of the congruent provisions of the Royal Titles Bill of 1953, introduced by Churchill's Government. 'We are doing this for the sake of those to whom the very names "Britain" and "British" are repugnant,' Powell claimed in the Commons. 'We are doing it for the sake of those who have deliberately cast off their allegiance to a common Monarch.'

This high notion of nationality, infused with a Burkeian reverence for the traditional bonds constituting a self-conscious historical community, can thus be seen as the premise for Powell's later protestations about immigration, the Common Market and Ulster. This helps explain the emphasis which Powell placed upon the intractable obstacles in the way of assimilating immigrants from India and Pakistan, with their strong sense of cultural identity, whereas blacks from the Caribbean might more readily come to conform to his conception of the requirements of British citizenship. 'I have set and always will set my face like flint against making any difference between one citizen of this country and another on the grounds of his origin,' Powell proclaimed in 1964, in words often used to reproach him subsequently. It was the same man who questioned the salience of 'black power' in the debate over immigration in 1971, declaring: 'Yet it is more truly when he looks into the eyes of Asia that the Englishman comes face to face with those who will dispute with him possession of his native land.' At the time this sounded like a paranoid fantasy harking back to G.K. Chesterton's dated novel *The Flying Inn*. It took a thoroughly modern novel, Salman Rushdie's *Satanic Verses*, nearly twenty years later, to get liberals to acknowledge what Powell was talking about.

In the years 1963–70 Powell shed the reputation of a remote, high-principled ideologue, only to be denounced as an opportunistic, vote-grubbing populist. There seems to be adequate evidence to dispose of some of the cruder calumnies against him. It is, after all, rather odd to charge a politician with careerism when he has on so many occasions put his career at risk in the name of principles which evoked little popular appeal or even understanding. It was Powell who resigned from his hard-won post at the Treasury in 1958, along with Peter Thorneycroft and Nigel Birch, in protest against Macmillan's unwillingness to push through the cuts in public spending which his Treasury team insisted upon as necessary. The actual sum in contention may in the end have seemed trivial to lax-minded sybarites who had never had it so good, but Powell protested: 'I do not personally regard £50 million or one per cent of national expenditure as a triviality.' Again it was Powell who, having climbed back into the Cabinet, staked his future upon a bid to thwart the manoeuvres which followed Macmillan's resignation in 1963. Butler thus had the ball at his feet. If he had shown a fraction of the resolution of Powell and Macleod in refusing to serve under Lord Home, Butler would have become Prime Minister. As Powell put it later: 'We handed him a loaded revolver and told him all he had to do was pull the trigger.' Powell may have been an intellectual in politics; but he was one who lacked judgement rather than courage in a visceral exercise of power.

When Powell became the Opposition defence spokesman after the 1964 General Election, then, it was his third stint on the Conservative front bench – and equally short-lived, as it turned out. Powell's Birmingham speech of April 1968, with its vision of 'the River Tiber foaming with much blood', brought his dismissal from Heath's Shadow Cabinet. This time he had pulled the trigger himself, and surely not without some premonition of the dangers, to himself as well as to others. For whatever the longstanding intellectual consistency of Powell's views on citizenship and nationality, the tone which he now adopted was undeniably new. He had suddenly entered a street discourse in which old ladies, besieged by 'wide-grinning piccaninnies', were wont to find excreta pushed through their letter-boxes. This speech, which marked a decisive moment in Powell's emergence as a popular tribune, simultaneously sealed his final exclusion from the political establishment. Thereafter his was the voice crying in a wilderness of his own making.

How important a figure was Powell in the politics of the years 1968–74? In the General Election of 1970, to be sure, he made a late intervention on the Conservative side and Heath unexpectedly won. But why? Nobody knew better than the old classical scholar not to fall for the old fallacy: *post hoc ergo propter hoc*. Whatever conclusion he drew, he now adopted a messianic posture over entry to the Common Market, which he subsequently made the touchstone of his political allegiance. Thus in 1974 he broke irrevocably with Heath's Conservative Party. With his long-reiterated claims to be a party man – 'I was born a Tory, am a Tory and shall die a Tory' – Powell was nonetheless impelled by his own logic to renounce his old party in view of what he saw as its apostasy over the Common Market. 'The elector votes not for a person but for a Party,' he explained, 'and not for a Party in the abstract but a Party majority in the House of Commons.' Hence the improbable spectacle of Powell voting Labour and urging his bemused followers to do likewise.

From this point onward, with his refusal to stand again in Wolverhampton, Powell appeared increasingly marginal in British politics. True, he had banged home his own nail into Heath's political coffin, albeit at a moment when the lid was already pretty effectively secured. True, Powell proved able to exploit the minority status of the Callaghan Government to some effect during his parliamentary reincarnation as an Ulster Unionist. But, as much as Heath or Callaghan, he was ultimately eclipsed by a politician whose style he had despised – 'that dreadful voice, and those dreadful hats' – but whose message appropriated from him, under his nose, much of his own following. Thatcher succeeded, moreover, in striking a populist chord not only with overt nationalist appeals but also with an assertion of the need for financial rectitude which, on Powell's lips, had sounded merely quaint and reactionary. Moreover, she understood about power: how to use a loaded revolver when handed one, how to avoid it backfiring, and how to hide a smoking gun.

In 1970 there emerged a more serious, if ultimately abortive, threat to the consensus on economic policy. After the increasingly interventionist experiments of the 1960s under Wilson's Labour Government, the Conservatives returned to office pledged to bring about 'a silent revolution'. Edward Heath as Prime Minister initially presented an abrasive image and seemed ready to face industrial confrontation. Indeed he saw trade-union reform as the real solution to Britain's economic problems, having renounced incomes policies as a means of controlling inflation. But Heath's non-interventionist stance soon buckled under the pressure of events. Major companies like Rolls-Royce were nationalized when they faced collapse; above all, in 1972, there was a major retreat on incomes policy, which henceforward became the foundation of the Government's economic policy. The fact that these abrupt reversals became notorious as 'U-turns', deeply damaging to the Government's credibility, was a lesson which Thatcher, Secretary of State for Education in Heath's Cabinet, took to heart. The world context of Heath's initiative was unfortunate; he found himself in power during the oil crisis of 1973–4 which bidded up energy prices – not least of coal. The sudden fall of Heath in 1974, locked in mortal combat with the coalminers in defence of his incomes policy, facilitated the sudden rise of Thatcher in 1975.

Thatcher's luck was to be a significant ingredient in her political success. She was lucky to emerge as the single credible alternative to Heath at this juncture. If only Heath had not played his cards so badly, if only Willie Whitelaw, his deputy, had not been so self-effacing, would the Conservative Party have been ready to move so sharply to the right, let alone to choose a woman? Yet it was she alone who bravely and openly challenged Heath for the leadership. It was said at the time that she had 'hijacked the party' – certainly she took it on a hazardous flight, fraught with unpredictability and suspense, to an uncharted destination of her own choosing. Few people fully realized what they were letting themselves in for. Thatcher was lucky, too, in the circumstances of the 1979 General Election. The 'winter of discontent' in 1978–79, when the minority Labour Government reeled under a series of public sector strikes, provided a vivid object lesson illustrating the need for radical change. This was a classic case of a government losing an election rather than an opposition party winning it. But again she seized the chance that was offered to her, this time to hijack the country. Reiterating that under Heath the Conservatives had lost three elections out of four, she declared in 1979: 'I'll only be given the chance to lose *one*. If we win, I'll have the chance of another.'

Thatcher's stance marked a complete repudiation not only of socialism but also of the approach of the Heath and Macmillan Governments: she denounced 'the policies that failed before' and affirmed that there would be no humiliating U-turns under her leadership. After the rebuff to Thorneycroft and Powell in 1958, and the disappointment with Heath's post-1972 phase, therefore, 1979 proved third time lucky for the Conservative Right. It was fitting that Thorneycroft was rehabilitated by being brought back to become party chairman.

Thatcher's monument has been the remaking of her party in her own image. No longer could the Conservative Party be said to be dominated by the traditional upper-class élite, once a grocer's daughter from a small provincial town was in charge. Alderman Roberts, the Methodist lay preacher from Grantham, with his Liberal roots in the shopocracy, thus achieved posthumous fame through his remarkable daughter, who gladly acknowledged the lessons she learned at his knee:

His simple conviction that some things are right, and some are wrong. His belief that life is ultimately about character, that character comes from what you make of yourself. You must work hard to earn money to support yourself, but hard work was even more important in the formation of character. You must learn to stand on your own feet.

Margaret Thatcher in due course moved on to the Church of England and the Conservative Party; she married a rich businessman and lived in a smart house in Chelsea. Like Gladstone, however, she looked beyond the metropolitan establishment and showed no snobbish embarrassment in appealing to the virtues of humble people in the provinces; though in practice, like Neville Chamberlain, her cultural world was more narrowly constrained by a respectable, upwardly mobile Nonconformist tradition. She succeeded, with deep conviction and wide success, in preaching the simple economic maxims of the corner-shop – the overriding need to balance the books, the dictum that the customer is always right, the virtues of thrift and hard work, and the moral that riches are the just reward of enterprise. One of the great strengths of Thatcherism lay in its claim to offer ordinary people what they wanted through free choice in the market.

It can be said that Thatcherism, like Bevanism, had to be

invented by a hard core of loyalists to legitimate the leader's essentially personal stance. There was, of course, Powell's lonely example to inspire the ideologically faithful; but by the mid-1970s he had revealed himself as, in partisan terms, unforgivably disloyal, not to mention unsuccessful. The role of Sir Keith Joseph, by comparison, was pivotal. With family money and social position to fortify his own academic gifts, Joseph became the right-wing answer to Tony Benn. Just as Benn discovered his conversion to socialism in the mid-1970s, after thirty years in the Labour Party, so Joseph experienced a complementary revelation. 'It was only in April 1974 that I was converted to Conservatism,' he wrote. 'I had thought that I was a Conservative, but I now see that I was not really one at all.' But Joseph's zeal was too uncompromising to make him an effective leader; he settled instead, like Hugh Dalton before him, for a tutelary role in his party and was happy to provide the intellectual powerhouse behind Thatcher's push for power. The Centre for Policy Studies became the think-tank of this revivalist movement; its director Alfred Sherman spread the word that Keynes was dead; and the Institute of Economic Affairs, which had been preaching the virtues of the free market since the 1950s, suddenly found itself fashionable. Keynesianism was certainly in a bad way in the late 1970s, when a simplistic policy of dosing sluggish growth with high spending more obviously increased inflation than it reduced unemployment. This was the Thatcherite opportunity.

It was in this context that the doctrines of Friedrich von Hayek, with his Austrian background, and Milton Friedman, with his Chicago pedigree, acquired a new verisimilitude in Britain. Hayek had spent much of his long lifetime in articulating what many Conservatives knew in their bones: that Keynesianism plus democracy was a heady mixture, fuelling an ever-accelerating slide into the political economy of inflation. If it is a mistake to regard Hayek as, in any strict sense, a Conservative, this does not detract from the curious affinities between the spare rigour of his thought, with its uncompromising conclusions and doctrinaire cast, and the homespun platitudes of Thatcherism. Hayek's outlook was closer to that of old-fashioned Liberalism, his terrestrial paradise 'an intellectual island where the tradition of Macaulay and Gladstone, of J. S. Mill or John Morley lives' – and where Disraeli and the Webbs would be equally unpopular.

Hayek's vision was of the spontaneous order of the free market, permitting individuals to achieve their ends within a framework regulated by price. 'This price is not determined by the conscious will of anybody,' he claimed. 'And if one way of achieving our ends proves too expensive for us, we are free to try other ways.' Hayek always recognized, of course, that competition needs to be *created*, within a framework of law; but its beneficent force could then be left to do the rest. Thus in his influential tract *The Road to Serfdom* (1944), which the young Margaret Roberts claimed to admire, he looked forward to making 'the position of the monopolists once more that of the whipping boy of economic policy' in the confidence that 'most of the abler entrepreneurs will rediscover their taste for the bracing air of competition!' Likewise he sought to explain, from his central European experience, 'why "liberal socialism" as most people in the Western world imagine it is purely theoretical, while the practice of socialism is everywhere totalitarian'. Acceptance of the impartial, unforeseen incidence of the law, combined with submission to the impersonal, unplanned forces of the market, thus paves the road to freedom.

Hayek's state is strong, but within narrowly defined limits. It upholds a regime within which individuals fulfil themselves through existential acts of responsible choice. The general consequences of their actions are visited upon them, but it is of the essence that the results should be specifically unpredictable. Conversely, there is an underlying assumption that the market can guarantee an optimal outcome, provided that prices are not distorted. (The Keynesian scenario of market failure is simply not contemplated.) Here is the only sense in which Hayek preached monetarism. For in his scheme of coordination money had to be 'neutral' and hence not increased in quantity so as to produce distortion. There were obvious differences between this once-for-all approach and the gradualist monetarism advocated by Friedman, who supposed that fine tuning of the money supply could gently squeeze down inflation in a predictable way, lagged by an interval of perhaps two years. Before Thatcher became Prime Minister, Hayek's all-or-nothing strategy was usually dismissed as economically cataclysmic and therefore politically unthinkable. In the end, however, Hayek proved a better guide than Friedman to what happened.

These technical arguments between Keynesianism and monetarism, and between variants of monetarism, were not the real point when it came to real politics. Monetarism was only an academic dogma until Thatcher infused it with her own moral and political values, thus clothing it in a popular idiom which made it sound like the economics of common sense. Moreover, the resilience of her Government derived from a sort of ideological second-strike capacity which enabled her to snatch vindication from apparent discomfiture, and to project her own vision in terms which still seemed persuasive.

It should be recalled that in 1979 the Conservatives were running as the sunshine party. Theirs was an appeal to optimism, as against those who declared Britain's economic plight to be intractable. Naturally Thatcher stressed that Britain was in a bad way, but only so as to point instead to a better way. The Thatcher Experiment was explicitly based upon the proposition that a government which controlled the money supply could thereby squeeze inflation out of the economy without impairing its vitality. Indeed, in opposition, such policies were presented as the means to prosperity, creating jobs by cutting prices. The fact that the unemployment figure stood at over 1 million was presented in the Conservatives' propaganda as a graphic indictment of current Labour Government policy. 'Labour Isn't Working' was the message which their advertising agency, Saatchi and Saatchi, plastered across a thousand hoardings. Thus the notion that the unemployment level could be taken to measure the success or otherwise of economic policy was not dreamed up subsequently by jaundiced critics of Thatcherism: it was endorsed by the Conservatives in their prospectus. It was their opponents who suggested otherwise. For the case against monetarism held that in so far as it was capable of throttling inflation it would do so by throttling the economy as a whole – under such conditions, inflation would indeed decline, along with the economic activity which generated it.

The Thatcher Government insisted that true prosperity could only come through sound finance and set about curbing inflation. Sir Geoffrey Howe, who happily combined marked ability with remarkable docility, was the Chancellor initially set with this task. He proclaimed, in conformity with Friedman, that a gradual reduction of the money supply (technically defined as M3) was the overriding strategy. In practice, as is now generally accepted, this objective proved unattainable. The targets for M3 were persistently missed. The Government's response was first to ignore what was happening. The chief secretary to the Treasury, John Biffen, could assure the Commons in July 1980 that inflation was not the result of wage increases but had been 'mainly determined by the expansion in the money supply', some two years previously. Later, as inflation fell regardless of the continuing monetary expansion, the Government began to query M3 as an appropriate measure of monetary growth. The appointment of a new Chancellor (the self-confidently unflappable Nigel Lawson) in 1983 helped to pass off the successive adjustments in the story, and in 1985, in his Mansion House speech, he publicly repudiated M3. Monetarism was by now a misnomer or alias for a policy which had abandoned specific targets in the money supply but which relied on harsher disciplines, notably the parity of sterling.

The squeeze imposed by high interest and exchange rates in 1979–81 had a devastating effect upon the economy, especially upon manufacturing industry. The Government could thus point to undeniable indications that the policy was beginning to bite. Whom it bit was indicated by a doubling of unemployment. But if it was difficult now to take monetarism seriously as an economic policy, it was erroneous to discount Thatcherism as a political strategy. Thatcher herself was undismayed by the slump. 'My job is to let the country begin to exist within sensible and realistic economic disciplines,' she said in the summer of 1980; and in the following year she explained that 'it isn't that I set out on economic policies; it's that I set out to change the approach, and changing the economics is the means of changing the approach'. This was the faith which saw her through the night of doubt and sorrow. 'Economics are the method; the object is to change the heart and soul.'

It certainly needed strong nerves to continue with these policies through the winter of 1981–2, when the Government's popularity declined to hitherto unprecedented depths, before signs of success were glimpsed. The rate of inflation, which had stood at 10 per cent in 1979, and reached over 20 per cent in 1981, fell sharply by 1983, to around 4 per cent – despite the failure to control M3. But unemployment had meanwhile doubled to over 3 million. If Keynesianism stood accused of buying employment at the price of inflation, Thatcherism could plausibly be accused of simply inverting the process. Defenders of the Government later explained this as an improvised resort to shock tactics which succeeded in winning the battle, albeit with higher casualties than had been foreseen. On this reading, Thatcher and Howe inadvertently became exponents of the doctrines of Hayek while purporting to implement the policies of Friedman.

At any rate, the Thatcher Experiment meant that the Keynesian plank in the post-war consensus was ditched overboard. Full employment was thus relegated as the primary objective of Government policy with an insouciance which few had thought politically feasible. To be sure, rising unemployment proved electorally damaging to the Government; but once the total had reached a plateau, albeit at a level unprecedented for fifty years, its political impact could be contained. Indeed, the lessons of the 1930s were reinforced, with an increasing segregation of experience between North and South, between smokestack and sunrise industries, between decaying inner cities and booming suburbs, and between redundant employees with little prospect of new jobs and people in work with rising incomes. But even in the blackspots the experience of unemployment in the 1980s was less searing than fifty years previously. 'I can manage on the dole, but it's not like having a decent wage,' said a young man in Newcastle-upon-Tyne in 1988. 'Those in work can spend 30 quid on a night out. I can't do that.' This was relative deprivation, not despair. Moreover, though the short-term effect of plunging so deeply into recession in 1981 was so bad that few politicians would consciously have opted for it, its long-term effect held many political dividends. Things could only get better; nowhere to go but up; improvement more or less guaranteed for several years. And since it was no end of a lesson, maybe it had done us no end of good.

Thatcher's luck held throughout her first Parliament as Prime Minister. She was maintained in power, at a critical moment, by a randomly fortuitous episode in the spring of 1982 which could easily have brought her downfall. Her Government had, for all its talk about the importance of defence, shown itself incompetent to defend even the Falkland Islands, but its gambler's throw in belated over-compensation for its neg-ligence hit the political jackpot on the rebound. It did for Thatcher what Narvik had done for Churchill, what Suez had done for Macmillan. She was clearly responsible for supporting her Defence Secretary, John Nott, in overruling the advice of the Foreign Secretary, Lord Carrington, who reiterated that the withdrawal of HMS *Endurance* from the South Atlantic would be construed by Argentina as a signal to go ahead. Faced with the invasion, Thatcher once more took her fate in her hands and staked her career upon her success. It was Carrington who had to go – an admirable air-raid shelter for the Prime Minister.

The military expedition to recover the islands from Argen-tina was a hazardous enterprise, but one which showed

Thatcher's courage and resolution to advantage. The Church-illian parallel made sense to many people on an unexpectedly wide spectrum. The frail figure of Michael Foot, the Labour leader, was reanimated by the spirit of the young author of *Guilty Men*, the brilliant tract which he had published in 1940, and he leapt up in the House of Commons to speak for England. David Owen, whose tenure at the Foreign Office had seen the Argentinians thwarted in their designs, realized that this was his finest hour. This was no time for doubts about whether the British action courted disproportionate risks in defence of a principle of sovereignty which the Foreign Office had been prepared to negotiate away.

When the barren South Atlantic island of South Georgia was taken by the British task force, Thatcher had a word for it: 'Rejoice!' When the Argentine cruiser *Belgrano* was sunk by the Royal Navy, the *Sun* newspaper, the voice of populist, loyalist Thatcherism, had its own word for it: 'Gotcha!' The outcome of the war was a personal triumph for Thatcher; the islands were recovered at the cost of 1,000 deaths, most of them Argentine, and the Argentine dictatorship fell. It was also the basis for a vicarious Thatcherite triumphalism which gave the Falklands factor a lasting resonance in British politics. 'We have ceased to be a nation in retreat,' Thatcher declared in July 1982. 'We have instead a new-found confidence – born in the economic battles at home and tested and found true 8,000 miles away.' When she used the pronoun 'we', as was increasingly remarked, she usually meant herself. Her self-confidence as a leader was permanently buttressed by this vindication, against all the odds, and she was increasingly taken at her own valuation as a Prime Minister who towered alike over colleagues and opponents.

The electoral impact of the Falklands factor has been disputed. It is true that economic expectations, as measured by opinion polls, improved so as to underpin the Conservative appeal in the 1983 General Election. But the great surge in this indicator (14 per cent up) came in the months April to June 1982, at the very time that Government popularity shot up by 15 per cent. This exactly coincided with the Falklands crisis, identified as 'the most important problem facing Britain today' by 39 per cent in mid-April and by 61 per cent two weeks later. At this point 40 per cent declared themselves more favourable to the Government than a week before, as against 15 per cent less favourable; and over 90 per cent of both groups cited the Falklands as the reason. The net result was to transform voting intentions. At the start of the conflict, MORI put the Alliance support at 34 per cent, the Conservatives at 33 per cent, and Labour at 31 per cent. At the end, in mid-June 1982, the Conservatives had 51 per cent, Labour 29 per cent, and the Alliance 17 per cent. It seems difficult to resist the conclusion that it was the Falklands factor which decisively scotched the broad-based but shallow-rooted challenge which the Alliance had mounted in 1981–2.

With the decline of the Alliance, Thatcher's chances of re-election dramatically improved. If the SDP had temporarily cornered a substantial section of the Labour vote, it was because this support had been alienated by Labour itself. The unprecedented voting trends of the 1980s indicate unique stresses on the two-party system, which made the outcome highly unpredictable. It is arguable that the only chance of dislodging the Thatcher Government came and went in the early 1980s with the rise and fall of the Alliance as a major electoral threat. As things turned out, the triumph of Thatcherism, with parliamentary majorities in three figures in 1983 and 1987, was achieved on a remarkably small, if consistent, share of the vote – little more than 42 per cent. Thus it depended upon the existence of a third party with a level of support that fell fortuitously into a particular range: at once insufficiently high to do itself much good but sufficiently high to lower the threshold of success for a major party. A more broadly based Conservative appeal of the traditional kind might not have needed this peculiar concatenation of circumstances. But the success of Thatcherism, more narrowly conceived, was the product of a political gamble in which the lady walked off with the SDP's chips.

The Welfare State, instituted as part of the post-war settlement, proved surprisingly resilient under the early years of Thatcherism. Indeed, total government spending on welfare rose for the simple reason that there were more unemployed persons who qualified for social security payments. Moreover, perhaps as a result of the widespread experience of unemployment, there was a softening of general attitudes towards the poor. Opinion polls suggest that in 1977, before Thatcher came to power, 35 per cent of voters thought that, if people were poor, their own lack of effort was probably to blame; but by 1985 that figure had fallen to 22 per cent, and 50 per cent now blamed outside circumstances. Likewise, when Thatcher became Prime Minister, the same number of voters were in favour of cutting taxes as in favour of extending welfare services. But after eight years, an increase in welfare spending was supported by six times as many people as further tax cuts. Possibly the reductions in income tax, which the Government had meanwhile implemented, were felt to be sufficient. At any rate, there is surprisingly little evidence of a fundamental change of attitudes on such issues. It is true that private medical treatment has increased and that this trend was encouraged by government. But Thatcher pledged that the National Health Service was safe in her hands. Proposals to reform it by introducing market-pricing criteria, put forward in 1989, aroused public suspicion rather than enthusiasm; and it became clear that this was a field in which the Government had to tread carefully if it were not to risk alienating much of the electorate, including many of its own supporters.

The third side of the familiar consensus triangle was the mixed economy. When this was dismantled by the Government there turned out to be little real opposition and Thatcherism found an unexpectedly popular theme in privatization. In retrospect it seems that the great debate over public ownership, which loomed large in British politics for thirty years after the war, was largely theatrical. The Labour Party pointed to nationalization as the path to socialism, which promised to emancipate the working class from capitalist exploitation; but in practice it meant the creation of large, remote bureaucratic structures. Coal, gas, electricity, railways, the airlines and steel were among the industries nationalized by Labour after the war – about 20 per cent of the economy – and since steel was the only important example of dena-tionalization, subsequent Conservative governments tacitly accepted this as defining a stable frontier between public and private enterprises. If nationalization was a contentious political issue, it was because the Left periodically promised to extend it. The sale of shares in public utilities – unlike monetarism – was not widely debated before Thatcher took office in 1979.

Privatization was a policy which acquired its own momen-tum, since it was a success for the Government in a double sense. The flotation of British Telecom, which ran the tele-phone network, led the way in 1984. Financially, the sale raised £4 billion, which was counted as revenue in the public accounts. This successful formula was repeated, notably with British Gas in 1986 (for over £5 billion) and the remaining state holding in BP in 1987 (for nearly £6 billion). It has been estimated that the sale of public sector assets in the years up to 1988 raised £24 billion. But privatization also developed a social and political dimension. It saw the purchase of shares, at knockdown prices, by an unprecedently wide section of the population, who made easy capital gains on their holdings within a short time. Thus many ordinary families acquired a tangible stake in the capitalist system; by 1990 there were 11 million shareholders. Only with the scheme to privatize water supply in 1989 was the popularity of this policy challenged, with fears now surfacing of a conflict between monopoly profit and consumers' interests. The most significant success was the sale of public housing, which many working-class families rented from local councils. Under new legislation in 1980, tenants were given the right to buy their homes at advantageous prices, and by 1988 over 1 million had done so, raising some £15 billion. More significant, the political dividend for the Conservatives became obvious in the 1987 General Election, when their gains in support were con-centrated among voters who had benefited in this way. Well might Thatcherites claim that they had created a people's capitalism and a property-owning democracy.

Perhaps the biggest single change produced by the Thatcher Government has been in the position of the trade unions. In the course of ten years they lost in every way. Legally, their activities were progressively restricted by a series of Acts of Parliament, implemented step by step. In this the Government learnt its lesson from the experience of the Heath era and was careful to mobilize public opinion behind each new measure. Economically, the trade unions found their bargaining power eroded by the slump of the early 1980s, during which membership declined sharply. Politically, trade-union leaders found themselves suddenly shut out in the cold after years in which they had been on easy terms with Cabinet ministers. The old relationship was symbolized by late-night crisis meetings at 10 Downing Street over beer and sandwiches, and its ending marked a real loss of public visibility and status for the unions. Thatcher claimed that she was giving trade unions back to their members, who certainly acquired more say through the requirements for secret ballots in union elections and before industrial action.

Many skilled workers benefited from returning prosperity as the economy began to recover from 1982 onward; but they often did so individually, through new opportunities in the market, rather than collectively as trade-union members. Traditional trade-unionism suffered major and well-orchestrated defeats. When, under Arthur Scargill, the National Union of Mineworkers, whose action had crippled Heath in 1973–74, went on strike in 1984–85, the miners found the Government both resolute and well prepared in resisting them. The result was a near-fatal setback for the NUM, traditionally regarded as the shock troops of the British working-class movement. Likewise, the position of the London newspaper printers, which had exerted a stranglehold upon the industry, concentrated in old Fleet Street, was now challenged. Tough-minded employers were now able to deploy not only new technology – installed on new sites in East London and manned by a new workforce – but also legal curbs, backed by police action, in a pincer movement which crushed the old printers' unions.

Wapping, the waterfront district below Tower Bridge, where this dispute was fought out, provided a neat symbol of transition. Formerly the home of impeccably proletarian dockers, who had lost their jobs when the old port closed, Wapping now emerged as the fashionable habitat of a new generation of 'yuppies', who had got rich quick on the back of a computer-aided revolution in the City. It was a far cry from the grocer's shop in Grantham but it was the public face of Thatcherism, representing the blatant prosperity attendant on entrepreneurial success in a free market now liberated of its chains. The Government certainly swept away many restrictions in economic matters. Its abolition of foreign exchange controls was an early move in this direction, and this enabled British investors to build up a large overseas portfolio. Financial deregulation ('the big bang') in 1986, which largely destroyed the conventional division of labour between financial institutions in the City, was a further example.

The record of Thatcherism remains full of paradox. Its own claim has been to have rescued Britain from creeping paralysis by creating an enterprise culture. The Government specifically helped people with high earnings. Its first budget in 1979 reduced the top rate income tax from 83 per cent to 60 per cent; by 1988 the top rate was down to 40 per cent. The basic rate of income tax was also reduced during these years – from 33 per cent to 25 per cent – though this was balanced by an increase in indirect taxation. In fact, the total burden of taxation did not decrease under Thatcher, but the amount paid by the rich was cut dramatically. For the Government this was a vital step in its 'supply-side revolution', rewarding enterprise through greater financial incentives, and thus hoping to regenerate the economy. It was no accident, there-fore, that economic inequalities widened under Thatcher. London and the South of England might be flourishing, but the old industrial North and Scotland felt ignored. The squalor and deprivation of the inner cities, many of them in regions of industrial decline, remained a problem which Thatcher acknowledged as a pressing task on her re-election for the third time in 1987.

In 1987–8 Thatcherism achieved its apotheosis. In this mood, the Prime Minister's scheme to replace local rates with a poll tax – the flagship measure of her third Parliament – was unstoppable. Lawson was hailed as the most successful Chancellor since the war, and the boom over which he presided was lauded as proof that an economic miracle had been accomplished, permanently transforming Britain's prospects. Unemployment fell below 2 million in 1989 – a long-awaited success for the Government but one mixed with bad news too. It is true that the economy had grown fast since 1981–2, but this was partly because it declined so sharply in 1979–81, and manufacturing industry failed to bounce back. To some extent this shortfall was compensated by wealth generated by North Sea oil, but with the production of oil now declining, there were increasingly adverse effects in train for both the balance of payments and the budget. A yawning gap in Britain's trade figures opened up during 1987–9, as the result of a surge in manufactured imports, sucked in by high consumer spending.

A measure of success in economic policy was thus undeniable, but the long-term prospects remained precarious and fragile. Lawson's perception of the situation, however, revealed an obliviousness made all the more vulnerable by his self-confident demeanour. In refusing to be rattled by the balance of payments, which he dismissed as a problem for the private sector which it could easily finance, he seemed to have swallowed his own propaganda about an economic miracle. His decision to go ahead with large cuts in the higher rates of income tax in 1988 testifies to the sincerity of his beliefs. But he was putting further purchasing power in the hands of people whose propensity to consume imported consumer durables was well known. This must to some extent have fuelled inflationary forces, which took the retail price index back to around 8 per cent, thus imperilling the Government's hard-won record on inflation. The question thus remained whether, once inflation had been beaten, it would stay beaten while unemployment was reduced.

Lawson's response was to rely on raising interest rates, since he was committed to the view that monetary policy remained the proper way to control inflation. In using this single policy instrument to manage the domestic economy he behaved as no Chancellor had dared since Churchill in the 1920s, and he faced the same problem in finding a level of interest which could simultaneously reconcile external exchange rates with the domestic needs of British industry. High interest rates not only added to the cost of living, especially now that so many people had borrowed on mortgages to buy their own homes: it also for a time kept the parity of sterling at a high level, which made a rectification of the trade balance even more difficult. The Government's own budget was still comfortably in surplus, though to a large extent this was a function of oil revenues plus once-for-all sales of public assets.

Lawson's abrupt departure from the Government in October 1989 starkly revealed the tensions in policy between 10 and 11 Downing Street. Talk of an economic miracle suddenly looked embarrassingly premature. The prospect of fighting the next election on a platform of prosperity, as in 1987, looked increasingly remote. The troubles of major companies which had ridden the boom of the 1980s were all too visibly revealed – even Saatchi and Saatchi found themselves in trouble. It was in this straitened context that the implementation of the poll tax evoked such a widespread howl of protest in the spring of 1990. If Thatcherism had indeed succeeded in reversing Britain's economic decline, the forces of wealth creation now unleashed would be sufficient to ride out these difficulties. But should the growth of the economy during the mid-1980s turn out to have been a transient boom, during which economic resources were squandered to no good purpose, the historical record of Thatcherism is bound to look very different.

'Impossible! Never use that ridiculous word to me.' Mira-

beau's exclamation captures one side of Thatcher's irrepressible personality and explains why she succeeded in
achieving so much. Thatcherism without Thatcher is difficult
to imagine. She dominated her Cabinet through executive
drive backed by electoral muscle, appealing over the heads of
her ministers for popular sanction in divining the way
forward. After Carrington's resignation, or perhaps Whitelaw's decision to step down, she had no really formidable
colleagues, ready and able to resist her. Those who stood in
her way had to go. The Westland affair, in January 1986,
blew up the affairs of a small helicopter company into a crisis
of prime-ministerial credibility, in every sense of the word,
which demonstrated Thatcher's powers of survival – at a
price. It seemed at the time that the price was paid by Leon
Brittan, whose resignation took the pressure off the Prime
Minister; but the decision by Michael Heseltine that he could
no longer serve in her Cabinet set up the first real rival to her
leadership.

Thatcher showed herself increasingly unimpressed by the
conventional notions of what was politically possible, not
least in her readiness to affront vested interests, as she perceived
them. With one swipe of her handbag, she discarded the
traditional Conservative wisdom of Salisbury, salvaging only
his aversion to sentimentality. An academic sympathizer,
Kenneth Minogue, spoke truly in celebrating her renunciation
of 'bourgeois guilt' and commending her immunity to the
rhetoric of 'caring, compassion and consensus, the three
fudging Cs'. Thatcher straightforwardly pitched her appeal
down-market in terms attuned to the tabloid press, to radio
phone-ins and to television chat shows. She showed herself
no respecter of persons – or at least, not of the persons whose
names figured on the establishment lists of the great and the
good. She appointed no royal commissions because that was
the last sort of advice she needed.

This was an abrupt end to the happy reign of what Beatrice
Webb once called 'an élite of unassuming experts'. The
Thatcher Government preferred to nominate businessmen to
positions of power and influence. The enterprise culture was

lauded as a return to Victorian values, and the historic professions – not only dons and clergy but lawyers and doctors – were firmly sat upon. The crusade against restrictive practices in the trade unions was finally extended to the legal profession, much to the annoyance of highly-placed lawyers, while the expertise of social workers became the butt of scorn. It can be argued that the backlash against these superior persons was a product of their own hubris; they had overplayed their hand in an era when each new member of the caring professions revealed the need for two more. For here a fracture line had opened up between those employed within the public sector or in non-profit organizations and those employed within the private market sector. Each sector may have been professionalized, but high taxes were seen as paying for the one while being paid by the other. Thatcher spoke to this problem. Hence the spectacle of conformist corporate executives, grown as grey as their suits, getting their tongues around the rhetoric of individual initiative and free competition.

There was no love lost between the Government and such institutions as the Church of England, the universities, or the BBC, all of which it treated with suspicion. Norman Tebbit, an ex-minister who remained a vociferous ideological Thatcherite, pithily summed up this sense of grievance in February 1990: 'The word "Conservative" is now used by the BBC as a portmanteau word of abuse for anyone whose political views differ from the insufferable, smug, sanctimonious, naïve, guilt-ridden, wet, pink orthodoxy of that sunset home of that third-rate decade, the 1960s.'

This was the authentic voice of the saloon bar, speaking for the 43 per cent of skilled workers (C2s) who voted Conservative in 1987 (compared with only 34 per cent Labour and 24 per cent for the Alliance). This represented a pro-Conservative swing since 1983 of 4 per cent, among a class whose radical credentials went back to the Victorian artisans who supported Gladstone and the craft unions which sustained Attlee. If their thwarted sense of social injustice had now been redirected, it was a tribute to the appeal of radical Thatcherism. Conversely, the Gallup exit poll in 1987 also showed that voters with a university education divided in the proportion of 36 per cent for the Alliance, 34 per cent Conservative and 29 per cent Labour. No longer were the professional classes axiomatically Conservative, as they had been from Salisbury's time to Macmillan's. Old class barriers and the snobbery of upbringing and accent had to some extent been undermined, and new opportunities for social mobility enhanced. It may be only a contemporary version of a recurrent clash in every generation between the new money and the old money, but the 1980s left little doubt that the new money – in all classes – identified with Thatcherism.

Thatcher capitalized on the growing belief in the 1970s that government failure was more likely than market failure. Neoliberals in the tradition of Hayek proclaimed that the inveterate greediness of voters under mass democracy led inexorably to escalating inflation. Thus human nature fed a debased Keynesianism, which its opponents regarded as simultaneously deplorable and inevitable. The great political coup of Thatcherism was not to change human nature but to redirect it – especially among the skilled working class – away from collective and towards individual gratification. Thatcherism thus appealed blatantly to strong bargainers in all classes, not excepting trade-unionists. Hence Labour's dilemmas, as a trade-union based party, in mobilizing a campaign on behalf of the poor. The historic posture of the political Left has been to champion the Have-Nots by assuring them that 'ye are many, they are few'. It took Thatcher to discover that a majority of Haves could be mobilized in a people's coalition of the Right.

In the Europe of the future, it was claimed at the Conservative Party conference in 1988, all the 'isms' will become 'wasms' – with one sole and significant exception. This is manifestly to exaggerate the achievements of Thatcherism. Other countries have adapted to the harsher economic climate of the 1980s with moves towards the free market; but that does not justify labelling them as examples of Thatcherism, which was not so readily exportable. Indeed, Thatcher's insularity was nowhere more unmistakably seen than in her attitude towards the European Community. True, in the early 1980s she never proposed, like Labour, to leave it. But her policy seemed to be to stay in with a bad grace – to rampage from summit to summit as a sort of fishwife Britannia demanding her money back. There were tactical successes here, but also surely some failure in strategic vision. Latterly she became so suspicious of moves towards European integration as to render Lawson's position as Chancellor not 'unassailable' (as she claimed) but untenable.

Like Neville Chamberlain when he lost Eden in 1938, she then purported not to understand his resignation and maintained that there were no policy differences. Indeed, it can be argued that her political style more closely resembled that of Chamberlain than that of Churchill, with whom she preferred to associate her name. At the beginning of each volume of *The Second World War*, the Moral of the Work is prominently stated. 'In War: Resolution.' It would be churlish to deny that Margaret Thatcher showed herself truly Churchillian over the Falklands. 'In Defeat: Defiance.' Her courage in times of political adversity amply proved that she was ready to fight on alone. 'In Victory: Magnanimity.' In this respect, however, Thatcher never made more than a forced effort against a natural instinct which was unforgivingly triumphalist. 'In Peace: Goodwill.' Here, too, she showed a deficiency which may have been as much a matter of public perception as of personal intention but which soured even her successes. Measured by the full Churchillian standard, then, she would be lucky to get more than half marks.

If she had little of Churchill's breadth of outlook, instead Thatcher's narrowness of focus enabled her to get things done at the risk of becoming blinkered in her perspective. She despised her political opponents, rarely crediting them with good faith or good sense. She dominated her Cabinet, with meticulous attention to detail as well as grim determination to see off the opposition at all costs, with news management concentrated on her own person in Downing Street. This was a formula which worked well for Chamberlain in the late 1930s and started to come unstuck only after Munich; but the spiral of disintegration then quickly unwound and the political revolution of 1940 changed perceptions for a generation. In retrospect the 1930s looked like a decade of wasted opportunities, not least in economic policy.

Just as there are historical parallels for Thatcher's own conduct of government, so Thatcherism is not wholly without historical precedents. The fact is that a century ago British politics was as much dominated and fascinated by Gladstonianism as it has been recently by Thatcherism. Gladstone too remade his party in his own image, with a peculiar amalgam of moral axioms projected through his charismatic appeal in an inimitable populist style. 'I am in politics because of the conflict between good and evil, and I believe that in the end good will triumph.' These were the characteristic words of the Prime Minister in 1984; but it could as easily have been 1884. It was the Grand Old Man who first threatened to 'go on and on' until he had served a fourth term as Prime Minister, greatly loved and greatly hated – ultimately leaving a very uncertain legacy for his followers. Gladstone was personally both complex and profound, displaying faculties of insight and imagination which Thatcher never matched to any comparable degree. Her sophisticated admirers spoke of her as a 'very limited woman', for all that she might also be 'a great historical figure'. Still, it is a mark of the profound impact which she has made that she can more readily be compared with Gladstone than with his great Conservative antagonist, Salisbury, whose vision and tactics Thatcher almost entirely repudiated.

For almost a century after Salisbury, the Conservative Party followed the path he indicated, offering a quiet life to the possessing classes at the price of renouncing strident ideological appeals. What Joseph Chamberlain tried – and ultimately failed – to do was to inspire the Right with an alternative vision, entailing a populist appeal to the mass electorate. Moreover, he sought to use fiscal means to achieve his broader ends of averting national decline and restoring national morale. He put Tariff Reform on the political agenda at a time when the Unionists were already running into electoral trouble. Chamberlain's hunch was that he could sell even this unpopular new tax to the British people – there ought, after all, to be gainers as well as losers from broadening the revenue base – all in the name of his grand design of national regeneration. Alas, Chamberlain was proved wrong. In the end his radical policy fell foul not only of Conservatism, when the party broke in his hands, but also of the conservatism of the British electorate, stubbornly resistant to change. The idea that ordinary people should stump up to finance this noble enterprise, though clothed in populist rhetoric, did not thereby become popular with them. They proved ready to vote in surprisingly large numbers for the Liberal Party, which had widely been written off as a serious contender even a few years previously.

When Margaret Thatcher imposed the poll tax upon her party, she faced the challenge of yet again defying historical precedent about her leadership. With the uncomfortable example of not only Joseph Chamberlain but also Neville Chamberlain before her, she nonetheless comfortably avoided comparison with Austen Chamberlain. Nobody will say of her that she always played the game and always lost.

The authentic radicalism of the Thatcherite project was testified in paradoxical ways. Her moral populism revealed Gladstonian echoes; her raging, tearing propaganda, consciously opting for the frontal assault, stood in the Chamberlainite tradition. Thatcher had recast the appeal of a party, nominally Conservative, but owing little to the tradition followed from Salisbury to Macmillan, whose essential task was to mobilize the sleepy and complacent classes. In the process the Tories have reached out to new sources of support, at once dynamic and unstable, especially through helping to create a majority of voters committed to buying their own homes on mortgages. Yet the Government maintained its strategy of regulating the economy by relying on monetary policy – a commitment reaffirmed in John Major's only budget in 1990. Thus the very constituency on which Thatcherism crucially relied became uniquely vulnerable to the high interest rates inflicted by the Thatcher Government.

For over a decade, Conservative support in the opinion polls had faithfully (though inversely) fluctuated with mortage rates. When around 45 per cent of voters identified themselves as supporters of the Government in 1983 and again in 1987, they did so at times when the borrowing rate had fallen to 10 per cent. Conversely, by 1990 the building societies were charging 15 per cent – and a rueful Government was collecting the political bill. Having appeased the vocal demands of its own fiercest supporters, Thatcherism thus faced the nemesis which has notoriously attended efforts at radical reform.

Following the Thatcher Government's steady decline in electoral support from the beginning of 1989, its prospects looked bleak in the spring of 1990. The unpopularity of the poll tax dominated the headlines and brought the Prime Minister's own position into question. The local council elections in May 1990 thus assumed unusual importance in purporting to serve as a referendum on this issue. Yet although the Conservatives experienced severe setbacks across the country, they succeeded in their own limited aim of holding the two show-case London boroughs (Westminster and Wandsworth) where low levels of poll tax had been engineered by Conservative councils. Headline hysteria about the Prime Minister was thus countered, point for point, pica for pica, by an ostensible vindication, ostentatiously flaunted. After this, Thatcher's leadership of the Conservative Party into a fourth successive General Election seemed to have been settled.

Whether she could pull off the unique feat of a fourth successive victory, however, remained the big question. Poll tax had been pushed off the front page for another year, but was likely to remain as a recurrent problem for the Tories, blotting out the early summer as an opportune season for successful electioneering. Throwing money at the problem might seem a simple palliative; but this sort of recourse to the Exchequer was made difficult by overall economic constraints. Above all, the Thatcher Government had to stand on its record of economic management while – somehow or other – tempering the rigours of a regime of high interest rates.

Nor could contingency be discounted, as the sudden eruption of the Gulf crisis showed in the summer of 1990. Hurriedly prepared maps showing the whereabouts of Kuwait were scrambled on to the front pages where, a few years previously, hurriedly prepared maps of the South Atlantic had enlightened readers about the whereabouts of the Falklands. The immediate impact upon British public opinion, however, did not result in any comparable electoral bonus for the Thatcher Government, though the dilemmas of the developing crisis posed a continuing test of leadership. Were the affairs of the Middle East to be dismissed, in the manner of Neville Chamberlain, as another quarrel in a faraway country between people of whom we knew nothing? Or were the Iraqis to be enjoined, with Gladstonian fervour, to clear out, bag and baggage, from the province which they had desolated and profaned? And, whichever way the agenda was stated, could political support be mobilized so as to make the policy effective in the long run?

Those who felt that the Thatcher Government had irretrievably lost the initiative by 1990 were challenged, too, by its decision to put sterling into the European Monetary System. Though carefully circumscribed as a commitment simply to the Exchange Rate Mechanism, this step inescapably raised wider implications. Hardly less than Harold Wilson's belated acceptance of devaluation in 1967, the Prime Minister's five years of resistance made hers a conversion replete with mordant piquancy. Refraining only from pledging that 'the pound in your pocket' had not been Europeanized, she reaffirmed her well-nurtured suspicion of the European Community, thus perpetuating division and vacillation at the heart of her Government. Like the retreat from monetarism, this was a grudging concession to pragmatism, not least to the promise of relieving the pressure on interest rates and thereby ingratiating the Government with the very property-owning democracy of which it was so fearfully proud.

Here was the making of the final crisis. Forced to accept a

commitment against which all her instincts rebelled, Margaret Thatcher could not and would not make the right noises about Europe – 'No, no, no,' she cried under questioning in the House of Commons. For the third time – as with Heseltine, as with Lawson – her style of leadership foundered on the submerged rock of Europe, and now it was the arch-loyalist Sir Geoffrey Howe who was pushed into yet another of those incomprehensible resignations. The real surprise was that he refused to go quietly. When he turned on the Prime Minister in his resignation speech, he set off an avalanche which swept her away. Michael Heseltine was prompted to make the challenge for the leadership of the Conservative Party which, ever since the Westland affair, had been inevitable, sooner or later. Coming sooner, it proved to be too soon to allow him to snatch the prize, but too late for Thatcher to retreive the position once a strong showing against her had been recorded in the first ballot.

Like Neville Chamberlain, her fall was staggeringly sudden and complete, precipitated by an overt withdrawal of confidence on the backbenches. Like Gladstone, she found herself isolated in a cabinet drawn from a younger generation of ministers, with their eyes already straying ahead to a stange new era after the departure of the Prime Minister who had made their careers. Though still overawed and overshadowed by the Grand Old Lady, the Thatcher Cabinet ultimately turned on Thatcher. Like Joseph Chamberlain, her ideological crusade threatened literally to overtax her own supporters; and like Tariff Reform after 1913, the poll tax now lived on as a ghost policy, with the party determined to draw its fiscal sting even at the price of vitiating its original rationale. If this was indicative of how much Thatcherism depended on Thatcher, the manner of her fall was also a back-handed, back-stabbing tribute to her success in remarking a party of which it used to be said that loyalty was the Tories' secret weapon.

Salisbury's insight had been to see that the party of reform creates the opportunity for the party of resistance. He would have appreciated the irony of a situation in which this maxim threatened to backfire upon the Conservative Party itself. His view that 'Mr Gladstone's existence was the greatest source of strength which the Conservative party possessed' could have been adapted and adopted as an inspirational text for the Labour Party by 1990. Conversely, with Thatcher gone, the opposition lost its pre-eminent target and the Conservatives surprised themselves by taking on a new lease of life, perhaps tempted to reassert their safe traditional role in place of the more risky strategy of radical populism. Thus in Thatcher's demise, as in her greatest triumphs, style and substance were wrapped up together so as to focus, concentrate and personalize the issue. It was, in short, a question of leadership.

BIBLIOGRAPHY

This bibliography contains the sources of all direct quotations in the text, with the books to which I am most heavily indebted marked with an appreciative asterisk. Books are listed under the first chapter to which they are substantially relevant, and may have been used also in subsequent chapters.

Chapter 1: Gladstone: The Politics of Moral Populism

Michael Barker, *Gladstone and Radicalism, 1886–1894* (Hassocks: Harvester Press, 1975).

Maxine Berg, *The Machinery Question and the Making of Political Economy, 1815–48* (Cambridge: Cambridge University Press, 1980).

Ian Bradley, *The Optimists: themes and personalities in Victorian Liberalism* (London: Faber, 1980).

Asa Briggs, *Victorian People* (Harmondsworth: Penguin, 1965).

Asa Briggs and John Saville (eds.), *Essays in Labour History* (London: Macmillan, 1960).

John Brooke and Mary Sorenson (eds.), *The Prime Ministers' Papers: W.E. Gladstone* vols. i and ii (London: HMSO, 1971–2).

Geoffrey Crossick, *An Artisan Elite in Victorian Society* (London: Croom Helm, 1978).

D. A. Hamer, *John Morley* (Oxford: Clarendon Press, 1968).

D. A. Hamer, *The Politics of Electoral Pressure* (Hassocks: Harvester Press, 1970).

D. A. Hamer, *Liberal Politics in the Age of Gladstone and Rosebery* (Oxford: Clarendon Press, 1972).

J. L. Hammond, *Gladstone and the Irish Nation* (London: Longman, 1938).

Royden Harrison, *Before the Socialists: studies in labour and politics, 1861–1881* (London: Routledge, 1965).

Boyd Hilton, *The Age of Atonement: the influence of evangelicalism on social and economic thought, 1785–1860* (Oxford: Clarendon Press, 1988).

Gareth Stedman Jones, *Languages of Class: studies in English working class history 1832–1982* (Cambridge: Cambridge University Press, 1983).

Patrick Joyce, *Work, Society and Politics: the culture of the later Victorian factory* (Brighton: Harvester Press, 1980).

F. M. Leventhal, *Respectable Radical: George Howell and Victorian working class politics* (London: Weidenfeld & Nicolson, 1971).

★H. C. G. Matthew, *Gladstone 1809–74* (Oxford: Oxford University Press, 1986).

★H. C. G. Matthew (ed.), *The Gladstone Diaries*, vols. ix, x and xi (Oxford: Clarendon Press, 1986–90).

John Morley, *The Life of William Ewart Gladstone* (London: Macmillan, 1903).

John Henry Newman, *Apologia Pro Vita Sua* (1864; Everyman edition, 1912).

J. P. Parry, *Democracy and Religion: Gladstone and the Liberal Party, 1867–75* (Cambridge: Cambridge University Press, 1986).

★R. T. Shannon, *Gladstone and the Bulgarian Agitation, 1876* (London: Nelson, 1963).

Richard Shannon, *Gladstone, vol. i, 1809–65* (London: Hamish Hamilton, 1982).

F. M. L. Thompson, *The Rise of Respectable Society: a social history of Victorian Britain, 1830–1900* (London: Fontana Press, 1988).

*John Vincent, *The Formation of the Liberal Party, 1857–68* (London: Constable, 1966).

John Vincent, *Pollbooks: how Victorians voted* (Cambridge: Cambridge University Press, 1967).

Chapter 2: *The Authentic Voice of Conservatism: Lord Salisbury*

Lord Blake and Hugh Cecil (eds.), *Salisbury: the man and his policies* (London: Macmillan, 1987).

Edmund Burke, *Reflections on the French Revolution* (Everyman edition, 1910).

Bruce Coleman, *Conservatism and the Conservative Party in Nineteenth Century Britain* (London: Edward Arnold, 1988).

James Cornford, 'The transformation of Victorian Conservatism', *Victorian Studies*, vol. vii (1963).

Maurice Cowling, *1867: Disraeli, Gladstone and Revolution* (Cambridge: Cambridge University Press, 1967).

R. F. Foster, *Lord Randolph Churchill* (Oxford: Clarendon Press, 1981).

A. L. Kennedy, *Salisbury* (London: John Murray, 1953).

*Peter Marsh, *The Discipline of Popular Government: Lord Salisbury's domestic statecraft, 1881–1902* (Hassocks: Harvester Press, 1978).

Michael Pinto-Duschinsky, *The Political Thought of Lord Salisbury 1854–1868* (London: Constable, 1967).

Roland Quinault, 'Lord Randolph Churchill and Tory Democracy, 1880–5', *Historical Journal*, vol. xxii (1979).

F. B. Smith, *The Making of the Second Reform Bill* (Cambridge: Cambridge University Press, 1966).

Paul Smith, *Disraelian Conservatism and Social Reform* (London: Routledge, 1967).

*Paul Smith (ed.), *Lord Salisbury on Politics* (Cambridge: Cambridge University Press, 1972).

Robert Taylor, *Lord Salisbury* (London: Allen Lane, 1975).

John Vincent, *Disraeli* (Oxford: Oxford University Press, 1990).

Chapter 3: Joseph Chamberlain: The First Modern Politician

Julian Amery, *Joseph Chamberlain and the Tariff Reform Campaign*, vols. v and vi of the authorized biography (London: Macmillan, 1969).

Peter Clarke, *Liberals and Social Democrats* (Cambridge: Cambridge University Press, 1978).

*Richard Jay, *Joseph Chamberlain* (Oxford: Clarendon Press, 1981).

*Denis Judd, *Radical Joe* (London: Hamish Hamilton, 1977).

*A. N. Porter, *The Origins of the South African War: Joseph Chamberlain and the diplomacy of imperialism, 1895–9* (Manchester: Manchester University Press, 1980).

Richard A. Rempel, *Unionists Divided: Arthur Balfour, Joseph Chamberlain and the Unionist Free Traders* (Newton Abbot: David & Charles, 1972).

Alan Sykes, *Tariff Reform in British Politics, 1903–13* (Oxford: Clarendon Press, 1979).

Beatrice Webb, *My Apprenticeship* (1926; Cambridge: Cambridge University Press, 1979).

Chapter 4: Asquith and Lloyd George: Misalliances

*Michael and Eleanor Brock (eds.), *H.H. Asquith: letters to Venetia Stanley* (Oxford: Oxford University Press, 1982).

*Bentley Brinkerhoff Gilbert, *David Lloyd George: the architect of change, 1863–1912* (London: Batsford, 1987).

John Grigg, *The Young Lloyd George* (London: Methuen, 1973);

John Grigg, *Lloyd George, the People's Champion* (London: Methuen, 1978).

*John Grigg, *Lloyd George, from Peace to War* (London: Methuen, 1985).

Roy Jenkins, *Asquith* (London: Collins, 1964).

J. M. Keynes, *Essays in Biography* (1933; vol. x of *The Collected Writings of John Maynard Keynes*, London: Royal Economic Society, 1972).

*Stephen Koss, *Asquith* (London: Allen Lane, 1976).

Kenneth O. Morgan (ed.), *Lloyd George: family letters, 1885–1936* (Cardiff: University of Wales Press and Oxford University Press, 1973).

Bruce K. Murray, *The People's Budget, 1909–10* (Oxford: Clarendon Press, 1980).

Martin Pugh, *Electoral Reform in War and Peace, 1906–18* (London: Routledge, 1978).

*A. J. P. Taylor (ed.), *Lloyd George: a diary by Frances Stevenson* (London: Hutchinson, 1971).

Chapter 5: The Businesslike Approach: Neville Chamberlain

*John Charmley, *Chamberlain and the Lost Peace* (London: Hodder, 1989).

Winston S. Churchill, *Great Contemporaries* (1937; London: Fontana, 1959).

Richard Cockett, *The Personal Touch: Chamberlain, the politics of appeasement and the manipulation of the press* (London: Weidenfeld & Nicolson, 1989).

Maurice Cowling, *The Impact of Hitler: British politics and British policy, 1933–40* (Cambridge: Cambridge University Press, 1975).

*David Dilks, *Neville Chamberlain, vol.i: pioneering and reform 1869–1929* (Cambridge: Cambridge University Press, 1984).

*David Dutton, *Austen Chamberlain* (Bolton: Ross Anderson, 1985).

David Lloyd George, *War Memoirs* (1933–6: 2 vol. edn, n.d., London: Odhams).

H. Montgomery Hyde, *Neville Chamberlain* (London: Weidenfeld & Nicolson, 1976).

Chapter 6: Churchill: Lost Empires

Winston S. Churchill, *The People's Rights* (1909; London: Jonathan Cape, 1970).

Winston S. Churchill, 'Parliamentary government and the economic problem', in *Thoughts and Adventures* (1932; London: Odhams, 1947).

Winston S. Churchill, *The Second World War* 6 vols. (London: Cassell, 1948–54).

*Martin Gilbert, *Winston S. Churchill*, esp. vol. v, *1922–39* (London: Heinemann, 1976) with companion volumes.

Robert Rhodes James, *Churchill: a study in failure, 1900–39* (London: Weidenfeld & Nicolson, 1970).

Robert Rhodes James (ed.), *Winston Churchill: his complete speeches, 1897–1963*, 8 vols. (New York: Chelsea House, 1974).

Keith Middlemas and John Barnes, *Baldwin* (London: Weidenfeld & Nicolson, 1969).

Henry Pelling, *Winston Churchill* (London: Macmillan, 1974).

Chapter 7: Keynes: Academic Scribbler or Political Dabbler?

Anne Olivier Bell and Andrew McNeillie (eds.), *The Diary of Virginia Woolf*, vol. v. (1984; Penguin, 1985).

John Campbell, *Lloyd George: the Goat in the Wilderness* (London; Cape, 1977).

*Peter Clarke, *The Keynesian Revolution in the Making, 1924–36* (Oxford: Clarendon Press, 1988).

David Marquand, *Ramsay MacDonald* (London: Cape, 1977).

*Donald Moggridge and Austin Robinson (eds.), *The Collected Writings of John Maynard Keynes*, 30 vols. (London: Macmillan for the Royal Economic Society, 1971–89); esp. vol. iv, *A Tract on Monetary Reform* (1923); vol. vii, *The General Theory* (1936); vol. ix, *Essays in Persuasion* (1931); vol. x, *Essays in Biography* (1933).

Robert Skidelsky, *John Maynard Keynes*, vol. i, *Hopes Betrayed, 1883–1920* (London: Macmillan, 1983).

Robert Skidelsky, *Oswald Mosley* (London: Macmillan, 1975).

Chapter 8: The Tutelary Politics of Hugh Dalton

Alec Cairncross, *Years of Recovery: British economic policy, 1945–51* (London: Methuen, 1985).

Elizabeth Durbin, *New Jerusalems: the Labour party and the economics of democratic socialism* (London: Routledge, 1985).

Ben Pimlott, *Hugh Dalton* (London: Cape, 1985).

*Ben Pimlott (ed.), *The Political Diary of Hugh Dalton, 1918–40, 1945–60* and *The Second World War Diary of Hugh Dalton, 1940–5* (London: Cape, 1986).

Chapter 9: Attlee: The Making of the Post-war Concensus

Alan Bullock, *Ernest Bevin, Foreign Secretary, 1945–51* (London: Heinemann, 1983).

*Trevor Burridge, *Clement Attlee* (London: Cape, 1985).

Bernard Donoughue and G. W. Jones, *Herbert Morrison* (London: Weidenfeld & Nicolson, 1973).

Jose Harris, *William Beveridge* (Oxford: Clarendon Press, 1977).

*Kenneth Harris, *Attlee* (London: Weidenfeld & Nicolson, 1982).

*Kenneth O. Morgan, *Labour in Power, 1945–51* (Oxford: Clarendon Press, 1984).

Henry Pelling, *The Labour Governments, 1945–51* (London: Macmillan, 1984).

Harold Wilson, *Memoirs, 1916–64* (London: Weidenfeld & Nicolson and Michael Joseph, 1986).

Chapter 10: Macmillan: The Lessons of the Past

Russell Davies and Liz Ottaway, *Vicky* (London: Secker & Warburg, 1987).

*Alistair Horne, *Macmillan*, 2 vols. (London: Macmillan, 1987–8).

Anthony Howard, *RAB: a life of R.A. Butler* (London: Cape, 1987).

Robert Rhodes James, *Anthony Eden* (London: Weidenfeld & Nicolson, 1986).

Harold Macmillan, *Memoirs* esp. vol. iv, *Riding the Storm* (London: Macmillan, 1971).

Anthony Sampson, *Macmillan: a study in ambiguity* (London: Allen Lane, 1967).

Hugh Thomas, *The Suez Affair*, revised edn. (Harmondsworth: Penguin, 1970).

*D.R. Thorpe, *Selwyn Lloyd* (London: Cape, 1989).

Chapter 11: Bevan versus Gaitskell: Splitting the Difference

V. L. Allen, *Trade Union Leadership: based on a study of Arthur Deakin* (London: Longman, 1957).

*John Campbell, *Nye Bevan and the Mirage of British Socialism* (London: Weidenfeld & Nicolson, 1987).

C. A. R. Crosland, *The Future of Socialism* (1956; rev. edn, London: Cape, 1964).

*Michael Foot, *Aneurin Bevan, 1897–1945* (London: MacGibbon & Kee, 1962).

Michael Foot, *Aneurin Bevan, 1945–60* (London: Davis-Poynter, 1973).

Stephen Haseler, *The Gaitskellites* (London: Macmillan, 1969).

Lewis Minkin, *The Labour Party Conference* (Manchester: Manchester University Press, 1978).

*Janet Morgan (ed.), *The Backbench Diaries of Richard Crossman* (London: Hamish Hamilton and Cape, 1981).

Philip Williams, *Hugh Gaitskell* (London: Cape, 1979).

*Philip Williams (ed.), *The Diary of Hugh Gaitskell, 1945–56* (London: Cape, 1983).

Chapter 12: The Decay of Labourism and the Demise of the SDP

Tony Benn, *Diaries, 1963–72*, 2 vols., in progress (London: Hutchinson, 1987-).

Ian Bradley, *Breaking the Mould? The birth and prospects of the SDP* (Oxford: Martin Robertson, 1981).

James Callaghan, *Time and Chance* (London: Collins, 1987).

Barbara Castle, *The Castle Diaries, 1964–70* (London: Weidenfeld & Nicolson, 1984).

*Richard Crossman, *The Diaries of a Cabinet Minister, 1964–70*, 3 vols. (London: Hamish Hamilton and Cape, 1975–7).

Susan Crosland, *Tony Crosland* (London: Cape, 1987).

Michael Foot, *Loyalists and Loners* (London: Collins, 1986).

Kenneth Harris, *David Owen* (London: Weidenfeld & Nicolson, 1987).

*Denis Healey, *The Time of My Life* (London: Michael Joseph, 1989).

Peter Jenkins, *The Battle of Downing Street* (London: Charles Knight, 1970).

Roy Jenkins, *European Diary, 1977–81* (London: Collins, 1989).

*Roy Jenkins, Dimbleby Lecture (1979) in Wayland Kennet (ed.), *The Rebirth of Britain* (London: Weidenfeld & Nicolson, 1982).

Peter Kellner and Christopher Hitchens, *Callaghan: the road to Number Ten* (London: Cassell, 1976).

Kenneth O. Morgan, *Labour People* (Oxford: Oxford University Press, 1987).

David Steel, *Against Goliath* (London: Weidenfeld & Nicolson, 1989).

Hugh Stephenson, *Claret and Chips: the rise of the SDP* (London: Michael Joseph, 1982).

Chapter 13: Thatcherism: The Remaking of the Conservative Party

David Butler and Denis Kavanagh, *The British General Elections of 1979/1983/1987* (London: Macmillan, 1980/1984/1988).

Contemporary Record, Autumn 1987 and Winter 1988, 'The Falklands Factor' (Lawrence Freedman and Helmut Norpoth).

*Patrick Cosgrave, *The Lives of Enoch Powell* (London: Bodley Head, 1989).

Maurice Cowling, Introduction to the Second Edition, *Mill and Liberalism* (Cambridge: Cambridge University Press, 1990).

Andrew Gamble, *The Free Economy and the Strong State* (London: Macmillan, 1988).

Kenneth Harris, *Thatcher* (London: Weidenfeld & Nicolson, 1988).

Stuart Hall, *The Hard Road to Renewal* (London: Verso, 1988).

F.A. Hayek, *The Road to Serfdom* (London: Routledge, 1944).

Peter Hennessy and Anthony Seldon (eds.), *Ruling Performances* (Oxford: Blackwell, 1987).

*Peter Jenkins, *Mrs Thatcher's Revolution* (London: Cape, 1987).

Denis Kavanagh, *Thatcherism and British Politics* (Oxford: Oxford University Press, 1987).

Denis Kavanagh and Anthony Seldon (eds.), *The Thatcher Effect* (Oxford: Clarendon Press, 1989).

William Keegan, *Mrs Thatcher's Economic Experiment* (London: Allen Lane, 1984).

William Keegan, *Mr Lawson's Gamble* (London: Hodder and Stoughton, 1989).

David Marquand, *The Unprincipled Society* (London: Cape, 1988).

Harold Perkin, *The Rise of Professional Society* (London: Routledge, 1989).

Robert Skidelsky, *Thatcherism* (London: Chatto & Windus, 1988); Ivor Crewe's essay updated in *Contemporary Record*, Feb. 1990.

*Hugo Young, *One of Us: a biography of Margaret Thatcher* (London: Macmillan, 1989).

Hugo Young and Anne Sloman, *The Thatcher Phenomenon* (London: BBC, 1986).

ACKNOWLEDGEMENTS

Parts of these chapters are adapted from writings which first appeared elsewhere, and I owe particular thanks to Karl Miller and Mary-Kay Wilmers, the editors of the *London Review of Books*, and Jeremy Treglown, the former editor of *The Times Literary Supplement*. Some of Chapter 4 was published in my essay 'Asquith and Lloyd George Revisited', in *The Political Culture of Modern Britain: studies in memory of Stephen Koss*, edited by J.M.W. Bean (Hamish Hamilton, 1987). Copyright illustrations are reproduced by permission of Dr Milo Keynes, Solo Syndication & Literary Agency, the *Observer*, and Times Newspapers Ltd.

I am grateful to the Master and Fellows of St John's College, Cambridge, who, for more than ten years, have facilitated my writing and research. My final debt is to the carefully constructed random sample of readers who commented on the manuscript in draft: Eugenio Biagini, Winifred Clarke, Stefan Collini, Ewen Green, Margaret O'Callaghan, John Thompson and Oliver Walston. They helped me to remove some errors of fact, but those of taste proved more intractable.

Peter Clarke
St John's College, Cambridge

INDEX

Politicians are listed under the names commonly used during their active career: e.g., Disraeli, *not* Beaconsfield. There are no entries for the Conservative, Liberal and Labour Parties as such.